UNFREE

Unfree

Migrant Domestic Work in Arab States

Rhacel Salazar Parreñas

Stanford University Press
Stanford, California

STANFORD UNIVERSITY PRESS
Stanford, California

Library of Congress Cataloging-in-Publication Data
Names: Parreñas, Rhacel Salazar, author.
Title: Unfree : migrant domestic work in Arab states / Rhacel Salazar
  Parreñas.
Description: Stanford, California : Stanford University Press, 2021. |
  Includes bibliographical references and index.
Identifiers: LCCN 2021007417 (print) | LCCN 2021007418 (ebook) |
  ISBN 9781503614666 (cloth) | ISBN 9781503629653 (paperback) |
  ISBN 9781503629660 (epub)
Subjects: LCSH: Women household employees—United Arab Emirates—
  Social conditions. | Women foreign workers—United Arab Emirates—
  Social conditions. | Foreign workers, Filipino—United Arab
  Emirates—Social conditions. | Contract labor—United Arab Emirates.
Classification: LCC HD6072.2.U5 P37 2021 (print) | LCC HD6072.2.U5
  (ebook) | DDC 331.4/8164095357—dc23
LC record available at https://lccn.loc.gov/2021007417
LC ebook record available at https://lccn.loc.gov/2021007418

Cover design: Angela Moody

Typeset by Kevin Barrett Kane in 10/14 Minion Pro

Contents

UNFREE

What Is Unfree Labor?

RUTHIE, A SKINNY, PETITE FILIPINA DOMESTIC WORKER in her late 20s, sits on the outdoor patio of a rundown villa in Satwa, a working-class neighborhood in Dubai, where she stays with her boyfriend from Thursday evening to Saturday afternoon every weekend. Ruthie sits slouched into an old discolored couch, with her feet up on a heavily chipped wooden coffee table. Pointing to the sheets hanging on the clothesline behind us, she complains that her work does not end when she leaves her employer for the weekend, as she not only has to do her boyfriend's laundry but also has to cook for him. Ruthie's weekend arrangement is unusual; most domestic workers are not allowed to spend the night elsewhere, let alone have an extended day off. In the United Arab Emirates (UAE), sexual relations outside of marriage are *haram*, meaning strictly forbidden, and considered a sinful act. Yet in Ruthie's case, her employer trusts in her discretion as an adult not to put her employer or herself in legal jeopardy. Most days of the week, Ruthie works for a 35-year-old single mother from Iran. Her employer was raised in the neighboring emirate of Sharjah, though she went to college in Canada. In a two-bedroom condominium in a high-rise luxury building near the Dubai Mall, Ruthie occupies one room while her employer and her employer's 8-year-old daughter sleep in the other.

According to Ruthie, her employer gives her a "light" workload. Her primary tasks are cleaning and helping with childcare, which she does with minimal supervision. When her employer leaves with her daughter at 7:30 every weekday morning, Ruthie is often encouraged to "just go back to sleep and wake up at 12 or 1." Rarely monitored, she usually decides how and when to do her job. While not expected to cook for the family, Ruthie still on occasion chooses to do so, which is a favor that her employer never overlooks. Ruthie shares, "Sometimes, when I know she is tired or when she is late, I will just go ahead and cook. She will then say, 'Thank you Ruthie for fixing our dinner.' That is what she is like." The kindness and consideration of her employer are not lost on Ruthie. Marveling over her generosity, Ruthie notes that her employer gives her free rein in the kitchen and even invites her to use whatever ingredients she might need to bake pastries for friends on weekends. Each month, Ruthie earns 2000 dirhams[1] (US$555), significantly more than the minimum monthly wage of US$400 stipulated by the Philippine government for this work. She also receives an annual one-month paid vacation to the Philippines, which she never fails to take so that she can spend time with her own children.

Ruthie's story does not fit the dominant assumptions of labor conditions for domestic workers in the UAE, presenting a counter-narrative to the stories of enslavement, entrapment, ill-treatment, and violent abuse that are frequently featured in the news bulletins, advocacy group reports, and scholarly accounts of domestic workers in the region.[2] Such accounts make Ruthie's story difficult to imagine. Indeed, negative public reports on domestic work in the region make it hard to imagine that employers could ever possibly recognize the humanity of domestic workers. Instead, one is more likely to assume that employers would infantilize, if not entirely dehumanize, them, as in the case of 47-year-old Joy, who is treated like a child and assumed to need constant supervision both at work and in her personal affairs.

Joy initially worked for a Yemeni family who maintained their dominant hold over her in multiple ways: they denied her any time off; overworked her, making her do "everything, cooking, ironing the clothes"; and refused to release her from her contract. After completing her two-year contract, Joy had repeatedly wanted to quit, but her employers would lure her with vacations to get her to change her mind. Though her employers' strategy often worked, Joy knew her situation had not been ideal. Infantilized by her employers, Joy did not have much say even in what foods she could eat, as her employers always made this decision for her. Further magnifying her infantilization was her employers' refusal to pay her on a monthly basis. Access to her salary was extended on an as-needed basis, such as sending remittances to her family in the Philippines only when her employers deemed the request justifiable. They were supposedly managing her money to ensure that she would not squander her earnings, but would instead return to the Philippines with sizable savings that she could then invest in a business. Yet withholding her salary only aggravated their hold over her, which in turn discouraged Joy from ever leaving her job. It was not until she visited the General Directorate of Residency and Foreigners Affairs, the office that was at that time in charge of monitoring foreign domestic workers in Dubai, that Joy learned that it was illegal for her employers to withhold her salary. This knowledge emboldened her to quit after five years of coerced labor, but, perhaps not surprisingly, this came at the cost of her unpaid wages. When she left, her employers still owed her seven months of back pay. While Joy had little recourse for retrieving her remaining salary, she used their nonpayment of her wages as leverage to ensure her "release" as opposed to "cancellation." Being "released" meant that she could seek another employer in the UAE, while being "canceled" would have forced her to leave the country.

Joy's experiences are far from the worst faced by domestic workers in the UAE. Some face more extreme experiences of dehumanization, such as being "treated like animals," expected to work like "robots or machines," and subjected to physical violence. Dehumanized domestic workers are usually also ill-fed, as was the case with 29-year-old Roda, who was fed only once a day by her first employer, an Emirati. She recalled,

> When I was new, I didn't eat before I will start to work. It is right thing to do, you eat first before working so you can have energy. With her, you finished first your work before you eat. What time will I finish? It is late in the evening. You will just find water so you can survive . . . it seems like they treat me like an animal. I am not an animal.[3]

Dehumanized domestic workers like Roda are often made to work for more than 18 hours a day. Many are physically abused. Some are slapped in the face, pinched on the arm, or smacked on the head for the most minor of infractions.

Other dehumanized workers are subjected to more brutal disciplinary measures, as was the case for JoAnn, a 25-year-old single mother, who only managed to escape the extreme violence of her Egyptian employer after he accidentally left his house keys on the dining room table when he fell asleep one afternoon. I met JoAnn at the Philippine consulate in Dubai, where she was waiting to be repatriated to the Philippines.[4] JoAnn told me that she had probably had the worst experience of the hundred or so women staying at the consulate, and the others did not contest her observation.[5] Removing the scarf covering her head, she showed me her uneven haircut, which she said had been cut by her employers, and then, pointing to the visible bald spots on her head, she explained that these were caused by their repeated pulling of her hair. She told me that even after a month at the consulate, her head still hurt. Describing the violence that she had fled, JoAnn solemnly recalled:

> At first, she would slap me, bang my head against the wall, spit on my face. I tried to endure everything because it was Christmas time. I want to send something for my child. She slapped me using a flat shoe and they even burned my face with a match. They even told me that if I don't work, they would put a stick inside my private part. They were so disgusting she told me that they, the husband and wife, would even help each other to do that to me. It's true, I don't lie. . . . How many hangers has she broken against my body? If you would just see my pictures. . . . Punches, slaps, throwing my head against the wall. Then December, that's when she started hitting me with a wooden hanger, end of January 30, I escaped, 2nd or 3rd week of January was the time she started hitting me with belts but the hanger still continued. The slaps, spitting on my face continued.

For the brutality they inflicted, JoAnn's employers were eventually punished: one received a one-month prison sentence, and the other avoided prison by paying JoAnn a *diya*[6] of 5,000 dirhams (US$1,388).[7]

⁕   ⁕   ⁕

What are we to make of the vast differences in the labor conditions for Ruthie, Joy, Roda, and JoAnn? Ruthie enjoyed relative respect and decent living conditions, while Joy was strictly limited by her employer's overbearing rules. Roda and JoAnn each lived under abusively controlling employers whose behaviors threatened the women's well-being. As domestic workers in the UAE, they were all subject to the *kafala*, meaning sponsorship system, under which they were required to work solely for their employer-sponsor, as a live-in worker, for the duration of their contract, which in the UAE is typically one year for foreign employers and two years for local employers, i.e., Emirati. By legally binding them to their employer-sponsor, the *kafala* ultimately subjects domestic workers to the arbitrary authority of the employers. This authority is what explains the different experiences of domestic workers from one household to another. Under the *kafala*, employers are the primary assessors and administrators of the law. In other words, the "employer's word is virtually law"[8] in their households. This remains the case despite the recent implementation of domestic worker laws across the region.[9]

Under the *kafala*, domestic workers are the legal responsibility of their employer. As such, they must secure the consent of their employer to transfer or to quit their job. In other words, they lack the right to freely participate in the labor market, as they are legally bound in servitude to their *kafeel*, or sponsor.[10] This suggests that domestic workers are in fact denied freedom, given that they lack the liberty to "determine [their] course of action or way of life."[11] As the official "sponsors" or "patrons" of their domestic workers, employers ultimately have the power to determine their fate and, if they wish, terminate their membership in UAE society. Employers can fire and deport them at will. Magnifying the servitude of domestic workers, employers can also, conversely, keep them from leaving the country by withholding the extension of an exit visa. Finally, absconding, which is defined as leaving one's job without permission, is considered a crime and is punishable by incarceration and deportation, even for domestic workers who are dissatisfied or abused at work.

How do the domestic workers themselves see their relationship of inequality with employers? For the most part, they are aware of the absolute power of employers not only to deport them but also to determine their labor conditions. At the same time, the domestic workers are complicit in this inequality, accepting whatever their situation is as the fate, or luck, that they have brought on themselves by choosing to work within this system. Josie, a 45-year-old domestic worker in the UAE who previously worked in the Kingdom of Saudi Arabia (KSA), Malaysia, and Hong Kong, noted: "It is really luck of the draw when it comes to getting a good employer. I can't help but feel sorry for some who you know are getting maltreated by their employer." Her sentiments were echoed by 28-year-old Jovie, a domestic worker previously employed in Lebanon and Kuwait, who said: "It is really just luck that determines your fate." However, it is not in fact luck that determines the fate of domestic workers. Rather, it is the arbitrary authority of employers under the *kafala* that subjects them to inconsistent labor standards and thereby renders them vulnerable to abuse. All domestic workers, including Ruthie, are subject to this vulnerability, as a sudden change in attitude by their employers can easily shift their terms of employment.

Variations in labor conditions across households in the UAE indicate that employers respond differently to their sponsorship and patronage of domestic workers. Given these differences, can we uniformly describe domestic workers as unfree? The vast differences in labor conditions among the 750,000[12] estimated domestic workers in the UAE speak of an absence of labor standards. This absence does not come from a lack of labor protection, which, although minimal, does exist.[13] Employers may not, for instance, withhold the salaries of their domestic workers. Nor may they physically harm them, and if they can be proven to have done so, it can land them in prison. However, under the *kafala,* employers do have arbitrary authority over the domestic workers in their employ, which is a condition that renders the domestic workers unfree in that it leaves them vulnerable to interference and restraint. This interference and restraint include the denial of adequate food, as experienced by Roda; the refusal to allow a change in jobs, as confronted by Joy; and subjection to bodily and emotional harm, as realized by JoAnn. However, it is not this actual interference and restraint that makes migrant domestic workers unfree, but rather the fact that the workers are left vulnerable to the possibility of its occurrence.[14]

Advancing this argument does not mean dismissing the very real and devastating consequences of abuse suffered by domestic workers. It does allow us to recognize that not all employers act on their ability to abuse, and to call into question the dominant claims that abuse of domestic workers in the region is near universal.[15] In other words, we can acknowledge that the *kafala* system need not result in the mistreatment of domestic workers while emphasizing that it facilitates abuse and that that must be mitigated. But how do we recognize the severe inequality that grants employers arbitrary power over their domestic workers while at the same time acknowledging the different ways they have responded to this power? Key to addressing this question is an understanding of freedom and unfreedom.

Unfree is an ethnographic exploration of the conditions of migrant domestic work in the UAE.[16] Relying primarily on in-depth interviews with 85 Filipina domestic workers and 35 employers in the UAE, as well as participant observation of government-required pre-departure orientation seminars for domestic workers in the Philippines, the book focuses on the experiences of migrants from the Philippines, as they comprise one of the largest constituencies of domestic workers in the UAE.[17] The book examines and explains the emergence of a wide range of labor experiences as an approach to addressing the question: *What is unfree labor?*

What is Free and Unfree Labor?

To be legally bound to one's sponsor is a status not exclusive to domestic workers in the UAE or other Gulf Cooperation Council countries, including Bahrain, the KSA, Kuwait, Oman, and Qatar;[18] in fact, it is shared by domestic workers in almost all other destinations, including Hong Kong, Israel, Lebanon, Malaysia,

Taiwan, and Singapore.[19] Numerous studies have accordingly paid attention to the "unfree labor" of migrant domestic workers and illustrated different ways in which their constrained legal status adversely affects their labor.[20] Most studies abide by a theoretical framework of freedom that foregrounds individualism, following either Marxian[21] or liberal understandings of freedom,[22] which are perspectives that advance the argument that the legal status of migrant domestic workers corresponds to human trafficking, forced labor, or slavery. Both of these understandings ultimately see freedom as the achievement of autonomy, though this utopian view can be argued to be impossible in a "complex society" where one must be accountable not only to oneself but also to others.[23]

In what follows I look at each of these theorizations of freedom in turn, culminating in an examination of the republican theory of freedom, which I have found to be the most appropriate and useful for my analysis in this book. It also entails an analysis of the mechanisms that mitigate and work against the unfreedom to which the domestic workers are exposed. A republican notion of freedom foregrounds societal membership over individualism and sees freedom as something that is achieved through non-domination, or the inability to dominate others.[24] In the case of domestic workers in the UAE, this conception of freedom sees as its goal the reduction of the arbitrary authority of employers.

It is crucial to note that refusing the categorization of the status of migrant domestic workers as human trafficking, forced labor, or slavery only means that a much more nuanced understanding of the unfreedom of migrant domestic workers is required. The question is: What does that unfreedom look like? How is it experienced? How can it be addressed? The analysis in this book uses the categories of dehumanization, infantilization, and recognition of migrant domestic workers as a framework for understanding their different treatments under the same system, and examines how appeals to morality can be an important counterbalance to that system. By accounting for the nuances in the experiences of migrant domestic workers and the varying forms of subjugation they confront in the course of their labor migration, this analysis makes it possible to think more clearly about relevant responses. Understanding the structure of domestic work as a relational system shows that solutions must be sought beyond the law.

Theorizations of Freedom

Social theorists and philosophers have been debating the meaning of freedom for centuries. While historical cases of "unfreedom"—such as slavery or genocide—seem to be self-evident, once we probe beyond the most severe violations and abuses of rights and try to find consensus about what freedom actually looks like, there is little agreement. Dominant discourses on the unfreedom of domestic workers generally follow Karl Marx's, John Stuart Mill's, and Robert Nozick's theorizations of freedom and unfreedom. Marx views unfreedom as the alienation of workers from their labor within particular socio-economic systems of exploitation. While Marx considers feudalism and slavery as the ultimate socio-economic systems of exploitation that result in labor alienation, that is unfreedom, he argues that in capitalism, wage workers are likewise unfree, because they remain separated from their means of production and compelled to sell their labor.[25] In contrast, Mill proffers a liberal notion of unfreedom, defining it as the inability to act without hindrance or restraint,[26] a perspective that agrees somewhat with the libertarian notion of freedom advanced by Nozick,[27] which is premised on the absence of obligation. Extending our understanding of liberal notions of freedom, Isaiah Berlin distinguishes between negative liberty, meaning freedom from interference and restraint, and positive liberty, meaning the possession of the power and resources to fulfill one's potential.[28] In the case of domestic workers, this would mean having the negative liberty to quit their job without needing the permission of their employer and the positive liberty to pursue the most rewarding job available to them. Those who adhere to these perspectives on freedom, with the exception of the positive liberty framework, conclude that the *kafala* system can only result in poor labor conditions, due to the unfreedom of workers, whether that be due to alienation or restraint.

MARX AND FREEDOM

Studies that follow Marx and his view of unfreedom describe how migrant domestic workers are embedded in socio-economic systems of exploitation that result in their alienation.[29] They underscore that workers do not control their own labor and are thereby denied social freedom.[30] This framework insists on identifying the distinct socio-economic systems underlying migrant labor in order for us to see how "people's experience of exploitation, abuse, powerlessness and restriction ranges along a continuum" under late capitalism.[31] As such studies point out, migrant domestic workers are alienated not only in the workplace but already in the process of labor migration, because it is mediated by labor recruitment agencies.[32] This makes migrant domestic workers twice removed from the means of production.[33] What further supports these arguments of alienated labor is that, in the case of migrant domestic workers from the Philippines, labor recruitment agencies determine not only the worker's employer but also their country of destination, with minimal input from the prospective migrant.[34] Scholars following Marx and his definition of unfreedom emphasize that these individuals, in order to survive, must not only enter into a wage economy but also undergo labor migration, which compounds their alienation.[35] Accordingly, migrant domestic workers are said to toil in Arab states due to "compulsion by necessity," which is an aggravated form of alienated labor, compelling them to sell their labor for survival as well as to enter into bound relations of unequal dependency with employers in the *kafala* system.[36] This compulsion is said to render them vulnerable to subpar working conditions.[37]

LIBERAL FREEDOM

Scholars writing on the unfreedom of domestic workers also adhere to the conception of freedom as negative liberty, abiding by Mill's notion of freedom as being the lack of external restraint, when they uniformly assert that interference, that is the inability of domestic workers to act without hindrance, results in some degree or type of exploitation.[38] In this definition, to be free is "not to suffer compulsion by force, coercion by threat, or manipulation by background stage setting; it is to enjoy the fact of noninterference."[39] Scholars adhering to a framework of liberal freedom would argue that migrant domestic workers under the *kafala* are made unfree by their inability to freely participate in the labor market. This interference is said to result in the greater ability of employers to maximize the labor of domestic workers.[40]

One of the first to advance this argument was the sociologist Bridget Anderson, who posited that the legal sponsorship of domestic workers by employers in England promoted a "master-slave relationship."[41] In accordance with Anderson, other scholars have illustrated how the bound status of domestic workers under the *kafala* leads to subjugation. It is assumed that the inability of domestic workers to change jobs free of direct interference, i.e., without the permission of their employer, has adverse effects on labor conditions. These scholars flatly assert that the legal dependence of domestic workers on employers under the *kafala* is nothing but a tool of oppression or a form of "structural violence" that results in human trafficking or contract slavery.[42] Abiding by the notion of freedom as being without restraint, some view domestic workers who are not bound to an employer, i.e., unauthorized workers, as free and argue, accordingly, that the absence of restraint inevitably leads to the positive liberty of improved labor conditions. They assert that illegality, in the form of the informal economy, leads to freedom and, following Marx, to less alienation and greater control of one's labor.[43]

The liberal view of unfreedom is limited, however, as it cannot explain the varying labor standards domestic workers face under the *kafala* system. This view advances an absolutist perspective that does not allow us to explain the three distinct treatments of domestic workers: as either *recognized, infantilized,* or *dehumanized.* Nor does it do much to explain how the effects of the *kafala* might be mediated by other laws, particular labor-protection laws such as those recognizing the human rights of domestic workers that have been enacted across Arab states since the passage of the International Labour Organization [ILO] Convention on Domestic Workers in 2011.[44] Another limitation of this view is its assumption of the worst intentions in employers, in spite of the fact that differences in labor experiences indicate that employers respond in a variety of ways to their arbitrary authority over domestic workers. Most do not abuse domestic workers, even though, as we have seen in JoAnn's case, some in fact do.

Based on reported cases of absconding, Philippine government officials in the UAE estimate that approximately 4 percent of domestic workers likely face severe abuse. However, the outrage elicited by this possibility dominates much of the public discourse,[45] thereby overshadowing the less brutal reality of most of the domestic work in Arab states. Mirroring this outrage, the majority of scholarship on domestic workers in the region, equating freedom with the absence of external restraint, likewise foregrounds the likelihood of abuse under the *kafala* system. This equation correlates autonomy with illegality and its absence with legality. It is commonly asserted that the absence of autonomy for migrant domestic workers under the *kafala* system invites oppression, specifically in the form of poor working conditions.[46] This framework, however, suffers from the fact that it blindly advocates the absence of any restraint as the ultimate solution: autonomy in this sense implies that any form of governance, including laws protecting domestic workers, entails interference.[47]

While scholars utilize the framework of negative liberty to establish the unfreedom of domestic workers, employers and government officials in the UAE, interestingly, turn to positive liberty to insist on the freedom of domestic workers.[48] They argue that domestic workers willingly choose to migrate and stay in the UAE for the reason that it provides them with respite from poverty in their country of origin. Unlike negative liberty, positive liberty is determined not by external restraint but by the ability of individuals to engage in self-reflection.[49] Observing a positive liberty approach, the anthropologist Saba Mahmood, in *Politics of Piety,* a groundbreaking study of cultural politics in the grassroots women's piety movement in Egypt, insists that we recognize women's adherence to patriarchal norms as determined by self-governing free agents.[50] Applying a positive liberty approach to migrant domestic workers, the assumption that they are automatically rendered unfree by their inability to quit their job prior to the end of their contract would be dismissed as overly simplistic, as that fails to recognize their autonomous decision to enter into a subordinated position of servitude, a conscious choice they made after weighing poverty in the Philippines against servitude in the UAE.

Approaching freedom from the perspective of positive liberty, or what its leading proponent, John Christman, refers to as "individual positive freedom,"[51] enables employers and government officials to argue that domestic workers in Arab states are not necessarily rendered unfree by the external restraints on their actions. Using a "positive liberty" argument against the assertion that the *kafala* leads to the enslavement of migrant domestic workers, an American employer, Maureen, argues: "I think that, if it was truly slavery, if it was really that bad, that they would not be here . . . people come from poverty, so the people that you're seeing here, who are in these domestic worker jobs or on the construction jobs, are coming from a country where they don't have anything. They have nothing. They're living in slums." Maureen's logic adheres to a positive liberty conception of freedom in that she assumes migrant workers in the UAE to be self-governing subjects who have made the conscious decision to seek employment in the UAE and, irrespective of the external constraints that restrict their labor market mobility, and of their own free will, have chosen to stay in their job, due to the rewards it brings them in the form of economic mobility.

Without question, a positive liberty framework can be applied to the situation of migrant domestic workers in Arab states and used to argue against the assertion that they are unfree, as the vast majority do consciously decide to stay in their jobs. Most choose not to quit. However, one can also argue against this framework by questioning the assertion that migrant domestic workers have the ability to make an autonomous choice, as the external restrictions imposed on them by the *kafala* system, including needing to secure the permission of their employer to leave the country or transfer jobs, limit their options. And yet we must acknowledge the ability of domestic workers to engage in "self-reflection" and recognize their decision to seek work in the UAE as belonging to their (admittedly constrained) choices.

And what if we consider that domestic workers are denied the self-autonomous decision to leave their employment? Under the positive liberty framework of freedom, we can acknowledge that migrant domestic workers in

Arab States have the autonomy to stay but are without the autonomy to leave, rendering them unfree. In the end, however, a positive liberty framework fails to account for the dynamics that determine the autonomy, or lack thereof, of migrant domestic workers. In particular, what is missing from a positive liberty framework of freedom is a consideration of the unequal relationships of power and domination that govern the *kafala* system.[52]

ARBITRARY DOMINATION: A THEORY OF REPUBLICAN FREEDOM

Offering a more productive definition of freedom and unfreedom is the political philosopher Philip Pettit, who advances a republican understanding of freedom and unfreedom, one that foregrounds societal membership over individualism.[53] In contrast to the dominant liberal view of freedom as being without interference (i.e., being able to do whatever one wants to do), Pettit defines unfreedom as susceptibility to arbitrary domination and freedom as non-domination, which is achieved through the minimization of arbitrary interference. According to Pettit, "What constitutes the power relationship is the fact that in some respect the power bearer could interfere arbitrarily, even if they are never going to do so."[54]

Domestic workers are unfree, then, not because they face restraint but because they are susceptible to it. In this scenario, unfree domestic workers face the possibility of having either unbearable or tolerable work conditions imposed on them and of being assigned either a tyrannical or a benign employer. Unfreedom in this sense is "being subject to the arbitrary power of another."[55] While unfreedom under the republican framework can result in a range of outcomes, we must realize that in that case positive experiences are not to be celebrated, as they do not in any way mitigate the continued susceptibility of domestic workers to abuse, a susceptibility that arises from the arbitrariness of their situation, which is their unfreedom. Under the *kafala*, we find that the most benign of employers could potentially unexpectedly lash out against their domestic workers.

If we view unfreedom as susceptibility to domination, then autonomy—that is, lawless autonomy—becomes an unviable solution. This libertarian solution to unfreedom,[56] i.e., freedom as consisting of complete autonomy, devoid of any accountability to a community, is, according to Karl Polanyi, impossible in a "complex society."[57] Shifting from a notion of "freedom [that] demands absence from a human community" and rejecting the freedom in the form of autonomy that is demanded by negative liberty, our solution should instead look towards the alleviation and reduction of the arbitrary domination of those in power, which according to Pettit requires the establishment of mechanisms of "antipower" through programs of regulation, protection, and empowerment.[58]

Indeed, mechanisms of antipower do exist for migrant domestic workers in the UAE, as the arbitrary domination of domestic workers by their employers is mitigated by protectionist policies instituted by sending countries such as Indonesia and the Philippines; regulatory efforts by the UAE government, such as Federal Law No. 10 of 2017 On Domestic Workers; and human rights discourses advanced by advocacy groups such as Human Rights Watch and the International Labor Organization (ILO). These mechanisms provide labor standards that employers can choose to acknowledge or not, which partially accounts for the variations in labor standards across households, as they help to suppress the ability of employers to exploit domestic workers.[59] Building on Pettit and utilizing republican notions of freedom, *Unfree* describes the ways in which migrant domestic workers in the UAE experience unfreedom. It does so both by identifying the conditions of their labor and by delineating the social processes that result in the variety of those conditions. It establishes the vulnerability of domestic workers to the arbitrary authority of employers as it enumerates the mechanisms of antipower that reduce the desire and ability of employers to act on this arbitrary authority.

Negotiating Unfreedom: Formal and Informal Mechanisms of Antipower

The diversity of their experiences in the workplace challenges any conceptual reduction of the position of domestic workers in the UAE to either slaves or trafficked victims. These domestic workers include workers both with and without a day off; those whose employers give them the leeway to take on part-time jobs in other households and those whose employers do not; those who are paid on time at the end of each month and those whose wages are withheld by employers who refuse to pay them until the end of their contract; those with a private bedroom and those without; those permitted to engage in sexual relations outside of marriage and those who are not; those given access to a mobile phone and Internet services and those who are not; those who work as little as 8 hours a day or less and those who work as much as 18 hours per day; and those who work without reprimand in contrast to those who confront extreme brutality at work, including rape, torture, and starvation. While these variations in employment conditions indicate arbitrary domination, they prevent us from using the framework of negative liberty, which reduces our understanding of unfreedom to external restraints. What these variable conditions invite instead is an exploration of the mechanisms that temper the urge or ability of employers to impose absolute power over domestic workers.

What neutralizes the ability of employers to impose arbitrary domination? According to Pettit, formal state initiatives of protection, regulation, and empowerment, what he refers to as "antipower," could diminish the susceptibility of the unfree to abuse.[60] First, he calls for the elimination of domination through the enforcement of protectionist institutions such as laws and systems (e.g. the criminal justice system). Second, he calls for the regulation of resources in politics (e.g. term limits) and economics (e.g. labor protection, the reduction of monopoly power). Lastly, he recognizes the need to empower those without resources by prioritizing "equality in basic capabilities"[61] via welfare-state initiatives. However, these formal mechanisms to combat unfreedom are potentially out of reach for domestic workers. This is because domestic work remains partially outside the domain of state initiatives due to the unregulated nature of the occupation.[62] Moreover, the nod to civil society that Pettit gives and his recognition that antipower can emerge from "informal social and political factors"[63] such as trade unions and civil liberties associations cannot easily apply to domestic workers in the UAE, where civic associations remain deeply repressed.[64]

Despite the seeming limit in the reach of formal mechanisms of antipower, however, it is still evident that there are forces mitigating the actions of employers. Our inability to reduce their actions to calculated instrumentality suggests as much. This in turn raises the question of how antipower operates informally. How does antipower extend beyond formal state initiatives? Antipower, I argue, also transpires through the moral mediation of domestic work and the existence of codes of ethics that guide individual behaviors. These codes of ethics emerge not only from the interior self of employers but also from the exterior forces of antipower enumerated by Pettit, i.e., formal state and civil society initiatives of protection, regulation, and empowerment. In the case of domestic work, these initiatives might not be enforceable policies, but they do establish ethical standards that potentially guide the behavior of employers. More explicitly, they include the labor conditions recommended by sending states and enumerated in the Standard Labor Contract signed by domestic workers and employers; the conditions established in the 2011 ILO Convention on Decent Work for Domestic Workers and the concomitant laws on domestic workers since passed across Arab states; and the labor standards recommended in reports released by advocacy groups such as Human Rights Watch. None of these standards are enforceable, but they likely translate to ethical norms on the treatment of domestic workers, encouraging a consensus that undergirds what the legal scholar Adelle Blackett refers to as the "law of the household workplace," meaning standards that emerge in the informal space of the household.[65]

Numerous examples among employers indicate that the formal mechanisms of antipower do function informally to provide them with moral guidance on the proper treatment of migrant domestic workers. Zoe, for instance, a British resident of Dubai for more than four years, explicitly referred to the guidance of sending states and the rules they have implemented for the protection of domestic workers. She reported that it was the clearer guidelines set forth by the Philippine government that made her decide to hire a domestic worker from the Philippines as opposed to Ethiopia. She noted, "You know what else I liked about having a Filipina maid is that I know that the council and the government in the Philippines make sure that they're paid correctly, and that they're looked after, and help them if anything happened." In contrast, she said that the Ethiopian government "doesn't say any minimum salary or anything like that . . . made me feel a bit uncomfortable." Guidelines set forth in civil society by nongovernmental organizations (NGOs), which are often relayed to the public via the news media, also inform employers of labor standards. As the Lebanese employer Mohammad noted:

> No, I just notice that on the news, Arabic news. Maybe not Arabic, maybe CNN. They were promoting workers' rights and so on. It's wrong if you keep her. It's creative. It shows that it's wrong to put her in a corner and make her sleep on the stairs or something like that. I don't know where I've seen that but it seems to be a campaign. It's wrong to mistreat the houseworker.

Mohammad added that domestic workers themselves are as much sources of establishing standards of employment as are NGOs, explaining that he agreed to raise the salary of his domestic worker when she informed him that he was paying her less than market rate. He relayed: "And when she moved here, she started socializing, and she found out that, she said, look according to the locals, the norm here is 1,500 [dirhams; u s $ 417]. So, I said OK, you will be treated like the others."

The question of why Mohammad is personally inclined to act morally, abide by the standards set forth by the mechanisms of antipower, and choose to diffuse his potential domination of his domestic workers, is notably beyond the scope of this study: I am unable to explain why individual employers are moral, immoral, or amoral. In some cases, as the Canadian employer Maureen (a different Maureen) noted, it could be that certain cultures are oblivious to their ill-treatment of domestic workers;[66] in other cases, employers do what they believe is "ethical;" and in yet other cases, it is the mere fear of reproach from others in the community that keeps employers in check because, as the Emirati employer Ali said, people "would talk." Finally, the recognition of market demand could also discourage employers from mistreating their domestic workers. As Ali explained it, one thing that potentially dissuades employers from behaving badly is their market dependence on the services of domestic workers:

> I am not going to say it's perfect here. I think the maid are treating the family the way we treat them you know. By the end of the day, you look at the majority. *The majority of the maid, if they have a problem with the people over here in the UAE, they have their embassy over here. They will report us. They wouldn't come anymore.* But look around you, I mean seriously, there are some areas in Dubai if you go you will think it's Manila. Seriously, because they are full of Filipino. Like Satwa, some areas of Discovery Garden, it's just full of Filipinos. 'Cause they enjoy it here, they are making good money, they have a good time, they're safe. I mean seriously, I have Filipinos friends and they tell me how safe it is here because back home in Manila it's dangerous. (emphasis added)

Regardless of motivation, it is difficult to deny that morals can potentially serve as informal mechanisms of antipower and that formal mechanisms of antipower, such as those enumerated by Pettit, can also provide a benchmark for informal moral standards.[67]

The Moral Mediation of Domestic Work

How do mechanisms of antipower informally take effect on the ground? Turning to economic sociology allows us to see how morals operate as a force of antipower and potentially mediate social interactions between domestic workers and their employers. Domestic work arguably encompasses what is called a "moralized market," meaning that it is an "explicitly moral project" that is simultaneously guided by rationalism and justice.[68] In other words, both the desire to treat others in society with decency, i.e., justice, and the desire to maximize labor, i.e., rationalism, could simultaneously motivate employers. This could be the case even in such a context of severe inequality as the *kafala* system.[69] Other scholars disagree, as they see the inequality of the *kafala* as inviting rationalism alone.[70] The *kafala*, they argue, is nothing but a tool of oppression, one that strips workers of the ability to directly resist or confront authority.[71] For this reason, the *kafala* is said to be a form of "structural violence."[72] Yet this framework, which views domestic work as a structure and not a relation, cannot explain why the *kafala* has not resulted in the universal abuse of domestic workers.

While foregrounding the arbitrary authority of employers, *Unfree* shifts from the assumption that migrant domestic work is a form of structural violence, recognizing it instead as a social relation of asymmetric interdependence. Seeing domestic work as a relation and not a structure allows us not only to acknowledge the different responses of employers to their power but also to recognize the ability of domestic workers to engage in direct negotiation with employers. This assertion questions a longstanding argument extended by the noted political scientist James Scott, who asserts that members of subordinate groups, such as domestic workers, would "avoid any direct confrontation with authority," more likely engaging in informal acts of resistance instead.[73] He argues that "relatively powerless groups" would resist by engaging in "foot dragging, dissimulation, false compliance, pilfering, feigned ignorance, slander, arson, sabotage and so forth," acts that "require little or no coordination or planning."[74]

Examining domestic work as a relation and not a structure allows us to account for the emergence of varied labor conditions across households in the UAE. Indeed, the question of how social relations produce varied economic outcomes is a key question among economic sociologists[75] yet is minimally engaged by labor scholars,[76] who instead focus on how economic life overdetermines social relations to produce inequality and exploitation[77] or how social relations of, for instance, race, class, and gender position workers as either exploited by cultural and structural processes or empowered to undermine employers via subtle forms of subversion.[78] Due to the pervasive assumption that economic relations overdetermine social relations in labor experiences,[79] minimal attention has been given to the ways in which social relations structure employment conditions.[80]

Foregrounding domestic work as a social relation questions a prevailing narrative in the literature: the existence of a pervasive and universal culture of employment in domestic work.[81] In the UAE, it is said to be one of dehumanization or, as argued in the literature, "structural violence," "slavery," and "labor trafficking."[82] In contrast, the view of domestic work as a social relation allows us to see how its negotiation can lead to myriad cultures of employment, in other words varied economic relations, across households. It helps us understand how various employers can either dehumanize, infantilize, or recognize the humanity of domestic workers.

Employers and domestic workers engage in what Viviana Zelizer refers to as "relational work," meaning the continuous negotiation of the interpersonal relations that constitute economic activity. In relational work, "economic transactions are fundamentally social interactions."[83] However, in agreement with James Scott, many scholars would argue that asymmetrical relations of power and inequality in domestic work would hinder or even prevent relational work.[84] Yet relational work is not necessarily a negotiation between two equals.[85] A relational work framework allows us to see how economic conditions for domestic workers may vary across households depending on the contours of the social relations between employers and employees, i.e., how each party perceives the meanings of their relationship, transactions, and media of exchange, and how they accordingly negotiate them.

Conceiving of domestic work in the *kafala* system as a relationship that is constituted by continuous relational work between employers and domestic workers forces us to investigate how morals inform unfree labor and how the conditions of unfree labor reflect "continuously negotiated meaningful interpersonal relations."[86] It also allows us to realize that in the context of their severely unequal relationship, domestic workers can mobilize the morality of their employers and engage in direct negotiation. When negotiating with employers, domestic workers are not necessarily seeking to upend their unequal relationship with employers, but merely improve their labor conditions. They do so through acts of moral claims-making, which might include requests for a raise, a day off, access to communication, and sufficient food. Validating these acts of claims-making is the circulation of multiple moral discourses on "fair" standards of employment for domestic workers that are produced by various stakeholders, including sending and receiving states, intergovernmental agencies such as the ILO, and migrant advocacy groups including Human Rights Watch. In other words, the formal mechanisms of antipower lend validity to the efforts of domestic workers to engage in relational work and put forward acts of moral claims-making in the workplace.[87]

In a way that contests the assumption that the *kafala* is nothing but a "destructive market,"[88] the relations cultivated by domestic workers and employers mediate their economic transaction. Z, an expat in a German-Indian household, reported:

> From my personal experience, I have always seen maids being treated very well. They are paid to do a job, and, as long as they are doing their job properly, they are treated well. They are left alone. They can do what they want, pretty much.

But I have heard stories of maids being abused. . . . I have never known anyone who has treated their maid badly.

While acknowledging that the arbitrary authority of employers in the *kafala* system allows employers to abuse domestic workers, Z insisted that most do not, suggesting that an underlying moral principle of "treating others well" informs the market transactions between domestic workers and employers. Indeed, employers, including Kat, a newcomer from the United Kingdom, claimed to maintain employment standards that aligned with their morals; Kat treats her domestic workers according to how she "hopes to be treated" and in a way that sets a good example for her young daughter, or, as she noted, "for Hazel to watch us behave ethically with someone." Gendered morals and the desire to protect female domesticity also shape the rules and regulations imposed by employers on domestic workers. This was the case for the Lebanese employer Mohammad, who explained why he hesitated to extend a day off: "I have one concern because her parents trust us as being her local family. And if she goes wrong route, I think ethically we should have played a role, supporting role, preventing things."

In insisting on the moral mediation of domestic work, I do not assume a normative notion of morals or claim that their mere existence implies fairness and egalitarianism. I recognize that while moral discourses, as sources of antipower, may mitigate the conditions of unfreedom, they also, as sources of power, have the potential to aggravate those conditions.[89] We should acknowledge the existence of moral, amoral, and immoral employers. Moral employers are those most likely to mitigate relations of inequality in domestic work. Amoral ones are those whose behavior is neutral with respect to those relations. And immoral employers are those who are likely to aggravate them. Futhermore, the principles guiding the actions of employers may be not primarily principles of humanitarianism but principles instead of instrumentalism, not of egalitarianism but of racism or sexism, and not of migrant inclusion but of exclusion.

Unfree seeks to show how employment standards in domestic work result not solely from arbitrary domination but also from moral mediation. The presence or absence of morals among employers can explain the various interpersonal relations of dehumanization, infantilization, and recognition that we find in unfree relations of domestic work. However, there are limits to the negotiating power extended by moral mediation, as it does not upset the asymmetric relationship established by the *kafala* system and thereby fails to question the arbitrary authority of employers. As employers continue to assess and administer the norms and rules in their households, they have the power to reject or retaliate against acts of claims-making extended by domestic workers. Indeed, this is likely to occur in the case of dehumanized domestic workers, who are those most in need of negotiating for better work conditions. This limit to direct negotiation and the mobilization of morality is in fact acknowledged by the Philippine government, which warns domestic workers bound for Arab states of the high likelihood that they will be raped upon migration. This looming threat of domination confirms that domestic workers are unfree.

From Ideas to People: Who Are Domestic Workers?

Migrant domestic workers in Arab states are some of the most vulnerable to human trafficking across the globe.[90] For this reason, they are considered a "hard-to-reach population" that can only be accessed via convenience sampling.[91] This study defies this assumption, drawing from interviews with a diverse range of domestic workers, including those without a day off; interviews with employers, including the elusive group of local Emiratis; and interviews with government officials and migrant brokers in the UAE and the Philippines. Enhancing these interviews was participant observation conducted in government-mandated pre-departure orientation seminars in the Philippines, as well as surveys conducted with outgoing migrants and return migrants in the Philippines and content analysis of media reports on migrant domestic workers in the UAE.

Migrant Filipino domestic workers in the UAE include Christians and Muslims whose hometowns represent a wide range of provinces, extending from the northern tip to the southern tip of the Philippines. Regardless of their region of origin, they tend to be poorer than their counterparts in other destinations, who have been described as educated and of the middle class.[92] In contrast, those working in the UAE generally come from poor, rural areas of the Philippines. They come from farming or fishing villages with stagnant economies and few wage-labor opportunities. They come from areas with poor infrastructures, including limited telecommunication towers, intermittent electricity, weak labor markets, and undeveloped roads. Prior to migration, most resided in wooden homes or nipa huts with thatched roofs, with no access to either running water or electricity.

They learn of the opportunity to migrate not necessarily from friends or family but instead from recruiters deployed to remote provinces by agencies that facilitate their migration. Yet they do not go abroad wearing blinders. The high risk of abuse that they will face is not unknown to them, because they likely hear of it not only through news reports but also in the compulsory pre-departure orientation seminars. Yet they choose to ignore and overcome the

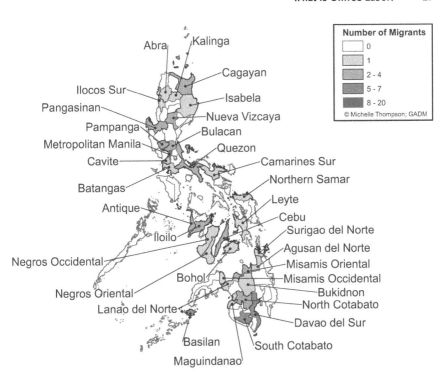

Number of Migrants	
☐	0
▨	1
▨	2 - 4
▨	5 - 7
▨	8 - 20
© Michelle Thompson; GADM	

Abra   Kalinga

Cagayan

Ilocos Sur   Isabela

Pangasinan

Nueva Vizcaya

Pampanga   Bulacan

Metropolitan Manila   Quezon

Cavite   Camarines Sur

Northern Samar

Batangas

Antique   Leyte

Cebu

Iloilo   Surigao del Norte

Agusan del Norte

Negros Occidental   Misamis Oriental

Bohol   Misamis Occidental

Negros Oriental   Bukidnon

Lanao del Norte   North Cotabato

Davao del Sur

Basilan   South Cotabato

Maguindanao

Map 1 Regions of Origin in the Philippines for Migrant Worker Interviewees in the UAE. SOURCE: Michelle C. Thompson.

fears elicited by such news and push forward with their migration. This for instance was the case for 30-year-old Roxanne, who still opted to migrate to the UAE despite learning of the likelihood that she would encounter some form of physical abuse. She explained: "At first, I want to back out, because I want to back out at first, because of what I heard. But I told myself that I know God has a plan, I told God give me a sign if I will back out or I will go. Give me a sign I told God. I prayed give me sign. If I am pregnant, I'm not go, if not this is your will to go." Why do women such as Roxanne suppress their fears of migration? Their disenfranchisement in the Philippines partially explains their determination to migrate. Lack of access to viable employment and the inability to avail themselves of government welfare, such as public schooling for their children or medical care, help to motivate their migration.

Many of the women I met in the UAE were young mothers who had struggled in the Philippines to find the means to raise their children.[93] Many had no access to the wage economy. To secure work, they would have had to relocate to the city and pursue employment opportunities in the informal sector, earning below-poverty wages as street peddlers or domestic workers. A handful had even started domestic work in their adolescence, the youngest starting at the age of ten, but most began as young adults with children to support. This included 37-year-old Lynn, who left her rural village for the small city of Taguegarao in the northeast province of Cagayan Village, where she found work as a laundrywoman (*laban-dera*). She earned significantly less than the recommended daily minimum wage of 350 pesos (US$7), taking home only 250 pesos a day (US$5).[94] Yet Lynn would have fared worse if she had stayed in her farming village, as she would have had no income, barely eking out a living selling vegetables.

As most domestic workers in the UAE had not completed high school, they were often limited to the informal wage economy prior to migration, as domestic workers, street peddlers, or agricultural workers. A very few had managed to attend college.[95] Those who had done so usually managed it through a scholarship or the sponsorship of a benefactor. This was the case for Manuella, a former laundrywoman whose college education was paid for by an employer who had impregnated her. In the Philippines, however, as Manuella learned, even a college degree does not get one very far without the right networks. Someone like her, whose benefactor passed away not long after she completed her education, would still struggle to make ends meet. Even if she were to secure a job, it would be unlikely as a regularized worker who could avail herself of government benefits in the Philippines, such as retirement and health care benefits. Instead, she would likely have become an unregularized, or contingent, worker in a factory or department store, as was the case for her counterparts who had completed some years of college. But in fact, Manuella could not find any job in the wage-labor market at all, not even as a contingent worker, due to the stagnant economy in her rural community. To survive, she resorted to selling cooked foods, like grilled hot dogs and bananas on a stick.

Understanding the experiences of domestic workers in Arab states requires that we consider their disenfranchisement and impoverishment prior to migration. This makes it clear that they represent the working poor, unlike the better-educated migrant domestic workers with capital, including the education needed to access higher-paying destinations such as Israel, Hong Kong, Taiwan, and Canada.[96] The absence of this constituency of migrant workers in the literature on women's labor migration speaks of the relative lack of research on south-to-south as opposed to south-to-north migration flows, even though the former constitutes a larger flow than the latter. There are now 90.2 million international migrants born in developing countries residing in the Global South, compared to 85.3 million in the Global North.[97] Their absence in the literature also speaks to the skewed focus of Philippine migration research, as migrant experiences in Arab states remain the least represented in the literature even though the vast majority of Filipino migrant workers are employed in that region.[98] Unlike their counterparts in other countries, Filipina migrant domestic workers in Arab states usually face two constrained choices in life: the unfreedom of poverty in the Philippines, or the unfreedom of indenture in Arab states. They choose the latter for its promise of financial mobility, despite the high risks of abuse.

Outline of the Book

This study establishes the absence of labor standards for domestic workers across households in the UAE, making it clear that this absence emerges from the arbitrary authority that the *kafala* grants employers vis-à-vis domestic workers. It is an authority that leaves domestic workers susceptible to abuse, which, according to republican notions of freedom, renders them unfree. *Unfree* illustrates how morals mediate and thereby mitigate this susceptibility to abuse; in so doing, it diverges from the more absolutist perspective on the unfree labor of domestic workers advanced by previous studies that subscribe to a liberal view of freedom and reductively equate our understanding of domestic workers' experiences to slavery, human trafficking, or forced labor.

Chapter 1 begins with an examination of the governance of migrant domestic workers by the receiving state of the UAE. It establishes the legal infantilization, and thereby unfreedom, of domestic workers under the *kafala* system. This occurs in two ways: first, workers are denied the independence of freely entering the labor market without the permission of their employer, and second, they are made the legal responsibility of their employer.

In chapter 2, the discussion then shifts to the role of the Philippine state, asking how it manages the migration of its citizens to enter highly vulnerable occupations without adequate labor protection. This chapter establishes that the Philippine state seeks to protect migrant domestic workers, while promoting their migration, by creating aspirational labor standards, seeing to the enforcement of these standards with the assistance of private recruitment agencies, empowering migrant workers by educating them about these standards prior to migration, and encouraging them to directly negotiate with their employers towards the recognition of these standards.

In chapters 3 and 4, I describe the labor conditions of domestic workers. While domestic work can be measured in a variety of ways, including the day off, workload, salary, food consumption, and freedom of communication such as access to the Internet, chapter 3 compares labor conditions across households specifically through a discussion of food consumption. Illustrating the different treatments of domestic workers, it establishes their recognition when given sufficient access to their preferred foods, infantilization when not given a choice about which foods they can consume, and dehumanization when allotted inadequate food provisions.

Chapter 4 then engages the question of what happens when employers reject the efforts of domestic workers to improve their labor conditions. This chapter enumerates the extreme vulnerabilities of domestic workers under the *kafala* system and describes the labor conditions of those who are unable to negotiate for "fair" working conditions. It focuses specifically on the plight of domestic workers who run away.

Chapter 5 explores the following questions: Why, given the risks, do domestic workers ultimately migrate to Arab states? What are their goals and aspirations? Do they achieve these goals? In other words, what forms of mobility does labor migration to Arab states provide? To address these questions, I turn to describing their "mobility pathways," meaning the socio-economic and geographic trajectories of their migration. This chapter illustrates the unlikelihood that domestic workers will ever escape the unfreedom of poverty that initially motivated their migration, making it clear that their labor migration is ultimately a story of immobility.

CHAPTER 1

Legal Infantilization and the Unfreedom of Servitude

ON JULY 21, 2018, Sondos Al Qattan, a Kuwaiti social media influencer with 2.1 million Instagram followers, posted a vlog vowing never to hire a Filipino domestic worker again.[1] Complaining about the new memorandum of understanding between Kuwait and the Philippines signed on May 11, 2018, she ranted in the since-deleted vlog:

> How can you have a servant in your house who gets to keep their passport with them? If they ran away and went back to their country, who'll refund me? I disagree with the law. And what's worse is they even have a day off every week! Honestly, this new law and these new contracts means I don't wish to hire a Filipina. She goes out one day a week and works for six days, which brings her total days off to four per month and we have no clue what happens during those four days when her passport is in her possession.

Qattan's dismay appears to stem largely from her view of the vulnerability that the memorandum imposes on employers. From her perspective, the memorandum[2] threatens the *kafala* system and weakens her position as a *kafeel* (sponsor),[3] as it prohibits her from keeping her domestic worker's passport in her possession and forces her to abide by the terms of Kuwait's new law on the employment of domestic workers,[4] which includes the recognition of a domestic worker's "right to a paid weekly break."[5] According to Qattan, a domestic worker who kept possession of their own passport would be able to quit their job easily and return home to their country of origin, putting employers like her at risk of losing the upwards of US$3000 that they pay a recruitment agency for the guaranteed two-year placement of a domestic worker in their home. This prompts her to ask "who'll refund me?"

Qattan triggered a public outcry among Filipino netizens who see the withholding of the passport and the denial of a day off as akin to modern-day slavery.[6] Other Arabs agreed, including the former Miss Lebanon, Nadine Wilson Njeim, who commented: "I feel it's very irresponsible of her to say what she said. You need to think twice before you post something because it's not your salon and you're not talking to your family. That's not restricting freedom of speech, but you're talking about enslavement. This is not me telling you not to say what you think, or some question of democracy. You're advertising modern day slavery—how can anyone be OK with that?"[7] Yet Qattan insisted that neither the withholding of her domestic worker's passport nor the prohibition of a day off concerned "humanity or human rights because I did not deprive the employee of her salary or beat her." She added, in a follow-up statement, "I have not on any circumstances in the present or the past have mistreated, degraded or in any way mistreated an employee . . . I consider all employees as equal human being with equal rights to that is of mine."[8]

Curiously, Qattan's popularity did not wane following her admission that she not only withheld her domestic worker's passport but also knowingly ignored Kuwaiti law and its stipulation of a rest day in the employment contract of domestic workers.[9] If Qattan experienced a backlash, it was short-lived. While several of her sponsors, including MAC and Max Factor, revoked their deals with her,[10] she later secured endorsements from other big-name brands, including Boots and Christian Dior, while releasing her own line of scents and eyelashes as part of the Sondos Collection. Within a few months, it was back to business for Qattan, who saw the number of her Instagram followers increase to 2.6 million.

We can speculate that the reason the public outrage over her vlog, even from other social media influencers in the region,[11] was short-lived was that it did not reflect the dominant sentiment.[12] In a qualitative study of 73 employers in Kuwait, the ILO found that many absolutely believed that they should withhold their domestic workers' passports and determine their labor conditions, including the provision of a day off.[13] Supporting these sentiments are the findings from a larger survey of local sentiment on *kafala* reform in Qatar. In a survey of more than 2,300 Qatari nationals on the 2016 reform of the *kafala*, the majority of respondents disapproved of migrant workers having greater control over their jobs. Moreover, 88 percent opposed the reform for the reason that it lessened the dependency of foreign workers on their employers.[14]

Qattan's vlog, and the debate it elicited over whether or not the absence of a day off signals modern-day slavery, raises a larger question concerning the complex legal system of the *kafala* that simultaneously engenders and restrains the arbitrary authority of employers. Her actions confirm the arbitrary authority of employers, including their ability to ignore labor contract stipulations with minimal penalties. At the same time, her vlog attests to the potential threat to her authority posed by the memorandum of understanding between Kuwait and the Philippines, as a mechanism of antipower.

What are the conditions that bolster the arbitrary authority of employers over domestic workers? What are the conditions that challenge this authority? The controversy over Qattan's vlog offers a springboard for examining the legal system that renders domestic workers unfree in the *kafala* system. This controversy foregrounds the legal paradox that confronts employers: while the *kafala* grants them arbitrary authority over domestic workers, various mechanisms of antipower diminish that same authority. These mechanisms include labor protectionist laws such as Law No. 68 of 2015 on Employment of Domestic Workers in Kuwait and Federal Law No. 10 of 2017 on Domestic Workers in the UAE, as well as memoranda of understanding on migrant domestic work between sending and receiving states. Drawing from interviews with a diverse group of 35 employers in the UAE, this chapter, using a discussion of the day off, describes the various ways that morals, and the interplay of rationalism and justice, determine how employers navigate the *kafala* system. It shows the dehumanization of domestic workers who are denied a day off by employers, the infantilization of those restricted to chaperoned excursions, and the recognition of those regularly granted a normal day off.

The Legal Infantilization of Domestic Workers

There are approximately 11.5 million migrant domestic workers across the globe, with the majority—8.45 million—being women.[15] The largest share, 27.4 percent, work in Arab states, followed by 20 percent in Europe and 19.4 percent in Southeast Asia and the Pacific.[16] In Arab states, the vast majority of migrant women—60 percent—are in fact domestic workers.[17] Most migrant domestic workers in Arab states come from Southeast Asia, specifically Indonesia and the Philippines,[18] but there are also sizable numbers from South Asia[19] and Africa.[20] Of the estimated 3.1 million migrant domestic workers in the region, the largest number can be found in the KSA, estimated at nearly one million, followed by an estimated 750,000 in the UAE, 620,000 in Kuwait, 250,000 in Lebanon, and 100,000 in Bahrain.[21]

Across Arab states, the *kafala* generally establishes the terms of legal residency for migrant domestic workers as well as centrally governs the dynamics of their relationships with employers. The *kafala* system makes domestic workers into mere visitors in their country of employment, who are only allowed to stay for the duration of their sponsored employment. They do not qualify for permanent residency (this is also true for migrant domestic workers across the globe, except in Canada and Italy).[22] Continuous employment with a sponsor does allow domestic workers to stay indefinitely, which is not the case in destination countries such as Israel, which has capped the residency of migrant domestic workers at 63 months, or Taiwan, which currently limits residency to 12 years.[23]

The word *kafala* derives from the Arabic *Ka Fa La,* which means "guardian, vouch for, or take responsibility for."[24] The *kafala* is technically a sponsorship system that assigns full legal responsibility for a foreign worker to their sponsor, who in the case of domestic work is the employer. This means that any legal violation, including crimes committed by a foreign worker, is the responsibility of the employer. To enable them to manage that responsibility, the *kafala* gives employers authority over domestic workers. And yet this responsibility also comes with its own set of pressures for employers, indicating that the *kafala* does not impose burdens only on domestic workers, as documented by other scholars.[25] The abdication of state responsibility for the labor conditions of domestic workers, as observed by the geographers Brenda Yeoh and Shirlena Huang in their analysis of the sponsorship system for domestic workers in Singapore, constitutes domestic work as a private household responsibility.[26] This responsibility, we could argue, places undue burdens on employers, one such burden being the potential punishment that employers face when domestic workers abscond, that is flee from their employment without permission. In the UAE, the government can fine employers of domestic workers who abscond up to 10,000 dirhams (US$2,778) if they fail to alert authorities. Employers can also be penalized if the domestic worker under their sponsorship is found to be working for another employer. Finally, as already noted, employers are liable for the crimes of the domestic workers that they sponsor.

Despite the constraints that the *kafala* imposes on employers, this legal system undeniably works much more to their benefit than to the benefit of the domestic workers. It gives the employers power over the domestic workers. As the British employer Matt observed, "there is an undercurrent in this country with everybody who works here and it doesn't really matter what level you work at. The same undercurrent remains that you are on someone else's visa." Matt admitted that he uses this power to his advantage, as he arbitrarily changes, and even cancels, his domestic worker's weekly day off whenever it suits him. The *kafala* also results in the legal infantilization of domestic workers, whose terms of membership in the UAE and other Arab states constitute them as mere household dependents of the employer rather than as independent workers. In Arab states, then, domestic workers are legally infantilized in two ways: first, they are denied the independence of freely entering the labor market without the permission of their employer, and second, they are made into that employer's legal responsibility.

The legal infantilization of domestic workers is not exclusive to Arab states. They share this legal status with migrant domestic workers across the globe. As Jolovan Wham, the former director of the domestic worker advocacy group H.O.M.E. (Humanitarian Organization for Migration Economics) in Singapore, mentioned in an interview, "We have our own *kafala* system here in Singapore." In almost all other destinations, the legal residency of migrant domestic workers is likewise contingent on their continuous live-in employment with their one sponsor. Like their counterparts in Arab states, migrant domestic workers in other destinations are restricted from terminating or transferring jobs. In Singapore, for example, they must secure the permission of their employer to transfer jobs; in Denmark, au pairs can only change employers twice;[27] in Canada, qualifying for permanent residency historically required the completion of two continuous years of live-in employment for one household in a four-year period;[28] in Israel, domestic workers can only transfer jobs thrice within their first five years of employment and must remain with one employer after those first five years of residency in order to avoid deportation;[29] in Taiwan, domestic workers do not qualify to transfer jobs unless the state deems their employer no longer fit to employ them;[30] and in Hong Kong, they must secure a new employer within two weeks of the termination of their last employment.[31] Only Italy allows migrant domestic workers to work for multiple employers.[32]

The conditions of legal infantilization are however different in important ways from one destination to another; in the case of Arab states, the infantilization is aggravated by the legal culpability of employers for the actions of domestic workers. This culpability places undue pressure on employers to discipline and monitor domestic workers, which likely contributes to the employers intensifying their control over the workers. This may be what we see in the actions of the now infamous social media influencer Qattan. While her actions may be motivated by nothing more than the rational urge to maximize the labor of domestic workers, we should acknowledge that the desire to mitigate her legal culpability might also influence her decision to deny her domestic workers a day off. This possibility is suggested by the concern she expresses when she states: "we have no clue what happens during those four days when her passport is in her possession."

State Protection of Domestic Workers

The *kafala* undeniably leaves migrant workers vulnerable to abusive work conditions. In response to mounting criticisms and pressures from human rights advocates concerning the vulnerabilities entailed by the *kafala*, various Arab states have revisited this legal system.[33] However, domestic workers remain exempt from existing reforms. While migrant workers in construction, retail, hospitality, and transportation can now claim some limited rights with respect to mobility in the labor market, domestic workers have gained no such ground.[34]

The exclusion of domestic workers from *kafala* reform does not mean that Arab states have failed to implement any protective measures to assuage the workplace vulnerabilities of these workers. The passage of the Decent Work for Domestic Workers Convention by the ILO in 2011 put pressure on the states to create protections, and they have accordingly attempted to establish minimum standards of employment and create a system for monitoring and reducing the risk of abuse in domestic work. They have implemented these protective measures in three central ways: first, through the passage of domestic worker laws; second, by cooperating with sending states in establishing standards of employment through memoranda of understanding; and third, by taking an active role in the management of migration. However, the *kafala* remains intact, thereby maintaining the arbitrary authority of employers over domestic workers and limiting the extent to which these various protective measures, i.e., formal mechanisms of antipower, can mitigate workplace abuse.

Domestic Worker Laws

Since the passage in 2011 of the ILO Decent Work for Domestic Workers Convention, countries in the region have passed national legislation on domestic work. In some countries, the regulation of domestic work in fact predated this convention. This is the case for Jordan and Lebanon.[35] Most other countries did not implement rules and regulations for domestic work until after the passage of the convention. However, the extent to which these laws establish minimum employment standards is put into question by the continued existence of the *kafala* system.

Across the region, the newly established domestic worker laws still give tremendous leeway to employers in determining labor standards.[36] For example, none of them imposes a minimum wage. In the case of the UAE, the 2017 Domestic Worker Law allows employers to establish the terms of employment, including the monthly salary, but grants domestic workers the right to 12 hours of rest daily, of which there must be 8 continuous hours; payment no later than 10 days after the completion of their work every month; 30 days of annual vacation; and 30 days of sick leave per annum.[37] However, the implementation of these labor regulations remains vague, making it easy for employers to ignore these standards of employment.

Memoranda of Understanding

Adding to the protection of migrant domestic workers are agreements initiated by sending countries for the purpose of instituting minimum standards of employment. This is usually accomplished through a memorandum of understanding as well as through a Standard Labor Contract. Typically enumerated in these agreements are minimum labor standards, including the provision of a minimum monthly wage, medical benefits, daily rest hours, weekly rest days, adequate accommodations, and paid vacations. The Philippines recently signed a memorandum of understanding that includes a Protocol on Domestic Workers with Kuwait in 2018, the UAE in 2017, and the KSA in 2013.

Yet the receiving countries are not necessarily spontaneously willing to agree to a memorandum of understanding or to uphold the terms of the Standard Labor Contract. Instead, sending countries such as the Philippines must compel them to do so, which they usually accomplish by taking drastic measures, such as imposing a complete ban on the migration of domestic workers.[38] In the case of the UAE, the Philippines had to threaten and then actually impose a ban to protect migrant domestic workers. In June 2014, the Philippines curtailed the migration of domestic workers to the UAE in response to the introduction of a unified contract for domestic workers by the UAE's Ministry of the Interior and the UAE's nullification of the Philippines' Standard Labor Contract.

In order to ensure that the conditions of employment for domestic workers met certain minimum standards, the Philippine government had put in place a system in which a labor attaché assigned to a consulate or embassy would review the terms of the Standard Labor Contract that had been agreed upon by the domestic worker and the employer prior to migration. The UAE eliminated this system in 2014. According to the UAE, the unified contract it introduced that year nullified the need for contract verification by the Philippine government. Because this new system restricted the ability of the Philippine government to protect the rights of its domestic workers and ensure that the terms of their labor met certain minimum standards, the Philippines decided to bar the migration of those whose contracts could not be verified by the labor attaché. In response, the UAE government refused to agree to the contract verification system demanded by the Philippines, and domestic worker migration came to a standstill. However, prospective employers bypassed this temporary stop by recruiting Filipinos as office cleaners and then moving them to domestic work upon arrival in the UAE or by sponsoring visit visas for prospective domestic workers, who would initially enter as supposed tourists.[39]

In 2017, the ban ended when the governments of the Philippines and the UAE came to an agreement and signed, on September 12, a Memorandum of Understanding on Labour Cooperation that included a Protocol on Domestic Workers. The agreement established a work contract that abided by the standards set forth by the UAE and at the same time met the minimum requirements of the Philippines.[40] Also reinstated was the ability of the Philippine government to verify the contracts of domestic workers upon their arrival in the UAE.

Migration Management

Lastly, receiving countries extend labor protection to migrant domestic workers by playing a more central role in their recruitment. This is the case in the UAE, which centralized the recruitment of domestic workers through the opening of Tadbeer Centres in 2018.[41] Operated by private corporations on behalf of the Ministry of Human Resources and Emirisation, Tadbeer Centres are intended to offer domestic workers greater protection not only by streamlining the hiring process but also by deterring illegal recruitment, including placements in households with prior cases of abuse.

Tadbeer Centres work with government-certified agencies in sending countries, which in key origin countries, including Ethiopia, Indonesia, and the Philippines, are required to facilitate the outmigration of domestic workers.[42] To fulfill its mandate, which includes the placement of the domestic worker in a viable job, the recruitment agency in the country of origin usually partners with a placement agency in the destination country, which in the case of the UAE could now include a Tadbeer Centre.[43] Emiratis historically paid recruitment and placement agencies approximately 12,500 dirhams (US$3,472) in fees to secure a two-year visa for a domestic worker. Expatriates paid more; for a one-year visa, they paid approximately 12 months of a domestic worker's salary, averaging 18,000 dirhams (us$5000), an amount that included 5,000 dirhams (us$1,389) in nonrefundable government fees. Tadbeer Centres, by contrast, charge a lower fee, of 3,500 to 8,000 dirhams (us$972 to 2,222), for their services (this does not include the transportation and processing fees incurred by domestic workers in the country of origin).

The migration recruitment system historically left domestic workers at a disadvantage, as the partnership between recruitment agencies in the country of origin and placement agencies in the country of destination resulted in competing interests for the agencies, who acted as advocates for both the domestic worker and employer. The fees paid by employers dissuaded agencies from allowing domestic workers to quit their jobs, even during the three-month probationary period stipulated in the contract. This is because that would put the agency at risk of having to return the placement fees paid by the employers. According to domestic workers, the agencies often fail to fulfill their responsibility as advocates; when trying to transfer jobs, the workers are usually discouraged from doing so and instead encouraged to stay and tolerate subpar working conditions. This same problem remains with Tadbeer Centres. The competing interests that hampered the adequate provision of services by private recruitment and placement agencies also resonate in a press release announcing the opening of the Tadbeer Centres:

> All basic rights of the worker will be taken care of by Tadbeer within the contract. The worker can raise a complaint or issue with the Tadbeer at any time, thereby ensuring that he or she is happy with her employer and work situation. However, Tadbeer also makes sure employers are happy with their choice. Families as employers can replace a worker immediately in case of disagreements.[44]

It remains to be seen how Tadbeer Centres will mediate conflicts between domestic workers and employers. Yet it is unlikely that these Centres will look favorably on domestic workers quitting their jobs, as the government recently extended the fee liability for recruitment and placement agencies from a probationary period of three months to the entire duration of the two-year contract. Employers are now entitled to a partial refund of the fees they have paid Tadbeer Centres if a domestic worker quits at any time within the contract without a legal or acceptable reason. Just as private agencies have done in the past, it is likely that the Tadbeer Centres will also pass this expense on to the domestic workers.

Limits of Protection

As mechanisms of antipower, the various efforts by receiving states to protect migrant domestic workers potentially constrain the arbitrary authority of employers. We can speculate that they impose some degree of moral pressure for employers to treat domestic workers with dignity. From minimum wage rates, to maximum hours of work per day, to paid vacations, the implementation of employment standards likely creates benchmarks for the measurement of decent conditions in domestic work. Yet are employers truly held accountable to these recently implemented standards of employment?

As the enforcement of regulation remains blurry in domestic work,[45] it is likely that the new laws will fail to dictate the actions of employers. Domestic workers still remain unfree under the *kafala* system, which limits the reach of these various protectionist efforts. Indicating that domestic workers are still vulnerable to the arbitrary authority of employers, we see that the implementation of labor laws across the region has not completely dissuaded employers from abusing them. This is illustrated in the case of 47-year-old Constancia Layo Dayag, who allegedly died of abuse at the hands of her employer in Kuwait. Her remains were returned to the Philippines on May 23, 2019.[46] It is likewise reflected in the case of 26-year-old Lovely Acosto Ruelo, who was allegedly tied to a tree by her employer in Riyadh as punishment after an expensive piece of furniture that she left outside was damaged by the sun. On May 9, 2019, Philippine government officials rescued her after a picture of her tied to the tree had circulated on social media.[47]

While the extent of the liability of employers remains unknown, recent actions by the UAE government indicate their intent to pursue criminal prosecution of employers who violate the law. In 2018, the Abu Dhabi Judicial Department set up a new special prosecution unit to try cases involving domestic workers and raised the potential fine imposed on employers and recruiters to 100,000 dirhams (US$27,778). Yet it is also highly possible that a greater number of domestic workers than employers will face prosecution, as data suggests that it is the domestic workers who are in fact more likely to be accused of crimes. A content analysis of newspaper articles published in 2013 and 2014 in two English-language newspapers in the UAE, *Khaleed Times* and *The National*, shows that domestic workers are more likely to be described as perpetrators than as victims of crimes. In that time period, 83 articles describe them as victims and 105 as criminals. The crimes ascribed to domestic workers include theft, child abuse, infanticide, murder, adultery, and absconding.[48]

Another pertinent question concerns the criminal liability of Emirati employ-ers. Common knowledge suggests that Emirati are unlikely ever to be prosecuted for crimes they commit against foreigners, including domestic workers. During intakes of domestic workers fleeing to Philippine government-run migrant shelters, case workers usually begin by inquiring about the nationality of employers; those with Emirati employers, regardless of the strength of their case, are advised not to pursue a civil or criminal case against their employer, while those with foreign employers are encouraged to do so and offered legal assistance. During the time of my research, two women housed at the shelter in the Philippine consulate in Dubai persisted on pursuing criminal cases against their Emirati employers. Both had been left in limbo, with no definite court dates for their cases: one had been in residence at the consulate for nearly three years as she awaited her case of wage theft, while the other had been in residence for 14 months while she proceeded with her criminal case against an employer's nephew who had physically abused her. Domestic workers who plan to pursue a civil or criminal case against an Emirati employer are discouraged from doing so not because they will lose in court but because of the likelihood that they will never even see their case in court.

It is said that the courts intentionally delay proceedings against an Emirati defendant with the expectation that the foreign plaintiff will eventually give up and choose to return to their country of origin. An important discouragement to foreigners from pursuing a court case is the fact that they are not allowed to work while their case is pending and must remain in the custody of their consulate or embassy. The strategic use of court delays to protect Emiratis from criminal or civil proceedings indicates what we can call their "legal absolution" by the state. The anthropologist Ahmed Kanna describes the contemporary feudal relation-ship between local Emirati and their rulers as constituting a "ruling bargain," in which local Emirati, who are non-voting citizens, are appeased by the provision of various state benefits including tax-free income, free health care, government-funded retirement pensions, free higher education even abroad, and cash gifts for Emirati couples who marry.[49] We can add legal absolution to this list of benefits that are part of the ruling bargain.

The protective measures instituted by the UAE and other countries in the region are ultimately limited by their maintenance of the *kafala* system. They do not fundamentally question the arbitrary authority of employers. Retaining the *kafala* also means that employers remain legally culpable for the crimes of domestic workers. This suggests that these measures do not eliminate the pres-sure on employers to closely monitor the actions of the domestic workers they employ. The *kafala*, and the responsibilities it imposes on employers, make it a challenge for employers to fully recognize the protectionist laws the UAE has put in place, including allowing domestic workers to hold their own passports; giving them access to communication, for instance through the use of a mobile phone or Internet; and lastly granting them a day off. All these conditions, employers fear, would open the possibility for domestic workers to pursue illicit activities, including absconding and having sexual relations. Because employers face legal culpability for these actions, they feel a corresponding pressure to deter them. It is in their interest not to trust their domestic workers. How, then, do employers negotiate the legal paradox between obeying the protectionist laws, on the one hand, and reducing the risk of their own legal culpability for the actions of domestic workers, on the other? The moral dilemma that this legal paradox engenders is clearly illustrated in the case of the day off.

Negotiating the *Kafala*: The Case of the Day Off

I told her, "If you get pregnant, I will send you back home. That's one of the terms of your contract." So, she cannot get pregnant. By anybody. You know? Her husband or otherwise. If she got pregnant with somebody else, she would be kicked out. Actually, she'd be put in jail here, which is crazy. I'd get in trouble as well for not supervising. Like she's a child, you know? That's how the government treats domestics. They treat them like children. Uhm, having extramarital affairs here, sex outside marriage, you get put in jail for it. I mean, it's, it's crazy. They will get put in jail and deported. Anybody will get put in jail. They seem to be particularly harsh with housekeepers and it's, it's, it's, it's not fair but that's the way it is. *So, we play by the rules that are, have been set out for us.*

—Maureen, an American employer (emphasis added)

I have always been strict with my maids because I sponsor them. I always say they are not allowed to be out of the house during the week. . . . I wouldn't dream of having anybody who was going to engage in sexual relations here to my knowledge because A, it is illegal, and B, if they did get pregnant, that is a whole load of hassle, and cost, and all the rest of it.

—Mohammad, a Lebanese employer

Maureen and Mohammad, in explaining why they monitor the outside activities of their domestic workers so closely, point to the burden of their legal culpability as employers responsible for the behavior of their employees. Prominent in their minds are the risks of illicit sexual activity, including pregnancy. According to Maureen, she could become liable for a fine of 50,000 dirhams (US$13,889) if a domestic worker under her sponsorship got into legal trouble, which is a claim I could not quite verify but which nevertheless circulated as true among employers in Dubai. Maureen also believes that it is against the law for domestic workers to become pregnant even by their own husband, which is why she refused her domestic worker's request to have her husband move into the apartment where she currently resides, in the same compound as Maureen's family. While Maureen is not alone in her opinion, other employers disagree with her. As her Canadian peer, also named Maureen, states: "I don't think that's an excuse for not giving somebody a day off. Keep them in because there's—you're scared they're going to get pregnant."

The question of the day off poses a moral dilemma for employers because it foregrounds a central contradiction in the legal governance of domestic workers. While the *kafala* system imposes the risk of criminal liability, thereby discouraging employers from extending a day off, the protectionist laws encourage but fall just short of mandating one. In other words, the fear of pregnancy may discourage employers from granting a day off, but the standards set forth by the protectionist laws encourage them to grant one. In the UAE, Federal Law No. 10 of 2017 extends "1 day of paid rest per week" to domestic workers but allows employers the option of financially compensating them, i.e., giving them "payment of the equivalent of a day's wage," in lieu of one. The law in other countries in the region likewise gives employers flexibility to determine the parameters of the "rest day," as they can either restrict the "rest" of domestic workers within the confines of their home or allow them to venture outside during their "rest" or "break."[50]

This still leaves us with the question of what causes employers to act in one way or another on the arbitrary authority extended to them by the *kafala* system. Are they motivated solely by rationalism? Many scholars seem to think so, ignoring the possibility that protectionist mechanisms, including for instance ILO's 2011 Decent Work for Domestic Workers Convention or the implementation by countries of a standard labor contract, might constrain employers from acting on their arbitrary authority to maximize the labor of domestic workers and mistreat them. Amrita Pande, for example, proposes that the *kafala* is akin to slavery because the legal dependence of domestic workers on employers under this system elicits "a misguided sense of possessing the worker" and is then used as "a mechanism of controlling and disciplining the worker."[51] Indeed, some employers do maximize their authority and impose inhumane labor conditions such as extended work hours, inadequate food provisions, and limited freedom. Some even admit to knowing they can verbally abuse domestic workers with minimal recourse. Caroline, a long-time British resident of Dubai, admits: "She put up with a lot of really abusive language from me but she just drove me crazy because she just didn't listen or didn't do what I asked her to do."

Yet employers do not always mistreat domestic workers. In some cases, a sense of humanity informs their behavior. Illustrating this sentiment is the moral guilt expressed by some employers over hiring transnational mothers. Sativa, an Indian employer, for instance, refuses to employ a domestic worker with small children and has established the moral boundary of only employing "someone with an older kid." Her British counterpart, Sarah, shares her guilt and has resolved the issue by ensuring the "good education" in the Philippines of her domestic worker's daughter, whose annual school fees of 5,000 dirhams (US$1,389) she covers on top of her domestic worker's regular salary. Employers such as Sativa and Sarah suggest that notions of moral justice could inform the work standards set forth by employers. This manifests in a variety of ways. For example, some opt to offer a salary that far exceeds the minimum monthly requirement of the sending country, which is 1,500 dirhams (US$417) for the Philippines, 1,200 dirhams (US$333) for Indonesia, and 500 dirhams (US$139) for Bangladesh. The monthly salaries reported by employers range from 1,100 (US$306) to 3,500 dirhams (US$972), with the median falling at 2,000 dirhams (US$556), which is higher than the minimum wage recommended by most sending countries but lower than the salary recommended in expat women's forums of 2,500 to 3,500 dirhams (US$694 to $972). A sense of moral justice likewise guides employers who refuse to give their domestic workers subpar accommodations. While some employers have domestic workers sleep in the pantry or hallway, others, like Mohammad, a long-time resident of Dubai from Lebanon, consider this inhumane: "Well we have a storage room but you cannot put a human being in this area." Finally, some employers insist on domestic workers having far more than "basic accommodations" and ensure their comfort by providing them not only with a television but also access to The Filipino Channel.

While the arbitrary authority of employers does not necessarily result in abuse, it does leave domestic workers susceptible to mistreatment. This still, however, does not mean that we can reduce domestic work to "structural violence" or, for that matter, slavery. This is because, as we see with the cases of Sativa, Sarah, and Mohammad, morals mediate the behavior of employers. For this reason, employers in the UAE acknowledge the burden of the legal infantilization of domestic workers with a variety of responses to the mandatory "one day of rest per week." Informed by an interplay of rationalism and justice, some employers recognize the personhood of domestic workers and grant them a day off, others infantilize them and restrict them to chaperoned excursions, while yet others dehumanize them and deny them one altogether.

Recognizing Domestic Workers

As we have seen, then, indicating that moral justice indeed informs the decisions of employers, some grant a day off to domestic workers. Some extend the day off to the entire weekend, allowing domestic workers to spend the night elsewhere, but most limit the day off to Friday, which is the designated day off for domestic workers in the region. While employers may impose a curfew and limit the length of the day off out of their own personal desire for relief from childcare and housework, it is likewise the terms of the *kafala* system and the responsibilities they incur as sponsors that motivate their decision. As employers admit, the provision of the day off does not come easily to them. Most have to repress their fear of the potential "misbehavior" of domestic workers. This is the case for the British employer Sarah, who knows of her domestic worker's boyfriend but chooses to let her be as she "does not want to not trust" her, although she admits that she "can't fully trust her because she is not a member of the family."

The Lebanese employer Mohammad, who imposes a curfew of 8 am to 8 pm and only allows his domestic worker one day off every other week, is like most employers in that he did not immediately grant his domestic worker the day off, extending it only after he felt that she had earned his trust. Still, he considers himself an open-minded employer. Explaining how he came to decide to grant the day off, he boasted that he was acting not out of fear of her potential pregnancy but out of his trust in her as an adult. Countering her legal infantilization under the *kafala* system, he noted:

> But I am not worried about her private life. . . . First, I respect her a lot and I trust her. Second, it's her life. Third, if you're saying, if there's something legally affecting you or something wrong, I don't think this is . . . because in modern days, if something goes wrong, we can easily find out. Like if she's pregnant from whom and all of that. It is not any more like 100 years ago that somebody is accused and can't prove.

Yet, in an indication of the limits to his humaneness and the fact that he is also very much motivated by rational calculation, Mohammad—not unlike other employers—only allows a biweekly, as opposed to a weekly, day off.

Even when they grant a day off, that does not mean that employers might not still act on their arbitrary authority after all. Many admit to suddenly canceling days off without warning. This occurs when they decide to go out with friends during the weekend, or when they forget to mention that they had planned a dinner party on the domestic worker's designated day off. One employer who admits to this practice is Sativa. This inconsistency probably occurs more often than not. As the Pakistani employer Fawsi observed, based on his more than thirty years of living in the KSA and the UAE, the requirement of the day off is a welcome change in the law but will remain difficult to enforce, giving employers the ability to recognize it selectively:

> I think it's great. But I think it's very difficult to implement because this happens within the house and we can't go knocking on the door. But I think we are moving in the right direction because I think human beings need a break. And I always give our maids a day off because I think they need it and they will be more efficient the other six days. So there is no point of depriving them of sleep and whatever and expecting them to be looking after your young children all day long because they can't. So the law is moving in the right direction but I don't know how they will implement it.

Fawsi gives the sobering reminder that the mandate of the day off does not indicate a diminishment in the arbitrary authority of employers. Even employers who are inclined to repress their rationalism for the recognition of the rights of domestic workers can still easily change their mind and opt out of extending the day off. As Fawsi observes, it is highly unlikely that they will receive any reprimand if they do so.

Infantilizing Domestic Workers

While many employers can repress their anxiety over the risks posed by the potential misbehavior of domestic workers during their day off, there are some who cannot altogether do so. For one thing, some employers cannot quite recognize domestic workers as trustworthy adults. Their gnawing fear over the repercussions of any misbehavior by domestic workers, particularly potential illicit sexual activities, deters them from providing a day off. As a compromise, they allow domestic workers to venture outside their home, but only if accompanied by a chaperone.

One Emirati employer, for instance, recognized the need of domestic workers to spend time outside the confines of the home, but admitted to not being able to see them as trustworthy adults. This employer resolved his moral dilemma by taking his domestic worker out on regular chaperoned excursions. As he explained,

> The hard part about housemaids is that they are in a house all day. When you don't see the sun, you are missing something inside. So they should have a day off. But if they have a day off, they don't have the money to do the nice things, only to find a boyfriend. They get pregnant then both the worker and the employer are in trouble. It's better to take the housemaid with you on errands, on vacation, but not day off. They will be much happier.

The desire to minimize the risk of any illicit activity by domestic workers is why employers admit to infantilizing them and restricting their time alone.

Employers faced with the moral dilemma that they see the need of domestic workers for a day off and yet fear the repercussions of their illicit activities while not under their supervision resolve that dilemma by infantilizing the workers. In addition to chaperoning excursions, some limit the hours domestic workers can spend outside the home to no more than one to four hours per week. Some restrict their time outside the home to religious activities. Some need to know exactly where their domestic workers will be and what they will be doing during the limited time they are allowed outside the house. Others insist on just bringing their domestic workers to family get-togethers, during which time they insist that the worker is receiving a "day off" in the sense that they are spending time with other domestic workers who are employed by members of their extended family. Finally, others admit that they are more comfortable allowing a day off "if it's an older lady." Employers who infantilize domestic workers are those who are most likely to take to heart their responsibilities as a *kafeel*. It is not only local employers, meaning Emirati, who hold this sentiment. Foreign employers likewise recognize the duties of being a *kafeel*. This includes the American employer Maureen, cited above, who feared that any criminal act by her domestic worker would land her in jail.[52] As she put it: "Technically, we are responsible for her. If she chose to rob a bank, we would be responsible."

Dehumanizing Domestic Workers

While employers may choose to minimize their liability for the illicit activities of domestic workers through close supervision, they can also choose to simply eliminate the risk by denying them a day off altogether. In such cases, domestic workers are confined to the home. This is the path taken by employers who dehumanize domestic workers and disregard their need to counter their isolation. This was the case for Tarik, an Arab-American, who described himself as "American-oriented." As he reported,

> About her going out, yeah there was a worry because she was under our responsibility. It's not like trust or anything but you don't know this person you know. It doesn't happen in any kind of job where you would let them take their work visa and go outside and do what they want to do. . . . And honest, they are from abroad and they don't know people around here, they don't know who they are going to go out with. And so we don't want them to have a boyfriend and have pregnancy and deal with all that.

Tarik's statement implies that employers who deny their domestic workers a day off are those who are least likely to trust the workers. As one Emirati woman flatly stated, when justifying why she did not permit her domestic workers a day off, "You can't trust them." An Emirati friend of hers agreed, explaining, "I wouldn't have a problem [with a day off], if I know they wouldn't be getting into trouble. And I know for the West that's perceived as slavery."

We could dismiss employers' lack of trust in someone who resides in their home and perhaps even cares for their dependents as hypocritical. Yet blame should also fall on the state for its legal infantilization of domestic workers and the moral dilemma this status imposes on employers who wish to minimize their criminal liability for the actions of domestic workers. Sharing his moral dilemma over the day off, another Arab employer, Ahmed, explained that while he wished his domestic worker could pursue romantic relations, he could not ignore the state policy that establishes that "domestic workers are not allowed to have a boyfriend." To minimize temptation and mitigate the risk of legal culpability for the crime of romance, he decided to deny her a day off altogether. Others agreed, including the Emirati employer Ali: "They didn't have the day off because they are worried that if she goes out, she gets you know . . . met the guy and they get pregnant and they are responsible. Most of the families here feel they are responsible for these girls. If it's the older lady, it's fine. But if it's a young girl and stuff, it is the city you know."

Does the fear of criminal liability warrant the denial of a day off? Or are employers who admit to this fear merely using it as a ruse to hide their real intention of wanting to maximize the labor of domestic workers? Employers repeatedly raised the subject of their criminal liability for the misdeeds of domestic workers, with the topic of pregnancy prominent in the minds of most, even including those who do extend a day off. This suggests that it is likely that employers who grant a day off are repressing this fear, that those who offer chaperoned excursions to domestic workers have resolved it, and finally that those who deny a day off are motivated by their fear to minimize the risk. When asked to describe their preferences for domestic workers, some even admitted to preferring a domestic worker who was not likely to get pregnant. As the British employer Zoe stated, "married so pregnancy is not going to be an issue." Caroline, also from Britain, echoed: "Frankly, I prefer a woman who is not going to get pregnant."

However, it was not only to avert the chance of pregnancy that employers decided to deny a day off. Some wished to minimize their domestic workers' interactions with others so as to deter them from gaining any knowledge that they could then use to negotiate for better working conditions. While none of the employers in fact admitted to doing so, plenty of domestic workers spoke of employers who banned them from talking to other Filipinos for fear that they might learn about working conditions and benefits that they could then demand from their own employers. Another fear is that domestic workers might learn of other job opportunities and then opt not to renew their contract. Domestic workers can in fact easily learn of other work opportunities from friends or other employers whom they meet in supermarkets or parks. While domestic workers cannot change jobs without the consent of their sponsor, they can bypass this restriction if, upon the completion of their contract, they leave the country for a neighboring country such as Oman and then return as the sponsored worker of another employer. (If a migrant domestic worker fails to complete their contract,[53] their employer can deport them and impose a one-year ban on their reentry for that offense; in that case, of course, they could not immediately turn around and take a job with another employer.) Regardless, the employers do try to minimize the presentation of such temptations to their domestic workers. In an interview with two female Emirati employers, one of them admitted as much. The other had shared the story of a friend whose domestic worker had threatened to leave after being offered 3,000 dirhams (US$833) in monthly salary by a French woman she had met in a supermarket. As the first summed it up, "And what happen to maid here is that they get access to people and they get approached. If I was to send my maid to the supermarket, they will be approached by other people who would offer them more money or leave the job . . . or pregnant."

And yet, regardless of the motivations of employers, can one argue that the denial of a day off is an indication that this arrangement is equal to modern-day slavery? Those who deny a day off do not think so. This is the case, for instance, for an Emirati couple whose home I had the occasion to visit for dinner one evening. According to them, their policy of not granting a day off was not an issue for their domestic workers, who received adequate daily rest as well as a weekly rest day, though confined in their home. On being called over to the dinner table, two Filipinas, dressed alike in housekeeping tunics, emerged from the kitchen to stand just outside the kitchen door. Asked how they felt about not having a day off, they smiled and responded "fine." Of course, a domestic worker is unlikely to embarrass her employers and complain about her working conditions to dinner guests. Still, what does undeniably support the claims of these employers regarding their employees' workplace satisfaction is the fact that each of these workers has renewed her two-year labor contract to work for this one family at least three times.

Others also argue against the assumption that confining domestic workers to their employers' home on their day off means that they are not receiving adequate rest. As one of the female Emirati interviewees reported: "They take rest periods, so on Friday our family usually go out so my kids and my husband, so they have no responsibility whatsoever. Nothing to cook, nothing to clean, nothing to do for the kids." Insisting that she treats her domestic workers humanely, she adds that she offers to send them back to the Philippines whenever her family travels, and that if they refuse her offer and choose to stay in the UAE, she ensures that they receive timely grocery deliveries. Nevertheless, it is unlikely that the workload of those without a day off ever ends, as numerous studies have established that its denial usually leads to overwork for the domestic workers.[54]

Curiously, employers who deny domestic workers a day off do not see this as abuse. They disagree with the correlation of the denial of a day off to modern-day slavery. Is this an indication that employers are unaware of their own abusive behavior? Indeed, some are. For example, some justify the low salary they offer domestic workers by gauging its value in relation to the life of poverty those workers had or would have in their country of origin, thus espousing a positive liberty conception of freedom.[55] As the British employer Caroline argued, "I think the other thing is that anyone who thinks that the maids here are exploited and underpaid does not realize how much the money they are paid is worth to them in their home countries. . . . I mean they live in rags in the Philippines, and you know, she is very, very wealthy in [her friends'] eyes."

Most employers spoke defensively against claims that domestic workers in the UAE were subject to human trafficking. Some even accused Human Rights

Watch of exaggerating the problem, arguing that all of the fuss was nothing but the magnification of the bad behavior of one or two employers that one hears of in the media.[56] Ali complained:

> If there is any abuse, they would talk. I mean you still get the people who . . . I mean one case happens, or two cases of like bad families that beat the maid blah blah blah, in general I just think people have to see the truth. I mean I'm not making it up, you can interview more people and you see by yourself because you are here in UAE, in Dubai. Look around you, I mean I don't see the slavery.

Yet Ali, like most employers who deny domestic workers a day off, only looked at the *kafala* from his own perspective. When deciding to deny a day off to mitigate their legal culpability, such employers disregard not merely their domestic workers' preferences but also their basic human needs, including for example their need to "see the sun," as one employer noted. While some domestic workers make the choice themselves not to take a day off, because they do not wish to spend money but would be forced to do so outside of their employer's home, most prefer to at least be given the choice. When they are infantilized and dehumanized, they are denied this choice.

Conclusion

The *kafala* legally infantilizes domestic workers. It leaves employers with the burden of legal responsibility for their domestic workers, including liability for any of their potential misbehaviors or misdeeds. This burden encourages the dehumanization of domestic workers, as it discourages the provision of a day off: those who want to recognize the human right of domestic workers to a day off are discouraged by the various risks, while those who do not want to provide a day off are given a justification.

There is a consensus among international advocates for domestic workers, including Human Rights Watch, that being denied a day off is akin to living in slavery. While employers who grant their domestic workers a day off are likely to agree, others beg to differ. This latter set of employers consists of those who do not see the day off as a human right of domestic workers. This includes Tarik, who denied his domestic worker a day off but claimed that there was "no reason for her to leave," as he supposedly treated her fairly and "without abuse." Likewise, the American employer Maureen did not see any wrongdoing in limiting the movement of her domestic worker outside the home, because she felt that the fact that she allowed her domestic worker's cousin to spend the night at their home adequately countered her isolation. Finally, others argued that the denial of a day off did not mean that their domestic workers were without rest, as they claimed that the workers were freed from work or given less work during their allotted weekly rest day, even if they were confined to the home.

Admittedly, it is not only morals, specifically the moral responsibility of a *kafeel* to shield domestic workers from harm, but also self-interest that deters employers from granting a day off. We see this in the case of Qattan, who worried about the money she would lose if her domestic worker absconded during her day off. The act of absconding does indeed pose a financial risk for employers. However, it poses even more constraints for domestic workers, as those who abscond will not be able to legally work elsewhere and face the threat of a lifetime ban from the UAE.[57] Another reason that employers deny a day off is because they have come to depend on the constant subservience of domestic workers. We see this in the case of the British employer Matt, who reported without embarrassment,

> We have often talked about starting a maid's school, you know? It has been a topic of conversation in many dinner parties. Someone needs to make the maid's school. Because what you are really looking for, and you wanna see, is the same level of service you can get in a hotel. That is what you actually, what you really want.

This sentiment of Matt's is shared by other employers as well.

According to the domestic workers, ultimate subservience is considered normal in numerous households in the region. 32-year-old Marjie, a domestic worker with three years of experience in the UAE, reported:

> And she [Emirati employer] is very demanding. She wanted us to serve their food with presentation. I was getting a headache trying to think of different ways to design their salad. She wanted flowers in the way I slice the vegetables. Then, she would get mad at me if there were no design in the food presentation. . . . . Then, she did not say anything to me except the words "faster" and "quickly." When she calls, that is what she says. I told her that it is not nice for her to always tell me to work faster. I told her that we work quickly so it is insulting when she tells us "faster." It hurts. She told me that that is the only word she knows in English and I told her that it hurts when she says that to us, "faster." I told her it would be better if she said "faster please." She responded, "why should I say please when I am a madam?" That is what she told me. So I did not say anything to her anymore, "why should I say please, when I am a madam."

Though aware of her subordinate position as a domestic worker, Marjie could still not help but be astonished at the extent of subservience her employer expected from her. Yet she should not have been surprised. I heard countless stories of employers refusing to lift a finger at home and expecting domestic workers to always be at their beck and call, including such specific stories as employers screaming at domestic workers to pick up a remote control that was within the employer's reach. We should recognize that Matt's desire for subservience, one that was clearly shared by Marjie's employer, emerged not from a vacuum but from the societal context of the UAE and neighboring countries, which have made the affordable labor of domestic workers available for the majority of households.

Regardless, the day off poses a moral conundrum for employers in the UAE. While the *kafala* system discourages its provision, various protectionist mechanisms encourage it. How employers respond to this burden varies, thus putting into question any reduction of their actions to "structural violence" or modern-day slavery. Instead, the various ways in which employers respond to this conundrum indicate that domestic work is a morally mediated relationship shaped by the interplay of rationalism and justice. Without question, it is most likely rationalism that undergirds the decision of employers to shorten or deny a day off. This is the case even if they reason that they do so to "protect" domestic workers. While employers who grant the day off are suppressing their rationalist urges and are informed by justice in their recognition of the basic human needs of domestic workers, those who dehumanize them by denying them a day off are presumably not suppressing this urge, and those who infantilize them by allowing only chaperoned outings are partially suppressing it.

CHAPTER 2

Managing Vulnerable Migrants

> You know the news about the Arab country. You know about the maid—
> they beat them, they rape, they hurt, they rape the maid. . . . So I [took note
> of these] suggestions about Gulf country. But [I thought] even in my own
> country, it will happen. Even my own people, it will happen. So where you
> go, it is on you. It is your decision how to stay safe.
>
> —Nhenski, a 37-year-old domestic worker in the UAE

STORIES OF THE RAPE, MURDER, AND STARVATION of domestic workers in
Arab states are common knowledge in the Philippines. They circulate in the
media and reach prospective migrant workers even in out-of-the-way areas of the
country. Two particularly brutal cases, both occurring in Kuwait, have haunted
the Philippine public in recent past. One was the discovery in February 2018
of the body of Joanna Demafelis, a 29-year-old domestic worker from Iloilo,
in a freezer in her employer's abandoned residence, more than a year after she
had been reported missing.[1] The other was the gruesome murder in May 2019
of Constancia Layo Dayag, a 47-year-old domestic worker from Isabela, who
was bludgeoned to death and found with a piece of cucumber stuffed inside her
genitals.[2] The UAE, however, is not exempt from news of the brutal treatment of
domestic workers. The plight of 31-year-old Jessica Dalquez, a domestic worker
from General Santos City, who was incarcerated for more than three years in
Abu Dhabi before being acquitted in 2017 of the murder of an employer she
had accused of attempted rape, is yet another story that cautions the Philippine
public, reminding them of the perils of migrant domestic work in the region.[3]

The known vulnerabilities of migrant domestic workers in Arab States raise
two questions. First, why do prospective migrants apparently continue to ignore these risks?[4] And second, does the state likewise ignore them and remain
complicit in the endangerment of migrant domestic workers? To address these

questions, this chapter examines the management of emigration by the Philippine state. Other scholars have claimed that the Philippine state fails to sufficiently address the vulnerabilities of migration.[5] They argue that the Philippines, because it considers labor migration to be a vehicle of economic development, regulates migration in order to maximize its economic returns, disciplining migrants to become "new [economic] heroes"[6] and streamlining their migration flows by creating an educational infrastructure that responds to labor shortages abroad[7] and marketing the skills of migrants.[8] These claims are undoubtedly true. However, they do not necessarily mean that the vulnerabilities inherent in migration are not being attended to.

Contrary to what other studies report, I find that the Philippine state operates not as a monolith but instead maintains multiple functions. It promotes labor migration while simultaneously seeking to protect migrant workers from harm. The state management of labor migration reflects a "moralized market," as it is guided not only by rationalism but also by justice.[9] To maximize the economic returns of migration, the Philippine state streamlines migration flows and disciplines migrant workers.[10] It creates markets for migration; regulates and monitors emigration; and produces migrant workers in compulsory training and orientation seminars. Yet nestled within these efforts there are also protectionist schemes that, in the case of domestic work, center on the implementation of minimum labor standards. The Philippine state markets but limits migration to destinations that meet its recommended labor standards; regulates migration so as not only to secure the smooth outflow of workers but also to facilitate the enforcement of its recommended labor standards; and lastly uses mandatory pre-departure orientation seminars to discipline migrant workers to become competitive workers but also educate them about the recommended labor standards so as to equip them with knowledge of their rights prior to migration.

These standards are however best described as aspirational. They are made aspirational by the fact that they are not enforceable outside the juridical territory of the Philippines. Employers in the receiving countries of migration need not recognize them. To enforce these standards, the Philippine state turns to a number of protectionist strategies, including securing memoranda of understanding with receiving states, institutionalizing migration by mandating the use of recruitment agencies, and disciplining migrant domestic workers to become self-advocating subjects in the mandatory pre-departure orientation seminars mentioned above.

In these compulsory seminars, the Philippine state disciplines domestic workers to be good workers, which, from its perspective, means workers who accede to the arbitrary authority of employers, because this surrender, i.e., the performance of subservience, is seen as being what will also make it possible for domestic workers to advocate for themselves and to question employers who do not adhere to the aspirational labor standards established by the Philippines, enforced in a memorandum of understanding with the receiving state, and enumerated in the Standard Labor Contract that is signed by the employer. For migrant domestic workers, empowerment is therefore conditional upon subservience. At the same time, the performance of subservience is not one devoid of empowerment, albeit an empowerment that is constrained and better fits what the anthropologist Juno Parreñas describes as "arrested autonomy."[11]

Contemporary Philippine Migration

With a count of 4,207,018 temporary labor migrants, the Philippines is one of the largest source countries of migrant workers across the globe.[12] Most of these migrants, an estimated 55.6 percent, work in Arab states.[13] The pipeline of migrant labor to Arab states was established not by accident but by design. The Philippine government's migrant employment program was established in 1974, when the government responded to the economic downturn caused by the rise in crude oil prices by promoting the labor migration of unemployed workers to oil-rich Arab states.[14] Since then, a steady stream of workers has continuously migrated to the region, including women, who are concentrated in domestic work.

Although the Philippine government does not provide specific numbers for migrant domestic workers, placing them instead under the broader category of "elementary occupations,"[15] we can reason that they constitute the bulk of women migrants. A 2018 survey of 2.2 million Filipino migrant workers has 37.1 percent reporting an "elementary occupation," with 9.8 percent of all men and 58.7 percent of all women holding such jobs.[16] Interviews with government officials confirm that domestic work is the job most pursued by migrant women. Data on level of educational attainment, regions of origin, and marital status of migrant domestic workers are also unavailable. Still, Philippine census data on migrant workers do suggest that most migrant domestic workers are likely to originate from rural areas of the country. While men far outnumber women migrating from the National Capital Region and its surrounding regions, by a ratio of 2:1,[17] women significantly outnumber men migrating from less developed regions, including the most northern provinces in the Cordillera Administrative Region and the most southern provinces in the historic Autonomous Region in Muslim Mindanao.[18] These are areas with higher levels of poverty than the urban center of the National Capital Region and have less developed economies, with higher unemployment rates.[19]

Most domestic workers from the Philippines migrate to Arab states; in the UAE, they comprise 20 percent of all migrant workers.[20] For this group of workers, migration means being funneled from one place of political and economic disenfranchisement to another. When they migrate, they escape an economically underdeveloped region with minimal labor market options only to enter a society where they have minimal labor rights. Migrant domestic workers in Arab states tend to come from areas with stagnant economies that are without wage-labor market opportunities, rural areas in impoverished provinces including Lanao, Magindanao, Basilan, and Agusan del Norte.[21] As members of the rural poor, they are unable to avail themselves of basic welfare provisions such as access to public hospitals or public education.

Indeed, many migrate to survive—to feed their children, clothe them, and reduce child mortality. If it weren't for the option to migrate, they would be unlikely to be able to afford the cost of antibiotics, for example, and might consequently experience the death of a child, as had happened to a handful of my interviewees. As 45-year-old Marilou explained: "Because it is very poor in the Philippines. Like my family is only farmer. I have two kids. I need to come here because I need to make money for my kids. We're only farmers planting rice." 30-year-old Jackie, who had also worked in Jordan and Kuwait, confirmed: "my family, we don't have working. Don't have work. My mom and my dad . . . I want to help them. Nobody can give my family help." Indeed, Jackie and other interviewees shared that their family would not have had sufficient food to eat if they (the interviewees) had stayed in the Philippines.

Prior to migration, nearly all of my interviewees had resided in a hut or wooden house with a thatched roof, which are residences that are prone to ruin by natural disasters. Most did not have access to electricity or running water. To get drinking water, they would usually have to haul it from a well or purchase it from a neighbor, at 4 pesos (8 US cents) a gallon, or 1 peso (2 US cents) a liter. Those without electricity usually relied on gas lamps or illegal access to electricity through a neighbor. Installing electricity in the rural Philippines is cost-prohibitive, amounting to at least 7,000 pesos (US$140) for labor and materials.[22]

Thus, migration to Arab states offered these poor rural women a mobility that they would not otherwise have had. Lynn described it this way: "For me, the income was not enough. I have two kids and then my husband is a farmer only. It is like our income is just sufficient for food, but not for the education of our children. That was our main goal, for our kids to be able to study. [*Pause*] . . . We were so poor." For Lynn, migration to Arab states was the most feasible way to gain access to a wage economy. As there were not enough jobs available in her rural community, she often resorted to bartering fish caught by her husband for rice to feed her family. Nor could she earn enough as a laundrywoman in the city, which was the final straw that pushed her to migrate abroad. Another interviewee, Haydee, a married woman in her 40s with three children in the Philippines, echoed the sentiment: "Life was hard and we see the future of our children. How can we send them to school if we do not have an income?"

Those who relocated to the National Capital Region likewise struggled to afford the education of their children. This includes 43-year-old Junna, who worked as a laundrywoman in Manila. She shared: "My goal was to be able to pay for my child's college education. I saw that my daughter is interested in studying. That is the reason why I went abroad. If I stayed in the Philippines, I was not going to be able to afford to send her to school." It is not only mothers but also older sisters who migrated to provide for the education of family members. Such was the case for 26-year-old Johnna, who had begun working as a domestic worker in the Philippines at 13 years of age and now sends a significant portion of her earnings in the UAE back home to cover the tuition fees of her younger siblings.

There is a long-standing assumption that migrants are not actually the poorest of the poor,[23] but many Filipino migrant domestic workers in Arab states, including Lynn, Haydee, Junna, and Johnna, do indeed arguably belong to that population. Many had been part of the 10 percent of the rural population whose households were without access to electricity.[24] The level of their poverty and membership in the rural poor is even reflected in the government's mandatory orientation for outgoing migrants.[25] Unlike other migrant domestic workers, many had never flown in an airplane. Accordingly, the orientation geared to domestic workers bound for one of the Arab states devotes at least an hour to travel logistics, informing prospective migrants about what they should do upon arrival at the airport, telling them how to identify the appropriate counter where they can check in for their flight, explaining to them why they should not worry when their bags are taken from them to be placed in cargo, illustrating what a boarding pass is, and warning them not to take the blanket provided by the airline with them when they leave the plane upon arrival in their country of destination. To further ward off any temptation to take the blanket, participants are even told that the airline would be able to track them down for stealing the blanket by checking which seat is missing one after all passengers have left the aircraft. In contrast, other predeparture seminars I observed did not devote any time to acclimating prospective migrants to air travel.[26]

State Management of Emigration

Sending states including Ethiopia, India, Indonesia, Nepal, Sri Lanka, and the Philippines monitor and manage the outmigration of domestic workers.[27] Of these countries, the Philippines arguably offers the most ideal case for examining migrant governance, due to its recognition by the World Bank as a "model for other sending countries"[28] and the fact that other countries have patterned their management of migration after that of the Philippines.[29] As is the case in other countries, the Philippines prevents prospective migrant workers from freely and independently exiting the country.[30] In order to successfully exit, prospective migrant workers must present a Bureau of Immigration officer with an Overseas Exit Clearance, which can only be obtained upon the completion of all government requirements for departure. Those who do not are at risk of being "offloaded," that is, prevented from exiting the country.[31]

The requirements for exit are established by the Department of Labor and Employment, which manages migration via two branches: the Philippine Overseas Employment Administration (POEA) and the Overseas Workers Welfare Administration (OWWA). First, prospective migrants must process new job placements through a private recruitment agency that has been certified by POEA. Using a government-certified agency is supposed to ensure that the migrant is placed in a secure and viable job that the agency, in partnership with an agency in the country of destination, has vetted and verified. Second, migrants must meet the skills requirement established by POEA for their specific occupation. For domestic workers, this requires the completion of 216 hours of skills training at a government-registered private training center that has been accredited by the Technical and Skills Development Authority.[32] Third, migrants and employers must agree to a Standard Labor Contract, which must be signed at the country of origin and verified at the country of destination. In the country of destination, these contracts are verified by the labor attaché in the Philippine Overseas Labor Office at an embassy or consulate. Fourth, migrants must also become a member of OWWA and pay the biannual fee of US$36, which qualifies them for a range of welfare benefits such as disability and dismemberment insurance and participation in education, repatriation, and reintegration programs. Lastly, they must complete a mandatory orientation seminar administered by OWWA.

These mandatory steps forge the collective identity of domestic workers and other migrants as "Overseas Filipino Workers" (OFWs), an identity that is premised on their shared experiences and rights. This collective identity is prominent in the UAE, where Filipino migrants, regardless of class or occupational status, expect to and do greet each other as *kabayan* (compatriots) on the streets. It is also common practice among Filipino migrants to help other *kabayan* in need, and runaways have turned to strangers for food, financial assistance, or shelter even though it is illegal to offer such assistance: those who provide it could be arrested and later deported for what would technically be considered the harboring of a fugitive. For domestic workers, their membership as a migrant worker in the collective identity of OFWs is also significant in that it counters their legal infantilization in the country of destination.

In the Philippines, the close monitoring of migration was instituted as early as 1974 with the enactment of the Labor Code, which officially recognized labor migration as a strategy of economic development. In its inception, a dual mission of promotion, i.e. providing labor market opportunities, and protection, i.e., "securing for [migrant workers] the best possible terms and conditions of employment," undergirded the state management of migration.[33] To ensure the meeting of these two goals, the government implemented "a systematic program for overseas employment" by mandating in the Labor Code the creation of two overseeing bodies—the Overseas Employment Development Board and the National Seaman Board. Together, they would be responsible for, first, regulating the involvement of the private sector, that is recruitment agencies, in overseas migration; second, maximizing overseas labor market opportunities; and, third, ensuring the "rights to fair and equitable employment practices" for Filipino workers.[34] In 1977, the state further expanded its provision of services for migrant workers when it established what is now known as OWWA, which is responsible for "protect[ing] and promot[ing] the welfare" of migrant workers and their dependents.

Notwithstanding changes in government policies concerning the role of the private sector in labor migration,[35] the organization of the emigration system has remained fairly consistent over nearly five decades, with the one drastic change being the reorganization of the two original governing boards, in 1982, into what is now known as POEA. Another significant change concerns the official stance of the Philippines on migration, which shifted with the passage of the Migrant Workers and Filipino Overseas Act of 1995.[36] This act officially declared that the guiding principle of overseas employment programs will no longer concern the

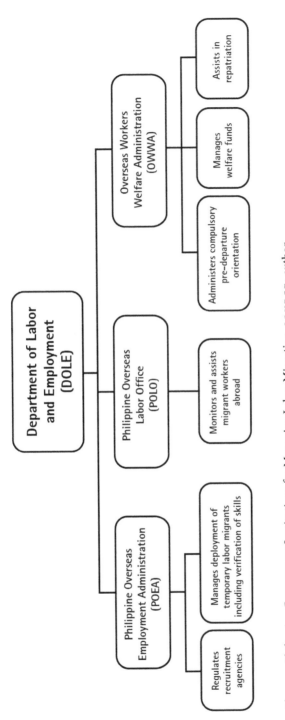

Figure 1 Philippine Government Institutions for Managing Labor Migration. SOURCE: author.

"promotion" of migration but solely the "protection" of migrant workers.[37] What prompted this shift was likely the need to quell public outrage over the Philippine government's inability to protect or save the life of the domestic worker Flor Contemplacion, who in 1995 was executed for murder in Singapore.[38]

The elimination of "promotion" as official government doctrine, as repeatedly proclaimed by government officials in interviews, is however at best symbolic. The existence of various government programs, such as the Medium-Term Philippine Development Plan 2004–2010, which set a goal of sending one million workers overseas every year, easily disproves it. Still, the establishment of this doctrine in the 1995 Migrant Workers Act and its reinforcement in the 2009 Amended Migrant Workers Act imply that the Philippine state has programs in place to mitigate the vulnerabilities of labor and migration.[39] It denotes that the state extends protection to migrant workers, which in turn enables the state to quell potential public outrage over its deployment of workers to high-risk destinations. Indeed, nestled within state policies and programs that promote migration are protectionist schemes geared towards mitigating the vulnerabilities of migrants. For migrant domestic workers, the state seeks to establish minimum labor standards when marketing migration; relies on government-certified labor recruitment agencies to assist in the recognition of these labor standards; and lastly both disciplines and empowers migrant workers to see to the enforcement of the standards.

Marketing Migration and Implementing Labor Standards

To identify potential labor markets, the Philippine state engages in "marketing missions," i.e., state-sanctioned visits to foreign countries.[40] Contradicting its denial that it promotes migration, the state uses these missions to assess its possible participation in the economic growth of other countries. Illustrating the wide extent of the Philippines' international labor migration market, state officials have conducted marketing missions in destinations as diverse as Kuwait, Lebanon, Malaysia, South Korea, Macau, Guam, Panama, Germany, Ireland, Norway, and Greece.[41] While other studies have been critical of these missions and their commodification of workers,[42] such analyses ignore how the protection of workers is embedded in state marketing practices. The Philippine state for instance limits labor migration to destinations "where the rights of Filipino workers are protected."[43] These destinations are those that have adequate labor and social laws for the protection of migrant workers, are signatories to multilateral conventions that are pertinent to migrant labor, and/or have concluded a government-to-government agreement with the Philippine state on the rights of Filipino migrant workers.[44] The Philippine state pursues government-to-government agreements if prevailing labor standards in a country of destination do not meet its recommended standards of employment (e.g. minimum wage) or if industry standards fail to adhere to its labor recruitment policies (e.g. employers bearing some of the cost of labor migration).[45]

In the case of migrant domestic work, the Philippine state sought to implement aspirational labor standards with the passage of the Household Service Workers Reform Package of 2006 which put into law the obligation of employers to cover the cost of migration, as well as the state's recommended minimum monthly wage of US$400.[46] This recommended minimum wage is significantly higher than those of other countries, including for instance the US$139 that Bangladesh has set for migrant domestic workers in the UAE.[47] To validate the elevation of its recommended labor conditions, the Philippine state committed to deploying only "skilled" workers, therefore requiring domestic workers to complete the 216 hours of skills training prior to migration that were mentioned earlier.

Demonstrating its efforts to protect domestic workers, the Philippine state has worked in a variety of ways towards the recognition of its aspirational labor standards. First, it sees to their enforcement by requiring the use of a Standard Labor Contract that stipulates the minimum labor standards set for the particular destination. These standards include the contract duration, monthly wage, medical benefits, terms of accommodation, mandatory rest periods, paid vacations, and travel benefits. Second, it imposes a ban on migration[48] to destinations that reject the terms stipulated in the contract or refuse to verify them. In the past, the Philippine state has imposed bans on the migration of domestic workers to Denmark, the KSA, Kuwait, Lebanon, Palau, and the UAE. Finally, the Philippine state turns to government-to-government agreements. In the case of Arab states, the Philippines has signed a memorandum of understanding with most destinations in the region and concluded an agreement on domestic workers with Lebanon in 2012, Jordan in 2012, the KSA in 2013, the UAE in 2017, and Kuwait in 2018.[49]

As noted earlier, receiving states do not easily agree to government-to-government agreements. They usually succumb to pressure, however, often through the threat of a ban, from sending states. In the case of the KSA, for example, the government balked at the efforts of the Philippines to implement an increase in the monthly minimum wage of migrant domestic workers from US$200 to US$400 in 2012. It initially rejected the stipulation of this new monthly minimum wage in the Standard Labor Contract. The Philippines responded by imposing a ban on the migration of domestic workers, which was subsequently lifted after the Saudi government conceded to the minimum wage hike and signed a bilateral agreement on the recruitment of migrant domestic workers.[50]

In an indication of the limited usefulness of relying solely on regulation for the protection of migrant workers, employers need not agree to the terms of government-to-government agreements. In the UAE, domestic workers have repeatedly complained about the refusal of employers to recognize the aspirational labor standard of a US$400 monthly minimum wage. Brenda, for example, noted that her employer never intended to acknowledge this wage: "[My employer] said that's only in the Philippines, that the Philippine government is lying to us, that it wasn't true, and that it's only a front so we could be approved to work here, such, and such." Brenda's situation, which is not an exception but a common experience among newcomers, reminds us of the challenge of enforcing policies for sending states.[51] As I explain in the next sections, the state addresses this challenge by turning to migrant institutions and the education of migrant workers.

Promoting Migration and Protecting Migrants via Labor Recruitment Agencies

Upon its establishment of labor migration as a development strategy in 1974, the Philippine state initially intended to bear sole responsibility for the job placement of migrant workers and gradually eliminate the participation of the private sector. However, the boom in the annual rate of migration forced the government to abandon this idea, as it realized that it did not have the staffing capacity to manage the growing volume of migration.[52] For this reason, the Philippine state, beginning in 1978, elevated its reliance on the private sector, specifically recruitment agencies, in the management of migration. Reflecting its position as a major stakeholder in Philippine labor emigration, one of the three nongovernment constituents on the five-person governing board of POEA represents the interests of the private sector. In 1995, the state expanded its partnership with the private sector, completely outsourcing the promotion of migration, including the tasks of identifying and advertising jobs to prospective migrant workers and creating job opportunities in state-approved destinations across the globe, to recruitment agencies.[53]

Today, the initial job placement of prospective migrant workers, including domestic workers, must be processed through a government-certified recruitment agency. For the protection of migrant workers, the state heavily regulates the activities of recruitment agencies. It delineates their responsibilities to include identifying and vetting prospective jobs, ensuring that these jobs meet the minimum labor standards of the Philippines, screening migrants for their job qualifications, facilitating their completion of pre-migration requirements including the completion of their compulsory training and pre-departure orientation seminars, and lastly ensuring the welfare of migrant workers by mediating workplace conflicts between domestic workers and employers and advocating on their behalf if employers fail to uphold the terms of their labor contract. The use of government-certified recruitment agencies is also said to deter "illegal recruitment," which according to government officials increases the risk of labor exploitation. Overall, recruitment agencies are responsible not only for the job placement of migrant workers but also for some portion of their welfare. Agencies that place migrant workers in bad job situations are penalized by having their license suspended or canceled. In the case of domestic work, agencies with more than one case of absconding may find their license suspended for failing to adequately vet employers.[54] While there are more than 2,800 recruitment agencies registered with POEA to facilitate land-based employment, fewer than 1,000 of these are in good standing.[55] Others are "forever banned," "delisted," "suspended," "canceled," or have had a "revoked license."

To minimize the risk of incurring such penalties from the state, therefore, the agencies closely scrutinize potential employers. In the case of domestic work, they vet them, with the assistance of local agencies in the destination countries, for their income and good character.[56] In the UAE, for instance, employers must not only meet the minimum household monthly income requirement of 10,000 dirhams (U S $ 2,778) but must also be cleared of past or pending cases of labor abuse.[57] Agencies that repeatedly place domestic workers in abusive households could lose their license. It is for this reason that agencies are unlikely to merely take the word of another employer when placing a domestic worker in a home. Doing so, according to a few agency representatives I met, would be equivalent to "human trafficking."

As the agent Mr. Mendoza explained:

We will never engage in human trafficking. This is how it works. Good example. Under my watch. This problem maid of mine was hired as a domestic worker and performed very well in Riyadh. So this person, without my knowledge, informed her relatives in Mindoro and told them to prepare because relatives of her employers need DH [domestic helpers]. We will send you the money. So papers need

to be fixed. So they came to me. They said, Mr. Mendoza, you sent that person
and so will you help us too. They are willing to pay. I told them that we do not
know the relatives of that employer we hired for and so that is human trafficking.

The situation Mr. Mendoza described does not technically fall under the definition of human trafficking, which would entail the transportation of a person
under some grounds of duplicity for the purpose of their exploitation.[58] Instead,
he described a situation in which a migrant worker might be liable for abuse
because the state or its representative, which in this case would be the recruitment agency, had failed to vet the prospective employer.

There is however a limit to how much effort the recruitment agencies put
into meeting the state's aspirational labor standards. What limits the extent of
their protectionist efforts is their financial interest. This has become something
of an issue for domestic workers wishing to quit their jobs. Those who hope to
do so are often dissuaded by the recruitment agencies, because in a transfer of
employment the agency risks forfeiting the fees it had received for the initial job
placement of the domestic worker. It is not unknown for recruitment agencies
to tell domestic workers facing workplace conflict, or even abuse, to *tiis*, meaning "to endure" or "toughen up." As one domestic worker notes, "They will tell
you to go back to your sponsor, but you are afraid because you don't want to go
back." The owner of a recruitment agency confirmed this. When asked if domestic
workers were able to quit their jobs, she responded, "Not unless you can pay for
the cost of your migration and training. Imagine your employer paid for all of
that and you signed a contract."[59]

It is also not unknown for recruitment agencies to ignore the cap the Philippine state has imposed on the fees they can charge prospective migrant workers,
namely no more than the equivalent of 40 percent of a worker's monthly salary.
Due to their relatively low salary in comparison to other workers, domestic
workers are regulated differently. Since 2006, recruitment agencies have been
prohibited from charging domestic workers any placement fee. It is, nonethe-
less, common practice for migrant domestic workers in destinations other than
Arab states to pay exorbitant placement fees.[60] Domestic workers bound for Arab
states usually incur no more than 5,000 pesos (US$100) in fees prior to migra-
tion because it is common practice for employers to cover the cost of migration
to this region.[61] Still, as poor rural women without access to the wage economy,
migrant domestic workers bound for Arab states find themselves having to rely
on a "fly now and pay later" scheme, a salary deduction arrangement used by

recruitment agencies, to cover this nominal fee. For other destinations, recruitment agencies charge prospective migrant domestic workers significantly more: it costs U S $ 1,000–1,800 to secure a labor contract in Singapore, U S $ 3,000–4,500 for a contract in Hong Kong, U S $ 5,000–7,000 for Taiwan, U S $ 7,000 for Israel, and U S $ 8,000 or more for Canada.[62] The decentralized organization of migration is what makes it possible for these agencies to impose such fees while avoiding government scrutiny.[63] The state does not closely monitor recruitment agency practices, checking on them only when someone lodges a complaint, including complaints of abuse in the country of destination.

Diminished Capabilities[64]

Recruitment agencies are supposed to protect labor migrants. However, their efforts to do so, including the most well-intentioned agencies, are constrained by their diminishment of the capabilities of labor migrants. The management of labor migration not only diminishes the ability of migrant workers to quit their jobs but also limits the ability of prospective migrants to select a destination country.[65] First, the system is set up such that migrant workers, including domestic workers, are unable to depart the country as tourists and independently enter a free market such as Singapore and the UAE, where they could secure a job locally and negotiate for more favorable terms of employment, such as a higher salary and guaranteed day off. Second, the use of recruitment agencies reduces the ability of migrant domestic workers to choose their own employers. Josie, a domestic worker in the UAE, observed: "If you go through an agency, you have no say on what employer you will get." This is the case not only for the UAE but also for other destinations, including Taiwan[66] and Hong Kong.[67]

The diminished ability of migrant domestic workers to choose their own employers is even worse for those migrating to an Arab state, because these workers are also unlikely to be able to select their country of destination. For domestic workers bound for an Arab state, their destination is instead determined by the "jobs order" available at the recruitment agency. Even using the same agency as one's friends and family does not guarantee that one will be placed in the same country. Cindy, a domestic worker in the UAE, learned of the opportunity to work in the region from a friend employed as a domestic worker in Oman. Hoping to follow her friend, Cindy visited the same agency, only to learn that it no longer had job orders for Oman but only for the UAE. Mishra, likewise, did not have the choice of following her mother to the KSA. Asked why she ended up in the UAE, she responded, "Because I applied to an agency, so that's it. I was sent here in Dubai." Similarly, Jocelyn, a recent migrant to the UAE, recalled how she initially landed in Jordan, where she worked for six years: "I did not pick Jordan. My first choice had been Dubai. It was not until I was in Manila that I learned that my destination was going to be Jordan. I wondered why Jordan. I did not know anything about the place." The determination by recruitment agencies not just of one's employer but even one's destination country means that domestic workers are unlikely to have friends or family in the country of destination who could cushion their transition to a new culture and shield them from potentially abusive employers. In other words, they are likely to be without social networks, which have been documented to be a primary source of support for migrant domestic workers.[68]

Being assigned to an abusive employer is a common fear among domestic workers. This is because the use of an agency usually involves an imbalanced exchange of information between employers and domestic workers, resulting in the latter not having much knowledge of their job specifications until they arrive in the country of destination. While employers receive some information about prospective employees from the biodata submitted by the worker to the recruitment agency, domestic workers are not told much about their employing family, including the size of their home and the needs of their household. As Jocelyn recalled about her job placement in Jordan: "It is just listed, their name in the contract. I had no iota of information about them. Strangers. I am sure they knew about me. Because I had to fill up a form that they forwarded to the agency in Jordan that they were able to read." In some cases, employers do share information, such as the number of children in a household, but they are also likely to intentionally hide information from both the agency and the domestic worker, for instance not informing them that the care of an autistic child or infirm elderly person will be a job responsibility of the domestic worker.

Fixers

Due to the vulnerabilities engendered by their dependence on recruitment agencies, migrant domestic workers have come to rely on informal recruiters, called fixers, to assist them in the migration process. Fixers are best described as hustlers, meaning aggressively enterprising persons, who must secure the cooperation of both the prospective migrants and the government-licensed recruitment agencies to assist in brokering the migration of individuals. Not all agencies willingly work with fixers, as they claim to already perform the services that the fixers offer and thus consider the fixers nothing more than an additional cost for prospective migrants. Fixers can often be found roaming the streets of Malate, a district of Manila with a high concentration of government-licensed recruitment agencies. A visitor to Malate is likely to encounter a fixer, as I did in a chance encounter with Narissa, a heavyset woman who stood out with her long, burnt-orange-colored hair and stomach bulging from her tight clothing. She had been standing in front of a photocopy shop adjacent to a recruitment agency that specializes in the deployment of migrant domestic workers to Arab states when I witnessed her pouncing on a woman who had stopped to read the job listings stuck to the storefront window of one recruitment agency in self-adhesive vinyl lettering. In a loud tone, she asked the woman, "*Gusto mo mag abroad? Ano yung trabaho?*" ("Do you want to go abroad? What kind of job?"). When the woman nodded her head in the affirmative and softly uttered "domestic," Narissa took that as her cue to begin her sales pitch: "Don't go to this agency. The jobs here are not good. They do not deploy to Kuwait. Kuwait is where the good jobs are. There the salary of $400 is guaranteed. Let me help you. I will take you to an agency that can deploy you to Kuwait. Fast."

Fixers do not just locate their prospective clients on the streets of Manila, however. Some travel to remote areas to identify prospective migrants and then personally escort them to the city offices of recruitment agencies. Some accompany the prospective migrant by bus to agencies in provincial cities such as Davao City and Iloilo City, while others travel with them by boat to Manila. Fixers that do this usually charge prospective migrants significantly more than those who just meet them on the streets of Malate, with some charging what a few agency staffers claim is as much as two months of a migrant's salary, an exorbitant amount that has led to the association of fixers with "illegal recruitment."

The presence of fixers does give prospective migrant workers with limited means access to migration. Fixers pay for all of the costs of travel from the remote area to the city, and some even extend loans to prospective migrants to cover the costs of obtaining their passports and other government requirements for labor migration. Fixers claim that they do not charge prospective migrants for these expenses but instead get the employers to pay for them via the recruitment agencies. Even if this is not true, it is likely a justification that fixers feel compelled to give, because it is frowned upon and considered unjust in the Philippines to saddle migrant domestic workers with fees. However, it is unlikely that recruitment agencies would cover those added costs, given that the agencies that admit to working with fixers claim to compensate them no more than US$100 for the referral of a prospective migrant.

To justify their presence, fixers insist that they provide a necessary service. They claim to do more than what the recruitment agencies do, describing themselves as "protectors" of migrant workers, particularly migrant domestic workers. For this reason, they usually charge more than US$100. Narissa, for instance, told me that she charges her clients US$500, which she claims is covered by the recruitment agency but is in fact most likely paid by the prospective migrant worker through a salary deduction system. Narissa claims that, as a "protector," she is there to ensure that they fulfill all the prerequisites of migration, from securing their passport to fulfilling the skills-training requirement, and, more significantly, that she assists them during the entire duration of their two-year contract, including advocating for them in cases of workplace conflict. Indeed, I once saw her negotiate with a recruitment agency on behalf of a client wishing to transfer jobs. In another instance, I saw her assist a migrant worker on vacation by giving her instructions on how to obtain the Overseas Exit Clearance she would need to exit the Philippines. The divided loyalties of the recruitment agencies between employers and domestic workers puts the latter at risk of not having what they call a "backer," or an advocate, which is a hole filled by the fixers.

To impress clients and to project an image of someone who knows the ropes of migration, fixers often portray themselves as successful return migrants who achieved financial security through migration. Narissa and other fixers I met often bragged about the residences they had managed to purchase through their stints abroad. To flaunt her accumulated wealth, Narissa regularly posts pictures on Facebook of one-hundred-U.S.-dollar bills spread out across a table. And yet it is questionable how wealthy Narissa truly is, as the home that she flaunts in pictures to all of her friends may indeed be cement in structure, but it remains unpainted and is lacking doors to separate the bedrooms. Still, fixers like Narissa flaunt their material success so as to seduce prospective migrants and convince them that migration is a viable means of achieving financial security.

Disciplining and Empowering Migrant Workers

The state does not rely only on the laws or institutions of migration to extend protection to migrant workers. It also turns to their education and empowerment. In compulsory pre-departure orientation seminars, the state equips migrant domestic workers with the knowledge of its aspirational labor standards for the purpose of empowering them to become not only "self-regulating"[69] but also self-advocating subjects. In these seminars, domestic workers undergo a process of disciplining to become competitive workers, so that their competitiveness will empower them, in the state's logic, to negotiate directly with their employers for better working conditions. For the Philippine state, a competitive worker is a compliant and docile worker. It accordingly uses pre-departure orientation seminars to discipline domestic workers to be subservient servants. At the same time, the state encourages them to resist employers who abuse their subservience.

On any given day, thousands of migrant domestic workers arrive at one of three OWWA buildings around Manila to complete their compulsory pre-departure seminars. One can catch a glimpse of them lingering and patiently waiting for the facilities to open. To avoid traffic, some leave as early as 3 am and arrive at 5 am, only to wait until the doors open, around 8 am. The buildings where these seminars are held are old, dark, and damp. The lack of government resources is visible in the absence of lights in some of the hallways, the broken elevators (which prospective migrants are barred from using anyway, even when they happen to be working), the lack of toilet paper in the restrooms, and the absence of central air conditioning. Safety does not seem to be a concern; white plastic chairs fill almost every inch of each classroom, preventing doors from fully opening and giving participants very little room to move. A room with a "maximum capacity" of 60 usually has 100 attendees in it.

The seminars hosted at OWWA represent a signature program of the Philippine state's management of emigration. This includes the pre-departure orientation seminar. Made compulsory for all prospective migrant workers in 1983, the pre-departure orientation seminar is a one-day, country-specific seminar that covers cultural and social norms in countries of destination and provides prospective migrant workers with advice on how to maximize the opportunities afforded by migration. As described on the official website of OWWA, it is "a one-day compulsory orientation to OFWs [Overseas Filipino Workers] consisting of modules on employment contract, country of destination, stages of the OFWs' life abroad, health and safety, financial literacy, travel tips and airport procedures, and government programs and services. This is attended by all workers (all skills) prior to their deployment abroad."[70]

While all prospective migrant workers must complete the pre-departure orientation seminar, domestic workers are required to take a more extensive seminar, due to their designation as a "vulnerable migrant population." For this reason, the mandatory seminars for domestic workers are administered separately from those for all other migrant workers. In addition to the pre-departure orientation seminar, domestic workers must also complete a stress management seminar and a language and cultural familiarization course.[71] The stress

Table 1 Modules of the Philippine Government Compulsory Pre-Departure Orientation Seminar.

Module	Contents
Working Overseas	Cultural Insights: Country of Destination (Facts), Stage of the Overseas Filipino Worker's Life Abroad
	Code of Discipline of Overseas Filipino Workers
Employment Contract	Rights and Responsibilities
	What to Do in Case of Contract Violations
Government Programs and Services	Benefits of Overseas Workers' Welfare Administration Membership
Last Important Reminders	Health Tips
	Financial Planning
	Travel Tips and Airport Procedures

SOURCE: author.

Table 2 Comprehensive Pre-Departure Education Program for Household Service Workers [CPDEP].

Seminar	Length
Pre-Departure Orientation Seminar	One day
Stress Management	Half a day
Language and Culture Training	One and a half days

SOURCE: author.

management seminars help prospective migrant domestic workers anticipate the demands of their labor, and the language and cultural familiarization course teaches them basic language skills that will enhance their ability to communicate with employers. In March 2009, all three programs were folded into what is now called the Comprehensive Pre-Departure Education Program for Household Service Workers (CPDEP), which for domestic workers bound for Arab states extends to three days.[72]

The administering of pre-departure orientation seminars for all migrant workers is a cross-sector collaboration, as OWWA has outsourced most seminars to the private and civil sectors. Skilled, technical, and professional workers can complete their pre-departure orientation seminar at either a labor recruitment agency or an industry association.[73] Since 1992, NGOs have likewise been permitted to host and conduct pre-departure orientation seminars for migrant workers entering a vulnerable occupation, including domestic work. While other workers can take their mandatory seminar in other regions of the country, this is not the case for domestic workers, as they must complete the stress management seminar as well as the language and cultural familiarization course at one of three OWWA facilities in Metro Manila. It is for this reason that the vast majority of seminars conducted at OWWA are dedicated to domestic workers. And reflecting the proportionally very large scale of labor migration to Arab states, most seminars conducted at OWWA are for domestic workers bound for this region.

CPDEP, in other words the pre-departure orientation seminars for domestic workers, are run by college-educated government employees, including foreign service workers currently between deployment assignments. These include both men and women, though the seminars for Arab states that I was directed to attend were all run by men. Their relationship to the prospective migrant workers is that of a helping professional who is assisting them in adjusting to a foreign environment. The government staff are assisted by NGO representatives who run the pre-departure orientation modules on "health tips" and "financial planning." Overall, there was not much consistency in the seminars I attended at OWWA. Not once did the teachers in the three seminars I visited refer to their seminar as CPDEP, calling it PDOS (pre-departure orientation seminar) instead. And because none of them ever shared with the class any overview of the modules they were to cover, it was difficult to follow the logic and order of instruction.

What was apparent in CPDEP was the extensive amount of time dedicated to instilling a worker identity among participants. Interspersed throughout the three days were reminders to domestic workers that their purpose in migration is to "work and not rest." Even the stress management seminar made a point of advising them to embrace their identity as a "worker." As one instructor noted, "You are not a helper, but a worker. Never say you are a domestic helper. Always say you are a household service worker or domestic worker. You are a professional. You are an ambassador of the Philippines." The language and cultural familiarization course is also justified as necessary for their training as "migrant workers," and instructors mention that the successful completion of the course will make them superior to their counterparts from Bangladesh, Sri Lanka, India, or Indonesia. After seminar participants performed poorly on a pop quiz on how to greet someone in Arabic, the instructor expressed his disappointment that they were "not performing to the level of someone who is of the highest paid group" of domestic workers. As he noted, they needed to perform better so as to justify the fact that their wages would be higher than those of their counterparts from other countries.

Instructors also used CPDEP to fortify the domestic workers' identity as "migrant workers" by outlining the minimum labor standards recommended by the Philippine state. In CPDEP, domestic workers are told of their right to a minimum monthly salary of US$400, as well as their right to three free meals per day, free clothing and toiletries, 8 hours of rest per day, a weekly rest day, a free roundtrip ticket to and from their hometown every two years, a one-month paid vacation every two years, and decent accommodations. Instructors enumerate these basic conditions during the discussion of the employment contract, but also repeatedly make mention of them throughout the three days. By instilling in domestic workers their collective identity as workers, CPDEP attempts to counter the lack of labor standards that participants are likely to confront once they arrive in their destination country.

In foregrounding the identity of domestic workers as "workers," or "OFWs" (Overseas Filipino Workers), the Philippine state counters their constitution as household dependents in the *kafala* system. It does not, however, question the *kafala* as a migration regime and its designation of employers as the sole assessors and administrators of the "law of the household."[74] Instead, the Philippine state cultivates the complicity of migrant domestic workers in this authority. As one instructor explained to his students, "You are a Filipino worker; you are the one who will adjust to the employer; you cannot change them; you need to get along especially with your madam. If they say, hurry up. Hurry up. Don't freak out."

For domestic workers bound for Arab states, CPDEP does not paint a rosy picture of labor migration, presenting instead the bleak outlook of a life defined by overwork, isolation, and physical violence. Not surprisingly, most interviewees describe CPDEP as nothing but a "discouragement seminar." "*Kaya mo ba*," meaning "can you take it?"; "*Kaya ba natin*," meaning "can we take it?"; and "*Kaya para sa pamilya*," meaning "can we take it for the family?" are questions frequently asked of participants, to which they are expected to respond in unison, "*kaya*," meaning "we can." In CPDEP, domestic workers are first made to feel "discouraged" by being reminded of their unequal power relationship with employers, which is captured in the following narrative presented by one instructor:

> If you are a cell phone, you are an open line. Everything depends on your employer—your work, your rest. They are awake at 2 am. You can ask for permission to sleep and they will say no. You can't tell your madam, "it is 10 pm, go to sleep now." [*Laughter in the room.*] You have no freedom. If you have no day off, you will look out the window and wave at people. Homesickness is often caused by isolation.

In CPDEP, domestic workers are taught to defer to the unequivocal power of their employers. CPDEP relays the message that it is acceptable for employers to control their most minute actions and behaviors, including when they should be awake and asleep and if and when they should have a day off. They are taught that being reprimanded is part of the job, as reflected in the demeaning but "widely used" phrases taught in their basic Arabic language training, which include *mafi mukh* (no brain), *haywan* (animal), *himara* (stupid/donkey), *ghabiya* (imbecile), and *kalb* (dog).

Participation in CPDEP ensures that domestic workers do not leave the Philippines with a blind eye to the vulnerabilities of their migration. In these seminars, domestic workers are repeatedly reminded of their subordinate status vis-à-vis their employers. They learn of their limited rights and the fact that their employers may ban them from using a cellular phone, deny them access to the Internet, constrain their "day off" to a rest day confined in the home, restrict their communication with the outside world including friends and family in the Philippines, and limit their food options. While these vulnerabilities are already known to many prospective migrants, some first learn of them in CPDEP. This was the case for Johnna, who migrated at the age of 23 years old. She recalled her surprise when first hearing of them: "OWWA reminds us that if you are experiencing bad conditions with your employers, you find a way to escape. [*Pauses.*] When I attended training in the Philippines, I thought to myself: 'What is this? I have to escape?'"

In CPDEP, domestic workers are consistently made aware of the inconsistency of labor standards from one household to the next due to the arbitrary authority that the *kafala* accords to their employers. As another teacher noted,

> Class number one, pray for your employer. Your employer is the key to your success. So pray for your employer. People ask if employers are rapists. Too negative. Positive thoughts. Pray you have a nice employer. OK with work and OK with food. Number two pray that your employer is wealthy because they can afford [the minimum monthly wage of] US$400. Number three pray your employer is religious. More likely they are good. If your employer is not good, you better study the house and escape routes. [*Loud laughter.*] Number one prayer, prayer for employer.

Prayer as a key strategy or coping mechanism is very much taken to heart by domestic workers; during breaks in the CPDEP orientation seminar, many of them shared that it was through prayer that they were able to repress their biggest fear about migration, which is their vulnerability to rape or murder. This was also the case for 29-year-old Onalyn, who had first migrated to the UAE ten years earlier. It was only through "pure courage" that Onalyn managed to board a plane after being forewarned during her government training of the likelihood that she would be raped by her employer: "Just pure courage. I just kept praying. . . . I just kept praying because I get to think of all those women raped . . ."

Without question, the advice to resort to prayer indicates the acquiescence of the Philippine state in the authority of employers. However, the state also discourages domestic workers from simply accepting any abuse of this authority. What if domestic workers are assigned to an employer who refuses to uphold the terms of the Standard Labor Contract? Instructors seem to universally advise participants to "talk to your employer." One instructor, for example, warned prospective migrants of the high likelihood that they would reach a tipping point and feel like "jumping out of a window." He immediately went on to tell them they should avoid doing that and "talk to your employer" instead, and think about the well-being of their children who were depending on their earnings. In another case, after the instructor advised seminar participants to pray that they would be assigned a good employer, they raised the hypothetical question of what they should do if faced with the misfortune of not being assigned one. He told the participants that they should "talk to their employers" and, if they were in the KSA, to go to the Ministry of Justice there. He proposed a few other options as well, including reaching out to their local recruitment agency, as staff there are supposed to negotiate with employers on their behalf; calling family and having them inform their recruitment agency in the Philippines of their problems so that they could likewise negotiate on their behalf; and, as a last resort, turning to the Philippine consulate or embassy. Notably, those who turn to the Philippine authorities tend to be the ones who are facing the direst situations, whether that be extreme overwork, physical beatings, starvation, or rape. In another class, the teacher gave the same advice: "talk to your employer or write them. Do not fight. Keep a copy of the letter. If not resolved, then go to the Philippine consulate or embassy."

The Philippine state walks a tightrope, promoting contradictory worker subjectivities as it cultivates both the subservience and the resistance of domestic workers by advising them both to concede to the authority of their employers and at the same time to question those who abuse their authority. In cultivating consent, it prepares migrant workers to meet the labor expectations of their employers, including subordination and subservience. In cultivating resistance, it trains them to question the abuse of this authority. However, the extent of this resistance is limited by the maintenance of the migration regime that grants employers arbitrary authority and renders domestic workers susceptible to extreme exploitation. Indeed, the Philippine state accepts and remains complicit in the susceptibility of migrant domestic workers to abuse, repeatedly warning them throughout the CPDEP seminars of the great likelihood that they will be mistreated.

All of the seminars that I attended for prospective domestic workers migrating to Arab states warned the workers of the likelihood that they would encounter rape and sexual assault and harassment. Disturbingly, most of these stories were based on real-life experiences, often the experiences of former students who had completed CPDEP with these same instructors in years past. In one class, the instructor shared the story of his former student, "Maria," seeing her boss naked: "Maria, Maria, a boss calls from the living room. Maria runs to the living room to see what Sir wants and sees that Sir is sitting on the couch naked. What would you do?" Though this story was initially met with nervous laughter, it was followed by a more serious discussion, prompted by the question of whether the threat of rape was causing any second thoughts about migration among the seminar participants. In response, the participants uniformly said "No." This was however followed by silence, suggesting the very real fear that this possibility raised among them. Yet what seemed to give participants the resolve to repress their fear was their faith in prayer. This is suggested by what one participant blurted to end the silence: "That is why it is important we all pray we have a good destiny."

Comparing the Compulsory Pre-departure Seminars

How does the Philippine state's subjectification of domestic workers bound for Arab states compare to the state's subjectification of other notable constituencies of domestic workers? Underlying the CPDEP seminars for Filipino domestic workers bound for Singapore was likewise their paradoxical disciplining as workers who are taught to both resist and be complicit in the authority of their employers. In the two seminars I attended, participants were advised to "be deferential to your employer" and to minimize their demands. For instance, they were told not to impose their own food preferences but instead adjust to the eating habits and practices of Singaporean households, such as following the common practice of having small breakfasts. As a domestic worker advised in the standard video shown in CPDEP seminars for Singapore, "at first you will be hungry, but you will eventually get used to it and your body will adjust." At the same time, domestic workers are encouraged to have their employers abide by the terms of the Standard Labor Contract, including paying their monthly salary in a timely manner. In one seminar, the instructor even shared various scenarios and strategies for how the workers could request their wages if they are not paid on time by employers. Then, to ensure that they would have access to proper resources, they were explicitly given the contact information for the Philippine embassy in Singapore.

The Indonesian state likewise requires its prospective emigrant domestic workers to complete a pre-departure orientation seminar. Other migrant workers, by contrast, are not required to do so.[75] With a more decentralized emigration system than in the Philippines, it is recruitment agencies, in partnership with the state, that administer these seminars in Indonesia. Still, the various agencies seem to impart a similar message of subservience, regardless of destination. Domestic workers bound for Malaysia are disciplined into docile subjects and taught to tolerate subpar labor conditions;[76] those bound for Taiwan, despite the heightening of their professional identity, are likewise taught to develop an "employer-first approach and tolerance for being confined in the employer's home."[77] In Ethiopia, the Ministry of Labor and Social Affairs administers a half-day pre-departure orientation seminar that likewise instills the values of obedience and subservience in domestic workers, instructing them to obey their employers and perform their work diligently.[78]

The Economic Heroism of Migrant Domestic Workers

Knowledge of the dangers of domestic work does not seem to deter workers from migration. Even past experiences of abuse do not serve as a deterrent from re-migration. Among the migrants interviewed in the UAE were some who had experienced trauma in other migration destinations, including forced deportation, displacement by war, human trafficking, forced labor, and physical and sexual abuse. For instance, physical abuse by an employer in Kuwait, followed by her experience of overwork and forced labor in Jordan,[79] did not deter 30-year-old Jackie from migrating next to the UAE. Likewise, the outbreak of war and the bombing of her neighborhood in Lebanon did not deter Jovie from migrating to Kuwait and then to the UAE not long after she had been rescued and airlifted. As she recalled, "I had lost a lot of weight. It is because you will be sleeping the morning then you get woken up by your bed shaking. Then, I wouldn't be able to go back to sleep because I will start imagining a bomb will go off at our actual residence. I remember crying and crying."

Experiences of rape also do not seem to deter workers from re-migration. During one of the many times the issue of rape was raised in CPDEP, a student seated next to me suddenly shared the story of her rape by an air-conditioner repairman in Lebanon. She had recently returned from Lebanon, but soon afterwards started her process of re-migration. She had attended CPDEP to finalize her migration to the KSA. Yet her rape had occurred only two months earlier, and only two weeks before her scheduled return to the Philippines. This prospective migrant, I learned during the break, had actually chosen not to tell her employer of the incident because her return to the Philippines would have been delayed by the legal requirement that she stay and testify against her rapist in a court in Beirut. Upon arriving in Manila, she then chose not to return home to her province but instead went directly to a recruitment agency, where she reapplied for a job to be a domestic worker in another country. A question I could not help but ask was how she was able to repress the trauma of rape and choose to be placed once again in yet another highly vulnerable situation, that is in a household where she had no ties or connections. She responded, "*may college pa ako*," meaning "I have a college student still."

As described earlier, migrant domestic workers bound for Arab states migrate not just for survival but also to achieve financial mobility. They wish to send children to school, build a house, or start a business, none of which, they report, would be possible if not for their access to wage labor as migrant domestic workers.

Suggesting that the state understands and acknowledges that the pursuit of migrant domestic work is likely the only means of mobility for those bound for an Arab state, CPDEP devotes a significant amount of time to reminding participants of the purpose of their migration, which is to "work and not rest." To solidify this message, CPDEP allots a few minutes for attendees to silently contemplate and reflect on their goals for migration, after which they are instructed to write them down on a piece of paper. They are then told to fold the piece of paper, hold it in their possession, keep it in a safe place, and take it abroad with them. The teacher explains that there will be moments, while they are abroad, when they are feeling overworked, battered, isolated, and homesick, and when they will feel like quitting or, worse, contemplate suicide. They are advised, during such moments, to take out the piece of paper and read its contents out loud to themselves, because doing so will remind them of their goals for migration and will accordingly give them the strength to overcome the challenges of their situation.

CPDEP devotes at least two hours of class to addressing how prospective migrants can ensure that labor migration becomes a means for achieving financial mobility. What these discussions do not address, notably, is why one would even need to pursue labor migration in order to become financially stable. By not acknowledging the absence of labor market opportunities in the Philippines, the government manages to deflect attention from its unfulfilled responsibility to create jobs for the working-age population.[80] Migration is instead presented as an individual choice and as an avenue chosen by the migrant towards financial mobility.

As part of its protectionist program, the state devotes these two hours of CPDEP to financial literacy, the first hour being reserved for a bank representative to give step-by-step instructions on how to fill out an application for a bank account. Because no initial deposit is required, applications are processed immediately: the bank representatives come prepared to take pictures of the workers' IDs and return before the end of the day with their bankbooks. The accounts they open cannot be accessed for withdrawals from their destination country. They can only withdraw funds when they are in the Philippines. As the banker explains, this is designed for their own protection; it protects them from the temptation of spending and squandering their potential savings while they are still working abroad.

The second hour is then dedicated to teaching participants the value of saving money. This segment is usually run by an NGO representative. In this session, participants are explicitly encouraged to develop goals for migration, and they are directed to make one of those goals be the accumulation of capital towards the launching of a small business in the Philippines. As part of the advice towards meeting this goal, participants are told to avoid remitting all of their earnings to their family in the Philippines. Instead, they are told that they should send no more than 50 percent of their monthly wages to the family, depositing the other 50 percent in their bank account. To convince them of the feasibility of this goal, the NGO representative then illustrates how a budget of US$200 is sufficient to provide for their family and even enough to allow their children to go to a fast-food restaurant once a month. Time is then spent on addressing how their dependents, including husbands and children, will try to emotionally manipulate them into sending more money; this is followed by an explanation of why they should not succumb to their demands. A primary reason given is the need to prioritize their long-term goal of capital accumulation.

Are migrants likely to heed this advice? My interviewees seem to have done so: most of them remitted a maximum of 50 percent of their monthly salary to their families, with those earning more than the minimum wage sending more, but still consistently allocating at least US$200 for themselves. Yet, at some point, most seem to have succumbed to requests from male relatives for money to purchase big-ticket items, almost always a motorbike, resulting in the depletion of their savings. Most interviewees in fact do not have any savings. This is not just because they have succumbed to the material whims of their families in the Philippines, but also because of the absence of any other kind of financial cushion against emergencies and catastrophes, including the cancer diagnosis of a parent or a tropical storm washing away their house. Instructions in the CPDEP seminars do not factor in the likelihood of these emergencies. The workers are merely told repeatedly to "save your earnings." At the same time, they are told to give as much priority to themselves as they do to their families. An impassioned speech is usually delivered in which they are told to think about themselves and their need to also prioritize their own personal well-being. When they are told that it is not only their families but also they themselves who should benefit from their migration, the ethos of individualism is being projected, along with their deservingness of a reward for their hard work outside the Philippines.[81]

The question of how they should invest the funds they have managed to save after completing a two-year contract is also addressed by the NGO representative, who does a calculation on the blackboard to show that if they diligently deposit 50 percent of their monthly earnings in their Philippine bank account, they should have secured at least US$4,800, or 240,000 pesos, by the end of two years. This is assuming that they receive the minimum-wage salary of US$400. It is then that the NGO representative addresses the likelihood that they will need to migrate at least once more, telling participants that this amount would not be sufficient to open and operate a small business.

Participants are then given a lecture on the difference between active and passive investments. They are encouraged to pursue the former rather than the latter. It is explained that of the two most common goals for migrant workers seeking to save money towards future financial mobility, one, the opening of a small business, represents an active investment, while the other, the purchase of a home, represents a passive investment. Migrant domestic workers are strongly discouraged from the passive investment of purchasing a home because such an investment would fail to generate any future income, which would in turn delay their return home to the Philippines "for good" as they and their family would have to continue to rely on their wages as migrant domestic workers.

In dedicating a sizable portion of the practical discussions in the CPDEP seminars to financial literacy, the state recognizes migrant domestic workers as a key source of the remittances that the Philippine economy relies on for foreign currency. After India and China, the Philippines is the third largest remittance-receiving country in the world.[82] And domestic workers, as the largest group of migrant workers from the Philippines, play a part in the inflow of foreign funds into the country. Yet the extent of their contributions is limited by their quite minimal minimum wage of US$400.[83] Nevertheless, regardless of the small size of their earnings, migrant domestic workers are discursively constructed as "bagong bayani," meaning "new heroes," whose remittances supposedly sustain the economy.[84] Initially proposed by then-president Corazon Aquino in a 1988 speech delivered to domestic workers in Hong Kong,[85] the notion of domestic workers as "heroes" affirms citizenship as the fulfillment of obligations as opposed to rights. Domestic workers have the responsibility to spur economic activity in their underdeveloped regions of origin. While the discourse of heroism might support the economic value of outsourcing labor, it deemphasizes a key dimension of the citizenship of migrant domestic workers. In particular, it cloaks how the state has disenfranchised a segment of the population by its failure to give them access to jobs in the local economy.

Conclusion

The Philippine state admits that migrant domestic workers in Arab states will face the risks of rape, isolation, and overwork. It has accordingly established a robust protectionist program premised on the admission and mitigation of these vulnerabilities, which emerge not only from the legal infantilization of migrant domestic workers by receiving states but also from their diminished capabilities vis-à-vis recruitment agencies. To address these vulnerabilities, the Philippine state has sought to establish aspirational labor standards via laws and government-to-government agreements; implement these standards through the work of labor recruitment agencies; and enforce these standards through the education, empowerment, and engagement of domestic workers in direct negotiation with employers.

Yet these efforts are limited by the challenges for the Philippines as a sending state in enforcing its programs and policies,[86] the competing loyalties and priorities of recruitment agencies, and lastly the "arrested autonomy"[87] of the domestic workers themselves, whose ability to question the conditions of their labor hinges on their subservience and acquiescence to the arbitrary authority of employers. Consequently, the enforcement of the state's aspirational labor standards is constrained by the ability of the receiving states to reject them, the recruitment agencies to ignore them, and the employers to refuse them. Do these limitations indicate that the protectionist efforts of the Philippines are undertaken in vain? Not necessarily, because, as I address in the next chapter, aspirational labor standards counter the absence of labor standards across households in the UAE and serve as a benchmark used by domestic workers to better their labor conditions.

CHAPTER 3

Mobilizing Morality

IN 2014, HUMAN RIGHTS WATCH RELEASED a scathing report on the labor conditions of migrant domestic workers in the UAE. The report describes the conditions of domestic work as including verbal abuse, physical abuse, the absence of a day off, working for large extended families, inconsistent salary payments, long working hours, and overextended duties.[1] It suggests that domestic workers are universally mistreated.[2] According to the report, the *kafala* and the unbridled authority it grants employers are to blame for the poor labor conditions of domestic workers in the UAE. Without question, the *kafala* renders migrant domestic workers vulnerable to abuse. However, it does not always result in their exploitation. As mentioned frequently by domestic workers I met in the UAE, there exist not only "bad employers" but also "good employers." Prior to migration, domestic workers are actually made aware of this "fact," as the Philippine state, in its CPDEP seminars, as we saw in the previous chapter, encourages them to pray that they will be assigned a "good" rather than a "bad" employer.

This chapter examines migrant domestic work from the perspective of workers. It describes their conditions of employment, illustrates the diversity of their labor conditions across households, and in its discussion verifies the existence of "good" and "bad" employers. It identifies how domestic workers themselves evaluate their employers and shows how, when faced with a "bad" employer, they negotiate with the employer directly to try to improve their labor conditions. The presence of "good" and "bad" employers is a testament not just to the diversity of labor conditions across households in the UAE but also to the absence of labor standards. It is an absence that reflects the arbitrary authority of employers as well as the unfree status, and vulnerability to domination, of domestic workers.

Due to the absence of collective bargaining opportunities, weakness of labor protection, and asymmetric interdependence between domestic workers and employers, other studies observe that domestic workers are unable to negotiate for better work conditions.[3] This chapter, however, demonstrates that, on the contrary, even as members of a subordinate group, domestic workers can directly negotiate with employers.[4] One thing that suggests as much is the story of Marjie, mentioned earlier, who sought to improve her labor conditions by asking her employer to stop telling her to work "faster" or more "quickly." When making such a request, domestic workers like Marjie are negotiating by mobilizing morality, meaning that they are relying on their employers' moral sense to establish fair labor conditions.

Because morals mediate how employers respond to their possession of arbitrary authority under the *kafala* system, domestic workers can mobilize morality in order to influence their employers' actions, including convincing them to ease their workload as well as providing a raise, a day off, rest and leisure, access to communication, and adequate food. Indeed, morals explain why the unfree status of domestic workers does not in fact universally result in abuse. To improve their labor conditions, domestic workers attempt to sway the moral sense of their employers and engage in everyday acts of what I call "moral claims-making."[5] This refers to the process by which domestic workers utilize the aspirational labor standards created by the Philippine state and shared with them in CPDEP to negotiate directly for what they believe are "fair" labor conditions. Embedded in this process is the mobilization of the morality of employers.

What, Then, Is a "Good Employer"?

Discovery Gardens is a solidly middle-class neighborhood comprised of a cluster of apartments in the newly developed southwest section of Dubai. It is adjacent to the free port of Jebel Ali. It is mostly middle-class professionals from the Philippines, India, Iran, and from other Arab countries such as Jordan and Lebanon who reside in this housing development. On weekday afternoons, I would visit the playgrounds in Discovery Gardens in hopes of meeting Filipina domestic workers. This is where I met Josie, a 45-year-old domestic worker who had previously worked in the KSA, Malaysia, and Hong Kong, and who had nearly completed her first two-year contract working for a Lebanese couple with one daughter.

In our many conversations, Josie repeatedly described her employers as "good." When asked what made them "good," she told me that they were considerate of her food consumption. As she reported it, "I am responsible for all the food, and what I want to eat. We go shopping at Geant [a supermarket in Ibn Battuta Mall]. *Whatever I want to cook, I get, and they will pay for it*" (emphasis added).

While Josie describes her employers as "good," organizations advocating on her behalf, such as Human Rights Watch, would likely disagree. As I got to know Josie, I eventually learned that her supposedly "good" employers did not provide her with the minimum monthly salary of 1,500 dirhams (US$417) recommended by the Philippine government but instead pay her only 1,200 dirhams (US$333). I also learned that she does not have a bedroom of her own but instead sleeps in a pantry not big enough to accommodate a twin-size mattress. What further puts into question the use of the term "good" to describe her employers is that Josie does not have a regular weekly day off. Yet these conditions, which would be described as subpar by migrant labor advocates, do not seem to bear the greatest weight in Josie's determination of a "good employer." Instead, it is their recognition of her as a person with her own food preferences, need for rest and leisure, and need for outside communication, and as someone worthy of daily acknowledgment, that makes her describe her employers as "good."

Not long after we met, Josie decided to renew her contract and commit to working for the same employers for yet another two years. The absence of a day off, bedroom, or minimum wage and the willingness of her employers to release her from her contract were not enough to persuade her to search for another employer. She admitted that what deterred her from doing so was the risk that she would land in the household of a "bad employer," meaning an employer with an undesirable moral character: "I am thinking that I might find an employer that is able to pay me more but it will be at the risk of me getting treated badly or not as well. Their attitude might be wrong. So that is what I am thinking about."

Analysis of what constitutes a "good employer" remains sparse in the literature. Instead, discussions of employer-employee relations tend to emphasize the vulnerabilities of domestic workers as precarious workers[6] with limited control over their labor and migration; as legally subject to structural violence;[7] and as victims of labor trafficking.[8] The discussions also use domestic work as a springboard to identify the constitution of status hierarchies among women in contemporary globalization by examining how employers impose boundaries against domestic workers and continuously discipline them.[9] Overall, the literature seeks to document how inequalities are inherent in domestic work[10] and establish that "household work emerges from, reflects, and reinforces some combination of hierarchical relationships of class, gender, race/ethnicity, migration, and/or age."[11]

A discussion of labor conditions that focuses on perceptions of "good employers" could glean a worker-centered perspective and foreground the occupational aspirations of domestic workers. While it has not been a focus of analysis, the topic of "good employers" seems to be prominent in the minds of domestic workers, as scholars regularly make mention of it in the literature. In *Maid to Order in Hong Kong*, for example, Nicole Constable mentions how domestic workers hope to secure a "good employer" and "not a dragon" for their second contract.[12] Likewise, in a study of domestic workers in Malaysia, Christine Chin cites a conversation in which domestic workers distinguish those who grant sufficient breaks as "good employers."[13] In the United States, Pierrette Hondagneu-Sotelo acknowledges the labeling of employers who communicate openly as "good employers" by domestic workers.[14] Finally, providing an employer perspective to the discussion, Pei Chia Lan mentions how an employer once asked her for pointers on how to be a "good employer" in Taiwan.[15]

The category of "good employers" serves as an "ideal type," providing a useful tool for understanding domestic work from the subjective perspective of workers. Moreover, assessing standards of employment via an analytic focus on "good employers" underscores the unique power employers wield in the determination of labor conditions. When asked to account for the lack of employment standards across households, domestic workers would repeatedly say "because it depends on the employer." As supported by the criteria Josie used to measure the qualities of an employer, the discussion in this chapter shows that a "good employer" cannot be easily categorized or reduced to the extrinsic conditions of employment but that, instead, a "good employer" also emerges from the intrinsic quality of the interpersonal dynamics between employer and domestic worker and the cultivation of a particular relationship in which an employer extends recognition to the personhood of the domestic worker, albeit one not necessarily premised on equality but instead, in the perspective of domestic workers, decency in the context of severe inequality.

Seeking recognition is not necessarily the same as seeking "dignity" within subservience, which is described by Bonnie Thornton Dill as the practice among African American domestic workers of making their "occupational role personally meaningful and socially acceptable"[16] and removing any negative associations with their job. Instead, it refers to securing humane treatment at work, which domestic workers measure in a variety of ways including via the consideration of not just their workload, compensation for their labor, freedom of communication with family and friends, and day off but also the recognition of their need for rest if sick and the need to eat adequately. Finally, "good employers" are not understood by domestic workers as meaning those who treat them as equals. In other words, the unequal relationship between employers and domestic workers is an unquestioned norm, with "good employers" being those who choose to mitigate but not eradicate that inequality.

Good Employers, Bad Employers, and the Absence of Labor Standards

Due to the unusual power of employers to determine conditions in domestic work, labor standards across households vary tremendously. In the UAE, domestic work suffers from an absence of standards. This is illustrated in the variations in the employers' management style and the domestic workers' schedule, compensation, accommodation, and ability to communicate with the outside world.

Hours of work vary for domestic workers. Some work as much as 18 hours in one day, while others have employers who would not dare have them work for more than 8 hours in any given day. Similarly, some have a set working schedule every day. At the same time, it is not unheard-of for domestic workers to be on call 24 hours a day, with some employers known to wake up a domestic worker and ask them to cook and prepare a meal at midnight, to have a domestic worker clean a car at 2 o'clock in the morning because the employers spilled food on the seats, or to expect a domestic worker to keep to their early morning schedule despite having kept them awake while they entertained friends the previous evening. These are just some of the complaints shared by domestic workers regarding the inconsistency of their schedule.

In domestic work, how tasks are to be done is decided by the subjective desires of employers. This results in varying styles of management. Some provide nothing more than a clear list of duties that they expect domestic workers to perform independently, while others micromanage domestic workers and delegate designated tasks almost daily. Analin, who is employed by a Scandinavian couple without children, works independent of instruction: "They let me do my job. I know what my daily task are . . . They just let me do everything." In contrast, Manuella is subject to micromanagement by her Lebanese employer. She complains, "Every day . . . my ma'am will remind me what to do. Every day, when She comes, ay when she came in the room and open the room, she will asked you what did you do during my absence. I answered her 'put video cam so you will stop asking me.'"

How domestic workers are expected to do their job also differs across households. For example, it is not unknown for some employers to dictate the order in which domestic workers must wash dishes, with some expecting domestic workers to clear the plate of food before placing it in the sink and others requiring them to soak the plates before washing them with soap. Others have a more hands-off approach, leaving domestic workers to do their job as they see fit. When domestic workers do their job is likewise differently dictated by employers. Some employers expect domestic workers to clean while they and their children are still asleep, and others insist that they complete the task of cleaning under their watchful eye. Junna, for example, is required to clean the house between 4 and 6 am, while her counterpart across town, Elanie, a 26-year-old worker who had previous contracts in Kuwait and Jordan, only cleans in the afternoon under the supervision of her stay-at-home employer.

The rest and leisure of domestic workers also vary drastically across households. Some are allowed to pursue romantic relationships while others are not. Days off are likewise inconsistent, with some workers allocated two days off a week, some given one day off a week, and others given no day off at all. Some have a curfew and some do not. While some are given an annual monthly vacation, some are only granted one every two years. There is likewise a diversity of sleeping arrangements, with some given a private bedroom; some made to share a room with other domestic workers; some expected to sleep alongside their ward, whether that is a child or infirm elderly person; some relegated to a pantry as their bedroom; and some, finally, without a bedroom and required to sleep in the hallway or kitchen. Access to communication also varies, with many allowed to use a cellular phone and Internet services, even if only during designated hours, but others denied access completely.

Styles of disciplining likewise vary. Most domestic workers claim to be spared physical abuse but complain of employers regularly screaming at them. Likewise, many are subjected to what they refer to as "adult abuse" by children: it is not uncommon for children of employers to hit domestic workers, as a number of interviewees complained:

The only thing missing is for the children to throw rocks at you. The children will just scream and scream at you. Your employers will tell you to ignore them because they are supposedly only kids. But I am thinking that they are not that young. The oldest is already 11 years old. That is why we were saying that child abuse is not what happens in that household but instead adult abuse (*Laughs*). *Marjie, employed by an Emirati family*

I told [my employer], "Look at what your son has done to me." I showed him all the bite marks. There were so many of them. I asked him to cancel my visa. I wanted to go home to the Philippines. The woman responded "Fine, there are so many maids looking for work." I told her, "yes let us hope you get to hire one who will be like me." They did not say anything. They saw so many bite marks. All over my arms and back. I told them I cannot take it anymore. They went back upstairs. They did not say anything. We did not talk for four days. *Kristy, employed by a Turkish family*

For domestic workers, the physical abuse by children is a reminder of their lower status in the family. It is a condition that they may complain about, but in the end must tolerate. Kristy, for instance, stayed with her employers, who did see to it, after she complained, that their son stopped biting her. For the most part, however, parents do not tend to believe domestic workers when they complain about children's behavior. Domestic workers are often expected to provide concrete proof. As Onalyn, who has worked for multiple families in the UAE, succinctly captures it, "The children here have bad attitudes because the parents always side on them. Of course, we are just housemaids and these are their children, what can we do."

Lastly, the lack of employment standards for domestic workers also manifests itself in their payment and the diversity of means and patterns of compensation across households. As the UAE has no minimum-wage laws, salaries differ drastically across households, with the highest-earning of the domestic workers I interviewed receiving upwards of US$1,000 per month and the lowest-compensated US$194 per month. Some households show consistency in recognizing the labor of domestic workers and accordingly extend annual raises. Others, however, do not. Cecille, for example, worked for a Greek household without a raise for four years, but opted not to insist on one as her labor conditions were otherwise favorable overall. Her employers provided her with her own bedroom with a bathroom, a refrigerator, and a laptop with Internet access and never made her work beyond her fixed schedule, which ended at 7 o'clock in the evening. However, most others who stay with one employer for four years fare better in salary than Cecille.

Other employers, unlike Cecille's, go beyond the minimum compensation and, in addition to providing an annual raise, recognize the labor of domestic workers by insisting on paying for the education of children left behind in the Philippines. Some also provide an annual bonus. Joy, for example, who was employed by an Australian pilot, received an annual bonus that corresponded with those of her employer. She reported, "if the bonus of the Emirates [Airline] are three months, I also have three months, my three-months' salary. This last bonus, I had a total of 4,500 (U S $ 1,250)." For Joy, this bonus made it well worth it for her to stay, despite only receiving a salary of 1,500 dirhams (U S $ 417), which is much less than what her friends receive who are likewise employed by pilots for Emirates Airlines and are paid upwards of 2,000 dirhams (U S $ 555) per month.[17] We should be clear, however, that not all domestic workers are adequately rewarded. After all, the minimum wage established by the Philippines is nothing but a recommendation that is not enforceable by law. Consequently, many domestic workers receive less than the salary stipulated in the contract approved by the Philippine government. Indeed, this is the norm for newcomers to the UAE.[18]

While the law does not specify a minimum monthly salary for domestic workers, it does establish certain parameters when it comes to their payment and compensation. Under the law, all employers must provide medical insurance to domestic workers, which they do tend to do consistently. The law also requires employers to compensate domestic workers within ten days of when their salary is due. This latter regulation is one that employers do not necessarily recognize, resulting in inconsistencies in payment for domestic workers. While most domestic workers receive a cash payment at the end of each month, allowing them to send remittances to friends and family in the Philippines, some have their wages withheld by employers who refuse to pay them directly until the end of their contract.

Employers do not necessarily intend to avoid ever paying the domestic worker, but as explained by some employers who admitted to withholding wages, they supposedly do so to ensure that the worker has accumulated savings at the end of their contract. Some employers who withhold wages open a bank account for the domestic worker, allowing the latter to monitor their payments.[19] Employers who insist on depositing the salary of domestic workers into a bank account do not necessarily give the worker access to their own monies but sometimes choose to hold onto their bankbook or bank card. In these situations of infantilization, domestic workers must ask permission to make a withdrawal. In other cases, employers who withhold wages do not open a bank account, leaving domestic workers in fear that they will not be compensated even upon the completion of their contract. This fear is not unwarranted. In 2012, 394 of the 2349 absconders reporting to the Philippine embassy in Abu Dhabi had fled due to "nonpayment of salary."

The diversity of employment standards for domestic workers in the UAE challenges the one-dimensional depiction of their work as nothing but subjugation. At the same time, it poses a challenge for how to fairly depict the diversity of employment standards without disregarding their vulnerability to abuse. In the UAE, the vast majority of domestic workers will not be brutalized, but it seems inevitable that some will face abuse including rape, torture, and starvation. Of the aforementioned 2,349 domestic workers who absconded and fled to the Philippine embassy in Abu Dhabi in 2012, 35 had been sexually assaulted and 104 physically abused. The largest group, however, of 598 domestic workers, had fled due to overwork. What accounts for the diversity of employment standards is the arbitrary authority of employers under the *kafala* system, a condition that leads domestic workers to hope and pray that they will have the "luck" of being placed with a "good employer."

Measuring Domestic Work via Food Consumption

Considering the wide range of employment conditions across households, how do domestic workers evaluate their working conditions? What conditions of employment bear the greatest weight in their evaluation? There are various extrinsic conditions of employment that domestic workers use to measure their working conditions. These include work responsibilities, such as duties and hours of work; salary and other material compensation, such as the provision of paid vacations, toiletries, and work clothing; the style of household management; the provision of a day off and adequate rest; the extension of privacy; access to communication such as the Internet; sleeping arrangements; and, finally, food consumption. However, domestic workers do not rely on an additive approach when evaluating their job, meaning that they do not assess their job based on the number of extrinsic measures fulfilled by employers. This is why an employer who pays less than the minimum wage could be considered a "good" employer by someone like Josie. Instead of taking an additive approach, domestic workers also judge a "good" employer based on the subjective factor of interpersonal relationships, specifically the attitude of the employer and their recognition of the personhood of domestic workers. For domestic workers, the meanings of extrinsic conditions vary according to the dynamics of their interpersonal relationship with employers and the infusion of kindness and consideration in everyday interactions between them.[20]

It is for this reason that domestic workers are unlikely to agree with the assessment by organizations such as Human Rights Watch that the denial of a day off is akin to slavery. Indeed, many do not even consider employers who deny them a day off to be inherently "bad." For instance, Marites, a 42-year-old domestic worker, insists on describing her Qatari employers as "good" despite receiving a salary of only 900 dirhams (US$250) per month and having no day off. Asked whether she agreed with not having a day off being equivalent to slavery, she responded: "I am not sure. I have not experienced that. My employers have been very good. That is why I cannot say anything about domestic workers getting abused." Domestic workers do not tend to equate the absence of a day off with slavery because they recognize that employers have a variety of reasons for denying them. Lynn, who had worked for the same Iranian family for nearly six years, reported: "the day off at first they didn't let me because their reason was there might be something bad that could happen to me . . . before if I am going to send money, they will accompany me and bring me wherever they go." This is not to say that the day off is insignificant to domestic workers. Many complained about not having one. This included 29-year-old Roda, who said: "me, I don't have off for 3 years. Think of it, sis, I can take no off, seems like I'm going crazy because no off. My [Emirati] employer will leave me. I'm alone in the house. It's very hard." Likewise, Jing, a domestic worker whom I interviewed in increments while walking the aisles of the supermarket Spinney's, used to cry over her lack of a day off. And yet, despite her complaints, she still opted to extend her contract for another two years. This is because her Emirati employer treated her well otherwise, never for instance screaming at her, and paid her more than the monthly minimum wage. Roda, in contrast, decided to leave her job, as she could no longer bear the isolation of never having a day off.

Instead of extrinsic conditions such as the provision of the minimum wage or a day off, domestic workers look primarily to the moral character of their employer when assessing the quality of their job. Strikingly, they frequently consider how employers manage the provision of food, an extrinsic condition, as the strongest determination of character. From the perspective of domestic workers, food provision centrally determines how employers see their personhood, and the allocation of food accordingly reflects the overall quality of their employment. According to them, if an employer is not only generous with food but also refuses to distinguish the food that they consume from that of the domestic worker, is mindful of inviting a domestic worker to eat before or simultaneously with them, does not simply give them leftovers, and considers their food preferences, that employer is seen as having positive moral attributes that will likely extend to other aspects of their management of domestic work.

One after another, domestic workers brought up food when asked to assess their employers. This was also true for Ruthie, with whose story I opened the introductory chapter of this book. She reported:

> My employer now is great. She buys everything for me. Food. Everything. When we eat, we eat at the same time. When she bakes cake, even if I am already laying down, she will come to my room and give me a piece of cake. . . . She is also not the type to order me around.

According to domestic workers, employers who are considerate of their food consumption are also likely to be sympathetic to their other needs, including their needs for rest, leisure, and communication with the outside world. Melanie, a 32-year-old domestic worker who earned 950 dirhams (us$264) per month for an Indian family, similarly sang the praises of her employers:

> My employers are very nice. They are not strict. If I want to leave with my friends, it is okay with them. As long as you are not doing something bad, then it is okay with them. They let me go outside if they are home. They do not look at me as a maid. They really see me as a family. *What they eat I also eat.* (emphasis added)

For Melanie, her employers' generosity when it comes to food was in harmony with their consideration of her other needs, including leisure.

When asked to assess what makes for a "good" employer, 29-year-old Jocelyn likewise included the provision of food in her assessment:

> They do not physically hurt their domestics. *What they eat, you also eat. They let you to cook whatever you want to cook.* They give you the things that you ask for. (emphasis added)

Providing yet another example, 30-year-old Ana defined a "good" employer as the following:

> It means they are good people. I have to say I am lucky. You see people here that are not treated well by their employers. *Their employers do not take them out to eat.* Then treating inside the house is like family. *They do not allocate what you can and cannot eat. They do not care what you eat and what you do and what you cook.* But

me I am not demanding, I will just eat what is there. I also adjust to them. What they eat, I will also eat. I am really lucky. I am not one of the unfortunate ones. That is why I have nothing to say against them. How they treat me is like family. It is not like others whose employers scream at them when they do not like what they are doing. That is why I feel really lucky. (emphasis added)

While Ana considered herself to be "lucky," anti-trafficking advocates such as Human Rights Watch or Freedom Walk would question her assessment, as they usually assess domestic work based on the extrinsic conditions of wages or days off. Ana earned only 1,000 dirhams (US$278) per month and was given no day off.

Drawing from the frequent use of food by domestic workers to measure the quality of their employment, an examination of food consumption allows us to describe labor conditions across households. In past research, food has been used to illustrate inequalities and the formation of status hierarchies in domestic work: scholars have noted the provision of inadequate food for domestic workers, the designation of distinct foods for employers and domestic workers (e.g. fresh food versus leftovers; the body versus the head of the fish), the separation of the eating spaces of employers and domestic workers, and the requirement that domestic workers eat only after their employers.[21] However, food is not just a mechanism of oppression; it also functions as a neutral category that can, in the diversity of its provisions, illustrate the various cultures of employment across households. Indeed, an inductive analysis of food consumption for domestic workers in the UAE shows that experiences in the workplace fall under the three categories of dehumanization, infantilization, and recognition. To be dehumanized means to be treated with indignity and inadequately fed; to be infantilized means to be without the ability to determine what food one should consume; and, finally, to be recognized means to be treated with dignity and respect and given access to food.

Recognized Domestic Workers

When it comes to food, the vast majority of households recognize the humanity of domestic workers. Most households provide domestic workers with the option to eat what and when they want to. There are three prevailing eating arrangements for domestic workers whose humanity is recognized. They are given 1) a food allowance; 2) free rein in the kitchen; and/or 3) the flexibility to add foods that they want for their own consumption to their employer's grocery purchases. Those without a food allowance are usually given the opportunity to purchase the foods, including snacks, that they prefer to consume. Josie, for instance, who was cited earlier, can freely include any item in the grocery cart that she wishes when food shopping with her employer. This is also the case for Jing, who shops daily for her employers' household and regularly adds potato chips for herself and her co-worker to the grocery cart that is mostly filled with her employers' requests.[22]

It is, however, the employers who establish the parameters of appropriate food consumption in their household. They do this without much input from domestic workers. For this reason, even domestic workers who are recognized tend not to be given their preferred food consumption arrangement, which would be the provision of a food allowance. This preference holds regardless of whether employers give them access to other foods available in the household. Domestic workers prefer a food allowance because they see it as an increase in their monthly earnings. Most of those who are given a food allowance receive 300 to 350 dirhams (us$83–97) per month, which they often maximize by limiting their food expenses to something like 100 dirhams (us$28) per month.

How they manage to limit their monthly food expenses to 100 dirhams speaks to their resourcefulness. 30-year-old Mariz Ann, who is employed by a Swedish-Canadian couple, explained how she can spend less than 100 dirhams for food per month by purchasing a whole chicken to eat during the entire week:

> Because I only eat milk, bread. I don't eat a lot of rice. I eat during weekends. So, I just buy milk, bread, sandwich, then I just make my sandwich. I don't eat—For example, I would buy chicken. One whole chicken is 15 dirhams (us$4). That's good for me for one week.

Mariz Ann claimed not to be starving herself just to save money. The 300 dirhams (us$83) that is allotted would not give her or other domestic workers with a food allowance much luxury in their food choices. Yet this is countered by the fact that some employers also choose to share their own food with their domestic workers. It is not unknown even for employers who provide a food allowance to also invite domestic workers to eat their food, to include the domestic worker when ordering takeout for the family, and to clearly earmark a portion of their dinner for the domestic workers. In these cases, employers provide the food allowance in order to ensure that the domestic workers are also able to consume the foods they prefer and not be constrained to eating only those foods that their employers like.

While some employers who provide a food allowance also give domestic workers access to other foods in their household, this was not the case for Mariz Ann's employers. Yet she claimed not to be bothered by their limited generosity.

While Mariz Ann did not think she ate too much, she noted that she ate more than her employers. She commented, "White people don't eat much, so you'd be ashamed to eat more than them." Mariz Ann prefers receiving a food allowance not only because it enables her to increase her monthly earnings but also because it allows her to eat away from the gaze of her employers. Eating in front of them would make her conscious of her consumption and, as she admits, would pressure her to limit her food intake. In addition to roasted chicken, Mariz Ann also consumes a variety of Filipino foods, which her employers allow her to cook with the exception of dried fish, due to its pungent smell. Mariz Ann could purchase Filipino food at one of the many Filipino mini-marts in the working-class neighborhoods of Karama and Satwa, but she often just patronizes one of the supermarkets where she works, in the affluent neighborhood of Dubai Marina, as they likewise offer a vast array of Filipino foods for the many domestic workers who live and work in the area.

An example of a recognized domestic worker with free rein in the kitchen is Dora Lynn, who works for a British family with three children in the middle-class neighborhood of Jumeriah Lakes. Dora Lynn has worked for the same family for five years, prior to which she was employed by a Dutch-French couple who only paid her 700 dirhams per month (US$194). Dora Lynn, whom I met in the food court of the Ibn Battuta mall one Friday morning, now earns 2,000 dirhams (US$555) per month and has an extended, 24-hour, weekly day off that begins on Thursday evening. Dora Lynn is employed by a family that recognizes all of her personal preferences when it comes to food and toiletries. As she reported,

> She treats me like a family. They give you our foods that you should be eating. In the Philippines, isn't it true that we eat rice three times a day? In contrast, my employers only eat bread. Then they just have tea. My employer told me, "Dora, everything and anything you want, please just make a list." So I told her pork, rice. I listed everything (*Laughs*). I wrote down "Likas Papaya." She said, "Oh Dora. What is this? Likas Papaya." It is the type of soap in the Philippines. . . . So, I told her "Sorry madam. Do not bother buying that. I will buy it myself. I will ask the Filipinos who are working in the mall on where I could get it." But she managed to find it.

Dora Lynn's employers are mindful not just of her personal preferences but also of her work preferences. They do not tend to dictate how she should do her job but leave it to her to determine how to perform it. Dora Lynn noted that their tolerance extends to her cooking any Filipino foods she wishes to eat, regardless of smell; she noted: "I cook my own food. I cook Filipino food. . . . I cook for my own. She [her employer] just wants to make sure that I get to eat what I like to eat."

While it might seem that domestic workers whose humanity is recognized in terms of food consumption would also be likely to have the mobility to leave their house freely, not all are in fact allowed to do so. Some are even denied a day off. This is often the case for those employed in households with conservative gender mores. Alma, for example, who now works for an interracial couple from New Zealand and Vietnam and in a household where she has free rein in the kitchen and full responsibility for the grocery shopping and cooking, was previously employed by an Emirati family that was generous with food but strict when it came to her interactions with others. They denied her a day off and limited her communication with the outside world. For instance, they did not give her access to the Internet or a cellular phone during her first months of employment, eventually giving her access only after they had learned to trust her. Yet Alma considered them to be "good people." As she said,

> They were local. They were good people. But the thing with them is they were cheap when it came to the salary and they did not give a day off. But they were OK when it came to food. Their food is your food. They are ok with food. But you did not have freedom of movement.

In that household, Alma had free rein in the kitchen. Her employers also allowed her to add her requests to their weekly grocery list, which Alma did, asking them to purchase the ingredients that she needed to prepare Filipino dishes. Wanting a higher salary, Alma eventually secured their permission to transfer jobs, which they willingly granted but only after they had personally vetted her new employers.

What is achieved in households that extend recognition to domestic workers is not equality. Racial and class boundaries might be mitigated, but rarely are they eliminated. An ideal household such as Dora Lynn's is quite rare. Yet even in the most generous of households, there is a limit to what domestic workers can expect to consume. For instance, Dora Lynn knows better than to request expensive foods such as salmon, exotic fruits, or imported American food products such as Skippy peanut butter. (She likewise knows not to make a habit of venturing outside the house too often even if she has already completed her daily housework.) For domestic workers whose employers allow them to add foods and other products to the weekly grocery list, they are aware of an unspoken rule regarding the limit to their consumption.

Pushing the boundaries of consumption would mean risking a blow-up.[23] This is the case because rarely are employers altruistic. Instead, many have a limit to the extent to which they will recognize the personal preferences of domestic workers. This is illustrated in the grievance shared by the British employer Caroline, who complained:

> Now they just expect to have free rein on your, your fridge. And you know, and when they are doing the shopping as well, like mine, you find they are buying things that they don't need, or they will buy shrimps or something to make their shrimp noodles. And I would never buy shrimps . . . And then they are buying themselves cans of Coca-Cola and things. And I am saying, "Look, you know, I didn't, I didn't say I was gonna keep you in bloody tin soft drinks, you know, I am not going to pay for that. You want Coca-Cola, buy it out of your wages." A lot of them are asking for toiletries as well and I am saying "piss off, I owe you, I pay you enough money to buy your own antiperspirant." They are pushing the envelope the whole time. They are asking for more and more.

Caroline's complaints are actually significant. They indicate a "hidden transcript"[24] among employers and confirm a ceiling to employers' generosity. Morals dictate that employers recognize the humanity, including personal preferences, of domestic workers. However, this moral pressure is not one that employers necessarily embrace, which is a warning of the precariousness of the recognition.

Infantilized Domestic Workers

Infantilized domestic workers are those who are fed at least three meals a day but are not given the option to choose what types of foods they can consume. In this regard, they are infantilized because employers ignore their cultural needs or individual preferences. Reflecting a common complaint, Marilou, a 45-year-old who works for an account executive of a cosmetics company, observed: "Filipinos are rice-eating people. We need to eat rice for breakfast, lunch, and dinner. Our employers only eat bread in the morning and think we will be fine also just eating bread. But we need to eat more than bread to do our work . . ." Examples of employers who have forced domestic workers to adopt their eating habits include Marilou's Iranian employer, who is always on a diet; Junna's Indian employers, who prefer to eat spicy vegetarian food; and a Lebanese family who feeds their domestic worker, Josa, "mostly Lebanese." The 31-year-old Josa claimed not to mind her lack of food preference, as she stated, "But it is fine and I have to thank God that all of their food is OK by me. There are some that are delicious and there are some that are not so delicious. But at least I can digest their food." Unfortunately, neither Marilou nor Junna shared her sentiments.

Why do employers disregard the eating preferences of their domestic workers? Sometimes employers can barely afford to cover their own food. In the UAE, the income requirements for a foreigner to sponsor a domestic worker are minimal—10,000 dirhams, or US$2,778, which makes it difficult to afford not just the salary of a domestic worker but also one's own living expenses. To put this in context, a middle-class couple residing in Discovery Gardens can expect to pay 50,000 dirhams (US$13,889) per year, or 4,166 dirhams (US$1,157) per month, for a one-bedroom apartment. If they are without an adequate housing allowance, this could leave them with less than 6,000 dirhams (US$1,667) to cover the rest of their monthly expenses, including the salary of the domestic worker, utilities, car payments, food budget, and the cost of leisure activities such as watching a movie or going out to eat. The challenge of covering the food expenses of a domestic worker becomes a burden. This is the case for example for Josa's Lebanese employers, who live in a one-bedroom apartment in Discovery Gardens and can neither afford to pay her more than 800 dirhams (US$222) per month nor accommodate her food preferences.

In other cases, it is not the lack of funds that precludes employers from recognizing the food preferences of their domestic workers. Some employers simply perceive and treat domestic workers as childlike. This is the case for Marilou, whose food preferences are not given any consideration by her employer. Marilou is given free rein in the kitchen. Yet she does not like most of the foods that are available to her there. Her employer, who is vegetarian, is also on a constant diet due to the appearance requirements of her job as an account executive for a major cosmetics company. While her employer's kitchen is always well-stocked, she only purchases healthy foods, such as quinoa, which Marilou cannot appreciate. Even though Marilou is fed three times a day and can avail herself of her employer's many "healthy" snacks, such as dates and energy bars, she does not feel as though she is adequately fed. She complained that she always has a headache because she is provided with "no chicken, no meat." This infantilization stretches beyond her employer's disregard for Marilou's food preferences. Her overall treatment as childlike extends to the monitoring of her friends by her employer, as she is only allowed to interact with other domestic workers in their neighborhood and explicitly barred from pursuing romantic relationships; is reprimanded and "bossed around" by her employer, who dictates how she should perform her job; and is limited to one day off a month, which is why she does not have much opportunity to purchase the foods that she would prefer to consume.

Cases of infantilization sometimes border on dehumanization. This is arguably the case for Junna, who has worked for the same employer in the UAE for nearly two years. Junna is employed by a wealthy Indian family that only consumes what Junna described as "spicy vegetarian Indian food." Because Junna finds most of their food inedible, she is forced to make do with just eating "rice and coffee," which is what her employers recommended she eat when she first complained about their food being too "spicy." To survive, Junna has resorted to sneaking in foods given to her by neighbors, but her employers do not allow her to consume any non-vegetarian foods. Junna complained:

> The problem is food. They are vegetarian. I am banned from eating our food. Meat I cannot eat because it stinks. Fish, chicken, all. Egg is the only thing available. I can't even eat canned food. One time my neighbor smuggled in some meat to me. She wrapped it really well but she [the employer] still smelled it, she screams "What is that smell Junna?"

> *What did they give you?*

> Pinakbet.[25] It was so good. (*Laughs*). I did not know they would be able to smell it even if it was wrapped so well and I was eating it outside of the window. She still smelled it. Since then, I have stopped trying to smuggle meat. Once she saw the picture of crushed shrimps on a packet. She asked, "what is that Junna? I do not like that. Throw." That is just a picture, okay? (*Laughs*) Sometimes I eat even if I do not like what I have available to eat. Everything is spicy. I would complain, "Madam, it is too spicy." (*Laughs*). So she said, "Oh Junna, just have rice and coffee." So rice and coffee is what I would eat instead of something I cannot stomach.

In order to get enough to eat, Junna has since resorted to sneaking in mild-smelling foods that she consumes at 4 o'clock in the morning, when her employers are still likely to be asleep and unable to smell the foods she prefers to eat. This disregard for the eating preferences of domestic workers indicates the lack of consideration that some employers have for their domestic employees' tastes and cultural preferences. As illustrated by the case of Junna, who claims she would likely go hungry if not for the generosity of her neighbors, this disregard sometimes extends to the dehumanization of domestic workers.

For Junna, this infantilization extends so far that she is required to ask her employers for permission to eat. While her employers have told her that she has free rein in the kitchen, Junna claims this to be untrue and says that she can in fact only eat whatever they offer her. This is for instance the case with fruit. As Junna recalled,

> They count the fruits. I can only eat when they offer it to me. What happened before was the ma'am looked for something I ate. So I told her, "Ma'am I thought you told me I can eat what I want." If that is the case, I told her, I would rather not eat their food. Then she responded, "Junna, it is okay but you have to ask." I told her, "Are you telling me that every time I eat I have to ask you? I would rather not eat."

The treatment of Junna as childlike is clearly foregrounded in the control and monitoring of her access to food; she has opted to resist and reject this treatment by purchasing her own foods and snacks and by relying on the generosity of her neighbors, including the employers of other domestic workers, who willingly share their food with her.

In general, the infantilization of domestic workers in the kitchen often extends to other aspects of their job and relationship with employers. In the case of Junna, she is given a curfew by her employers and must return by 7 o'clock in the evening on her day off. In the case of Josa, likewise, it is not only in the disregard for her food preferences that she is infantilized, suggesting that it is not just a lack of funds that motivates the behavior of her employers. Josa is also infantilized in other ways, including in her lack of a day off and in the mistrust of her employer, assuming that she would associate with the wrong people; in the disregard of her personal preferences in toiletries, which her employers purchase without ever asking what brands she prefers; and, finally, in their lack of regard for her expertise as a domestic worker. As Josa complained about their household management, "Everything was listed. She had a notebook. She had listed everything I needed to do, when the baby should eat, when the baby should sleep, everything."

The plights of Junna and Josa indicate that the infantilization of domestic workers extends beyond the management of food to involve almost all aspects of their job. It occurs not only in the disregard for their food preferences but also in their absence of options to choose their own brand of toiletries; the disregard for their skills and the micromanagement by their employers; and, perhaps worst, in the case of other households, the decision by some employers to withhold the wages of domestic workers until the end of their contract, which they supposedly do in order to ensure that domestic workers accrue savings while working abroad.

Dehumanized Domestic Workers

> You wake up at 5:00 o'clock. At 6:00 o'clock, you need to prepare their
> breakfast. They just watch you. *You can't eat. It's okay to drink water.* But
> there was no food because they didn't give anything for you. It's like, you
> fry an egg, one egg for you and one bread. But you only get to eat those at
> 12:00 noon. Then, your lunch is at 4:00 o'clock in the afternoon. Whatever
> is left in the fridge, and whatever is left over, that's what's for you. Then, they
> take out the bad ones, right. And those that were a little—They say, "Maybe
> this one we can't eat anymore." They take those leftovers outside, outside
> at the veranda, and leave it there. Then, he'd tell you, "That's your food for
> later when you eat." But you won't eat then. They just put it there to melt
> the ice. You only get to eat at 4:00 PM and then their dinner is at 10:00 PM.
> Then, you get done cleaning up at 12:00 AM. So, you sleep after 12:00 AM.
> Twelve, 1:00, 2:00, 3:00, 4:00, 5:00, the old woman wakes you up when
> it's time for them to pray. They wake you up to prepare breakfast, because
> coffee needs to be ready at 6:00 AM. After coffee, breakfast.
>
> —Mariz Ann, describing her first employers in Dubai, a Lebanese family

Dehumanized domestic workers are those whose employers limit their food
consumption. They do so by feeding them less than three meals a day, restricting
their food portions to small amounts, or distinguishing the foods they are allowed
to consume from the food for the rest of the household. In its worst form, the
dehumanization of domestic workers occurs when they are subjected to forced
starvation and limited to no more than one meal a day. In its mildest form, it
occurs when employers deny them access to particular foods. A common occurrence is denying domestic workers access to "expensive" foods such as exotic
fruits (e.g. blueberries) or imported cheeses (e.g. Manchego). Dehumanization
also occurs when employers only feed domestic workers their leftovers.

In some cases, employers deprive their domestic workers of food quite publicly. A frequent sight in Dubai is of domestic workers standing outside restaurants while their employers eat a full meal inside, or of domestic workers sitting
with employers in a restaurant or at a food court but clearly not eating while
their employers are doing so. When I first arrived in Dubai, front-stage Filipino
workers whom I told of my research often responded by expressing pity for
domestic workers. More times than I can count they had the same observation

as those shared by the counter worker at my favorite falafel stand in the Dubai Mall, "It is so important you study them. They are treated horribly. You see their employers deprive them of food when they go out to eat." While this likely occurs, I did also learn that it is sometimes the domestic workers themselves who are choosing not to eat with their employers. On one occasion, I saw a domestic worker sitting on her own outside a restaurant in the Dubai Marina, not far from a boisterous party with children eating in the restaurant. I approached her to confirm my suspicion that her employers were depriving her of food, but to my surprise she told me that she had already eaten, at another establishment, and that she preferred to be away from her employers while they were eating as she would otherwise be the one watching over the children during the meal. Sitting outside was a respite from her work. I share this story not to deny that employers deprive domestic workers of food in public, but to acknowledge that that is not always what is happening even when it looks that way.

Why do employers deny food to their domestic workers, or distinguish their workers' food from their own? It would be difficult to argue against the assertion that it is likely because they see them as their subordinates. This is certainly the case for 36-year-old Juliet, whose wealthy Swedish employers remind her of her lesser social status when they deny her access to blueberries. In some cases, employers perceive their domestic worker as subhuman. Maricar, a 28-year-old runaway who came to the UAE to support seven siblings, reports that when she complained to her female employer about needing to eat more than once a day, "her madam" told her: "You can survive on just water . . . dogs only need to eat once a day, so why can't you?" Then, when she complained to her male employer, telling him that if she did not get fed more, she would likely die, he replied, "If you die, I will just throw you in a garbage can. You are from the Philippines. You are not Emirati." Who are these openly racist employers? While they tend to be Emirati, they are not representative of the local population. Instead, they are likely to be older Emirati, who remember a time prior to the abolishment of slavery in 1963, and non-cosmopolitans, that is, individuals from places such as Al Ain, Fujairah, and Ras Al Khaimah, remote isolated Emirates with small populations.

Yet, as indicated by the plight of Mariz Ann with her Lebanese employers, it is not only Emirati who dehumanize domestic workers to the point of starvation, even though they are the ones who are most likely to get away with acts of abuse against domestic workers without any legal repercussions.[26] It is for this reason that Maricar will not pursue a case against her employers. In contrast, her counterpart Analisa, whom she met at the migrant shelter run by the Philippine government, will likely pursue a case against her Lebanese employers, even if only for the nonpayment of her salary.

The 35-year-old Analisa is a runaway who was underfed by her employers to the point of starvation. According to Analisa, she was only fed coffee and one piece of *kubos* (pita) in the morning. For both lunch and dinner, she would only be fed rice. When she complained to her employer about her lack of *viand*, meaning a meat, seafood, or vegetable dish that accompanies rice in a typical Filipino meal, she was told that rice should be sufficient for the reason that "it is your staple food." Analisa could not reason with her employer, who considered her not only a subordinate but arguably subhuman. For this reason, she absconded. As she reported,

> I told her, "Madam, if you don't want to give me food just send me back to the agency, my agency told me I have free food." She called the agency and said your housemaid is asking for *viand*, she was told then give her even just Indomie,[27] egg or tuna, but said she doesn't want to. No, because when her children eat and I ask for food, she gets mad. She says the food budget is for the children and that doesn't include me, that I can only have rice. Exactly what I did is I would mix, just ask for, coffee and put it in my rice. She said that is the way of eating in the Philippines, put coffee on rice. I told her how can I possibly eat rice without *viand*.

In general, the dehumanization of domestic workers is rarely restricted to food. Those who forcibly starve domestic workers are also likely to subject them to overwork. In the case of Analisa, she was not only underfed but she was also overworked, denied a day off, denied access to a cellular phone and the Internet, locked in the house by her employers, and made to sleep in a storage room.

✢   ✢   ✢

When asked to evaluate the current state of their employment, domestic workers repeatedly turned to patterns of food consumption. Indeed, as their observations establish, food provides tremendous insight into the moral character of employers. How employers decide to feed their domestic workers is usually telling in terms of how they perceive them and is accordingly likely to be reflected in other conditions of their employment. Recognized domestic workers are likely to be given a day off, if they are not employed by a conservative family with traditional gender mores or employers who are fearful of criminal liability, and given ample time to rest each day; infantilized domestic workers are likely not to have their priorities met by employers, who will not consider their other needs, for instance for a regular day off; and dehumanized domestic workers, finally, are likely not only to be denied food but also to be devalued in other ways, including in the denial of a day off and provision of an inadequate salary. Given that domestic workers are attuned to the significance of the moral character of employers in determining the conditions of their employment, how do they act on this knowledge?

Advocating for Good Employers

To counter the absence of regulation and the concomitant lack of standards in domestic work, a variety of advocacy groups are working on creating and promoting aspirational labor standards for domestic workers. These advocacy groups operate across different scales and include intergovernmental organizations such as the ILO, international advocacy groups such as Human Rights Watch, and sending states including the Philippines. Morals play a key role in the legitimation of the labor and human rights discourses that these groups attempt to advance in their advocacy efforts towards bettering the treatment of domestic workers.[28]

One could argue that these various stakeholders operate as "moral entrepreneurs," which are defined by Howard Becker as individuals or groups that establish and/or enforce rules against behaviors that they come to define as deviant.[29] In the case of domestic work, this deviancy would pertain to the actions of those who are labeled "bad" employers. In Becker's framework, moral entrepreneurs include both "rule creators" and "rule enforcers." Due to the efforts of moral entrepreneurs, there are moral discourses in existence that domestic workers, as central actors in the determination of their labor, can utilize to improve the conditions of their employment. In order to identify the process by which morals can function as a tool of "antipower"[30]—which, as I discussed extensively in the introduction, refers to the forces that would deter employers from acting on their ability to subjugate domestic workers—we need to understand how rules are constructed and enforced by moral entrepreneurs in such a way as to shape the workplace and the "moral subjectivities"[31] of employers.

Rule Creators

On June 16, 2011, the delegates of the ILO passed the Decent Work for Domestic Workers Convention with overwhelming approval, thus setting the stage for the establishment of labor standards for domestic workers. This convention calls for universal employment standards for domestic workers, including the enactment of state provisions for their protection, state recognition of their right to privacy, the use of a written contract, and the implementation of fair working conditions including one 24-hour rest day per week and proper remuneration. What was key to the passage of the convention was the mobilization of the morality of the delegates. As documented by Jennifer Fish in *Domestic Workers of the World Unite*, it was the establishment of the need to recognize domestic work as a "moral necessity for the elite"[32] that led to the passage of the Decent Work for Domestic Workers Convention. In debates, domestic workers and their allies would underscore employers' "moral responsibility for global justice."[33] The president of the International Domestic Workers Network, Myrtle Witbooi, herself framed the Decent Work for Domestic Workers Convention as a "moral fight"[34] and demanded that elites "recognize their moral accountability to 'the women in the backyard.' "[35] The utilization of morals also took place at an individual level, as International Domestic Workers Network activists directly interrogated ILO delegates about their own personal reliance on domestic workers, using moral grounds to make delegates personally accountable for the outcome of the convention vote.[36] At the end, as Fish observes, "this issue of moral accountability was present in the larger discourse framing the domestic-work convention as an anchor for human rights and the protection of the world's 'most vulnerable workers,' "[37] and the passage of the convention inevitably became a "moral responsibility" that was placed on the ILO.[38]

The moral grounds behind the push for "decent work for domestic workers" have undeniably continued to exert pressure, pressing receiving countries to create laws for the protection of domestic workers. Further fueling this moral pressure are efforts by Human Rights Watch to shame the UAE and other Gulf Cooperation Council countries into improving labor conditions for domestic workers. Since 2001, Human Rights Watch has regularly published and disseminated country-based reports on the worst treatment of domestic workers across the globe and in the region, releasing a report on Bahrain in 2012, the UAE in 2014, and Oman in 2016.[39] Finally, anti-trafficking campaigns have placed a spotlight on the worst conditions for domestic workers in the region, resulting in the continuous placement of countries in the region in the lowest tier of the *Trafficking in Persons Report* that is released annually by the U.S. Department of State.[40] These reports are usually covered in the local media, resulting in the creation of a moral discourse on bettering the treatment of domestic workers.[41] From the ILO to Human Rights Watch to the U.S. Department of State, the efforts of various "rule creators" have imposed moral pressure on receiving countries to improve the labor conditions of domestic workers and minimize their vulnerability to abuse. Indicating the effectiveness of these efforts, various Gulf Cooperation Council countries, as noted in chapter 1, have passed laws regulating domestic work.

Rule Enforcers

How are rules on domestic work enforced? Since the enactment of Federal Law No. 10 of 2017, the UAE has allowed unannounced inspections of households to ensure the better treatment of domestic workers. Yet, as demonstrated by the absence of standards across households, enforcement remains weak. One important hurdle against enforcement is the maintenance of the *kafala* system, which grants employers arbitrary authority over domestic workers. Still, the enactment of labor standards via legislation may pressure employers to see to their enforcement, especially as domestic workers are likely to encourage them to do so. Domestic workers, who are not simply passive recipients of the arbitrary rules imposed by employers, utilize the existing moral discourses about their fair treatment in order to improve their labor conditions. One of the things that empowers them to do so is the efforts by the Philippine government to educate them about their rights, including giving them knowledge of employment standards, prior to their migration.

From the ILO to Human Rights Watch, the efforts of various moral entrepreneurs as "rule creators" have legitimized efforts by sending states to establish employment standards for domestic workers. However, these standards usually operate as mere recommendations that are not necessarily enforceable by law. This is for instance the case when it comes to the salary of domestic workers in the UAE; while the Philippine government recommends a minimum monthly salary of US$400, there is no minimum wage legislated for domestic workers in the UAE. Still, the dissemination of aspirational labor standards for domestic workers by the likes of ILO and Human Rights Watch does pressure employers to recognize certain conditions of employment for domestic workers, as they undeniably create a particular moral discourse around rights-based standards of employment. Additionally, the existence of aspirational labor standards paves the way for domestic workers to become "rule enforcers." Culture, as Ann Swidler argues, operates as a toolkit to be used and drawn upon and accordingly informs our behavior and decision-making.[42] In this sense, the aspirational labor standards produced by moral entrepreneurs operate as toolkits that domestic workers can draw upon to construct and negotiate for "fair" standards of employment.

For domestic workers, the process by which this takes place begins with their disciplining by the Philippine government to be self-accountable for any potential harms of migration. As discussed in chapter 2, the Philippine state forewarns migrant domestic workers of the risks of labor migration, which lessens the state's own perceived culpability for any risks that the domestic workers may eventually confront once outside the country. One such risk is the failure of employers to adequately provide sufficient food to domestic workers. For this reason, the theme of food is quite prominent in CPDEP seminars, where prospective migrant domestic workers are repeatedly told of their entitlement to three meals per day. Types of food they can expect to eat are also described, as well as sizes of meals. For example, in one seminar, the teacher asked a roomful of seventy hopeful migrants, "who here likes to eat chicken? Raise your hand if you like to eat chicken." On cue, all the participants raised their hands, inviting the teacher to continue to make his point about the appropriate food consumption for domestic workers. He proceeded:

> In Saudi Arabia, there are a lot of chickens, big chickens, fat chickens. Who here likes to eat every part of the chicken? Raise your hand. Great that you like to eat every part of the chicken, because in Saudi Arabia you will get to eat the head, the neck, the wings and the butt of the chicken. Now repeat after me, what parts of the chicken will you eat? [*Pauses.*]

Almost predictably, each and every participant then responded and screamed in unison, "The head, the neck, the butt, and the wings." The teacher then ended the discussion by emphasizing his point once more, saying, "Remember that you will not eat the breasts and thighs. Those are for your employers." I use this narrative as an example because it resonates with the general lessons on food consumption shared in other seminars, suggesting that the Philippine government perceives domestic workers as subordinates but simultaneously reminds them that, despite their subordinate status, they are still human and thus are entitled to three decent meals per day.

As part of its protectionist agenda, a key goal of the Philippine government is to empower domestic workers and educate them about their rights. Prior to migration, as discussed extensively in chapter 2, domestic workers are educated about what the Philippine state has determined to be fair labor standards. In CPDEP seminars, they are encouraged to use these standards to gauge the quality of their labor conditions and instructed to "talk to your employers" if they refuse to recognize these standards. What are we to make of the reliance of the Philippine state on the workers themselves for the enforcement of their own labor rights? While it confirms the observation of the International Organization for

Migration that sending states including the Philippines face the challenge of enforcing its policies and programs,[43] it also points to the reliance of the Philippine state on the morals of employers for the implementation of fair labor conditions. When instructing domestic workers to "talk to your employers," the Philippine state is encouraging domestic workers to mobilize the morality of their employers. Indeed, domestic workers repeatedly used the aspirational labor standards set forth in their CPDEP seminars when describing and assessing their labor conditions, indicating that these standards provide them with the foundation for engaging in acts of moral claims-making.

Acts of Moral Claims-Making

My sponsor told me I am not allowed to speak to other Filipinos. I asked her why. I told her that when she sees an Arab, she greets them, and told her that we are like that as well. I am hard-headed. I fight back. Do you know my two years with them? One day did not go by that we did not fight. One time we were fighting. My job there was to take care of the child. She has a niece who is a liar. When she got home, I was surprised as she started just screaming at me.

I could not accept someone screaming at me. I told her "I did not come here to be treated like this. If you want my service, use it. If you are not content with my service, send me back to the Philippines. I will go back anytime." She did not want to buy me a ticket. She asked me if I am not satisfied with what she is paying me. I told her that I was not satisfied. 700?![44]

I told her to think about what time I start my work and when I end. I start at 6 am and sleep at 12 midnight. If it is Ramadan, we sleep at 3 am. They told me that they are afraid that the Filipina will run away. The Filipina, we are fighters and we escape if we do not like the situation. They probably experienced something and so they want to discourage someone from running away. It is because they paid so much for their visa and travel. But little do they know that even if they keep the papers, the Filipina will still run away. . . . That is what I learned from them. What I learned is you have to talk back when you know you have to, because if you do not, they will abuse you. You have to show that you know how to fight back so they get scared too. They will eventually change their behavior.

Alma, 33-year-old domestic worker

According to the British sociologists Sarah Irwin and Wendy Bottero, the ability of groups to make claims depends "on their position within a structure of

advantage," and on "the way in which particular claims draw upon socially ap-
proved obligation, appeals to collectivity, validated beliefs of justice and fairness,
and the persuasiveness of arguments of the inevitability of outside constraints."[45]
Applying their argument to the case of domestic work, it is clear that domestic
workers draw primarily from "validated beliefs of justice and fairness," rely on
the constitution of "bad" employers as deviants who would be confronted by
outside constraints, and appeal to the obligations set forth by aspirational labor
standards. Due to their position of structural disadvantage in the *kafala* system,
however, not all abused domestic workers can and do engage in acts of moral
claims-making. Those who are likely to do so are those with a "structure of
advantage," even if only a limited one. They include domestic workers who can
legitimize their claim using prior experience in other households; those with
access to other domestic workers who can confirm the validity of their claims;[46]
and, lastly, those with some bargaining chip, whether that is the emotional at-
tachment of a ward or the desire of the employer to renew their contract.

Acts of moral claims-making are common practice among domestic workers.[47] Even Maricar, the domestic worker whose Emirati employer likened her
to a dog that need not consume more than one meal per day, defiantly engaged
in acts of moral claims-making. Recall that she informed both of her employers
of her need to consume more than one meal per day and only resorted to running away after she realized that the risk of her death from starvation was of no
concern to them. In her case, she was clearly not able to mobilize the morals of
her employers. Others, too, in addition to Maricar, shared stories of how, in their
own ways as well as in their own time, they engaged in acts of moral claims-
making and attempted to mobilize morality in requesting the implementation
of particular work standards, standards they had learned from CPDEP, whether
those were a day off, a higher salary, more food, a lighter workload, or even access to a cellular phone.

Let me add a few more examples. Josie, the domestic worker who wisely
observed the existence of "good" and "bad" employers, recalled how she had to
"demand" a salary of no less than the minimum wage recommended by the Philippine government: "That is because I demanded. First, it was 1,000 (US$278).
That was the first seven months. Then I really talked to my employers. I told
them that I will not recontract at the end of my first year." She managed to secure a raise only after her employers decided that they wished for her to stay in
their employ for two more years. Manuella, weary of her employer's constant
nagging, pushed back by inviting her to install a webcam. Yet, not one to invite

confrontation, Manuella also admitted that she avoids talking back and usually makes her requests by writing a letter to her employers instead. One letter she wrote, for example, was a request for them to purchase a regular plane ticket, as opposed to a "non-revenue" ticket that forces her to fly standby, for her annual vacation to the Philippines. Kristy, who could no longer tolerate the tendency of her employers' child to bite her, had no qualms letting her employers know of the problem and that she had reached her limit. Junna, likewise, does not passively accept her employers' strict rules about providing only spicy vegetarian food. When her employers invite her out to eat at a restaurant, she declines if they insist on limiting her to vegetarian foods. She reported, "Sometimes when they go out, I accompany them and I ask if she would allow me to eat at my own table, away from them. I told her that if she won't let me eat meat, I would rather just stay home and not come with them. (*Laughs.*)" Finally, we should recognize Analisa's refusal to tolerate her subpar labor conditions and her insistence on her right to be provided with *viand*. Engaging in acts of moral claims-making is not an exception, then, but a pervasive practice among Filipino domestic workers in the UAE.

Conclusion

Without question, domestic workers in the UAE are vulnerable to the worst forms of abuse, due to their relationship of asymmetric interdependence with employers under the *kafala*. And yet, I found that domestic workers are unlikely to passively tolerate this abuse. Instead, they frequently turn to mobilizing the morality of their employers. They use morals as a tool of "antipower" to mitigate and deter their subjugation in the workplace. Paving the way for them to do so are the efforts of various moral entrepreneurs. In the absence of protective legislation for domestic workers and given the difficulty of enforcing what legislation there is, moral entrepreneurs have set aspirational labor standards for domestic workers, created a moral discourse in order to pressure employers to somehow meet these standards, and emboldened domestic workers to negotiate for better working conditions.

Because morality operates as an informal mechanism of antipower, there is no blueprint for how it can potentially shape labor conditions in domestic work. Instead, morals represent a toolkit that domestic workers can utilize to counter the imposition of subpar labor conditions. However, efforts by domestic workers to mobilize morality are admittedly limited by the unbridled authority of employers under the *kafala* system and the weakness of legislation in the UAE. With minimal penalties, employers can ignore the efforts of domestic workers to improve labor conditions. And indeed, many do so. Like Maricar, Analisa, and their many counterparts who likewise abscond, some domestic workers come to learn that no act of moral claims-making can ever mobilize the morality of their employers, which is a reality that can and has resulted, for some, in murder.[48]

CHAPTER 4

Escaping Servitude for the Unfreedom of Criminalization

SATWA IS A WORKING-CLASS MIGRANT NEIGHBORHOOD with run-down villas, old dark buildings, and cracked sidewalk pavements. It is adjacent to Jumeriah, one of the wealthiest neighborhoods in Dubai, where the multimillion-dollar homes of wealthy expatriates and Emirati boast the opulence of infinity pools, multi-car garages, and multilevel landed properties. The proximity of Satwa and Jumeriah magnifies the stark class differences that make up Dubai and reminds us of how the very poor and extremely rich live side by side in this city known for its opulent wealth.[1] In the blistering heat of June, I waited anxiously at a picnic table outside of a Filipino restaurant in Satwa. I was waiting for Mishra to arrive. Our meeting had been arranged by one of her employers, whose apartment she cleans. Ignoring the sweat dripping down my temples and the stickiness of my clothing, I waited patiently. Twenty minutes after my arrival, I saw a woman walking hesitantly towards me. I took note of her lack of confidence as she walked with her veil-covered head lowered and her eyes staring at the ground. Not long after she arrived to stand in front of me, I realized that her entire body was visibly shaking. She remained silent as I introduced myself, and I could only assume that meeting me, a stranger, had elicited an uncontrollable fear in her. Deeply bothered by her visceral reaction, I offered not to proceed with the interview, even though I very much wanted to interview her: she would have been the first unauthorized migrant domestic worker in Dubai whom I would successfully interview. Yet to my surprise, she insisted that we go forward with the interview. She explained that she wanted to help me with my research in hopes that I might, in return, be able to help her in the future. She explained that she had recently felt a lump in her breast and feared that she might have cancer. As an unauthorized migrant, she was without access to health care. She was hoping that if she was indeed sick, that I might aid her in returning to the Philippines.

Eventually, 36-year-old Mishra did indeed become the first unauthorized migrant domestic worker I managed to interview in Dubai. Women like Mishra are the most challenging to access, not only because of the clandestine nature of their work but also because of their criminalized status as unauthorized workers. The *kafala* system demarcates a clear boundary of membership for foreign domestic workers: they must be continuously employed as a live-in domestic worker, they must work solely for the household of their sponsor, and they cannot transfer jobs without the consent of their sponsor. Women like Mishra are criminalized because they have chosen to exceed the terms of their membership in the UAE. For foreign domestic workers, quitting a job without the consent of their employers means becoming illegal. Absconding migrant domestic workers are at risk of imprisonment if they do not manage to reach their embassy or consulate within 48 hours after they escape. What happens when migrant domestic workers choose to exceed the boundaries of their membership under the *kafala* system?

In various ways and to different extents, domestic workers continuously challenge the terms of the *kafala* system. There are domestic workers who abscond and leave their job without their employer's permission. While some avoid imprisonment by fleeing to their government's embassy or consulate, others, like Mishra, take a greater risk by going underground and becoming unauthorized workers in the UAE. But even domestic workers who stay with their sponsors sometimes push the boundaries of the *kafala*. Some do it by taking jobs on the side. With or without their employers' consent, they take on other work during their free time. This includes Manuella, who finds that her monthly salary of 1,700 dirhams (US$472) barely covers her son's college expenses. To augment her earnings, she works on the side, ironing a neighbor's clothes once a week. Some women engage in informal peddling of food and other goods. On her day off, Veneer, who retired at the age of 64 years after working for 16 years in Dubai, used to sell *balut* (fermented duck egg), which she purchased from a supplier in the working-class neighborhood of Satwa, as well as *tinapa* (smoked fish) and *relyenong bangus* (stuffed milk fish), which she prepared at home. Veneer would offer these goods to other domestic workers in order to offset the costs of her *merienda* (snack) and other expenses that she incurred on her day off. Veneer would also sell Avon products and Triumph lingerie, which she purchased in the Philippines during her annual vacation, to other domestic workers. In some cases, domestic workers take even greater risks. Some engage in intimate relations with boyfriends, risking pregnancy, which may lead to their deportation or, for those who are unmarried, imprisonment.

This chapter focuses on the plight of domestic workers who have escaped servitude by absconding from their employers.[2] They include those who flee to the Philippine consulate or embassy, where they wait to have their repatriation processed, as well as those who flee to an ethnic enclave such as Satwa, where they hope they can secure work in the shadow economy. Escaping servitude this way does not necessarily protect migrant domestic workers from a life of unfreedom. Those who seek shelter and government assistance for their repatriation back to the Philippines are likely to return to the same unfreedom of poverty that initially compelled their decision to migrate to the UAE. Those who stay on indefinitely as unauthorized migrants confront a different configuration of unfreedom—criminalization. As criminalized members of society, they are rendered unfree by their susceptibility to interference. Those who choose to exceed the boundaries of the *kafala* system as unauthorized workers in the UAE confront severe structural constraints that hamper their labor market opportunities, geographic mobility, and the recognition of their human rights. Unauthorized workers often find themselves with limited job options, geographically segregated in working-class migrant neighborhoods, and without legal recourse when unpaid or underpaid by employers.

The view of unauthorized domestic workers as unfree diverges from the insistence of some other scholars that illegality is liberatory under the *kafala* system.[3] They assume that for these migrant domestic workers, becoming "free from" the constraints imposed by their sponsor in the *kafala* leads to the negative liberty of being free from external restraints. This chapter, however, eschews the binary of migrant domestic work as either "free illegality"[4] or "indentured servitude," building on Julia O'Connell Davidson's observation that migrant contract workers confront a "continuum of exploitation"[5] and acknowledging the insistence of other scholars that we recognize the spectrum of "unfreedoms" or exclusionary conditions of membership confronting migrant domestic workers.[6] In accordance with these observations, in this chapter I recognize and identify the criminalization of undocumented workers as another form of unfreedom that defines the experiences of migrant domestic workers under the *kafala* system.

When Servitude Becomes Unbearable

As described extensively in chapter 2, Filipina migrant domestic workers are not blind to the possibility of their abuse when they agree to work in the UAE. In the compulsory government-run pre-departure seminar, they explicitly learn of their legal obligation to complete their contracts regardless of work conditions that might include long hours, the possible absence of a day off, limited communication with the outside world including family in the Philippines, a life of subservience, and the risk of physical abuse including rape. Still, they venture to the UAE. Migrants' willingness to risk the hardship of domestic work in the UAE stems from the absence of opportunity in the Philippines. They emigrate to escape the unfreedom of poverty, suggesting that for these women, migration from the Philippines to the UAE is a means of survival. Migration is thus a decision made under "compulsion by necessity."[7] Absconding is therefore not a preferred or strategic choice among domestic workers, due to its disruption of their livelihood. With the exception of two dismissed domestic workers who absconded to avoid forced repatriation to the Philippines, all of my interviewees had run away due to inhumane work conditions. These runaways were physically exhausted from overwork and had been starved and/or physically abused, all of which had put their lives at risk.[8] In other words, it is not servitude per se but instead the abuse of servitude by employers or the extreme maximization of labor under servitude that pushes domestic workers to abscond.

"I was made to work like a machine" is a comment one frequently hears from domestic workers who have absconded, usually followed by stories of overwork. Those who escaped had worked 12 to 18 hours a day. They cleaned, cooked, and cared for children or infirm adults. Most had not only one but two living rooms to clean. Some cleaned not houses but rather mansions. One, for example, had to clean seven bedrooms and seven bathrooms on a daily basis. This was Cherry, who shared her astonishment at seeing her employer's monstrous home for the first time: "I was shocked because the house was huge . . . there were seven bedrooms, then living room, two living rooms, seven bathrooms." While Cherry had to clean seven bedrooms per day, her friend Mishra, who likewise fled, had to clean seven cars every morning. Intensive cleaning had been the daily norm for those who eventually absconded. In more than one case, those who escaped servitude had been so overworked that more than once, they had collapsed out of sheer physical exhaustion. This includes Elanie, who fell down a flight of stairs and sustained a spinal injury after being required to carry a heavy Turkish rug up three flights of stairs. Recalling her accident, she reported:

It was incredible. The carpet that they made me pull was so incredibly big. They wanted to dry it upstairs. That is how I got into an accident. They wanted me to carry the carpet upstairs but their house is so big with so many floors. On my own, I had to carry the carpet all the way to the third floor. I fell and broke my spinal column. I told my Madam that I need to go to the doctor. I couldn't take it anymore. I lost my vision and I saw black. I asked my Madam if I could go to the doctor. I told her that I felt like I was dying. I kept on thinking that I cannot die here in the UAE because my father, my mother, they do not know what I have experienced. My Madam told me, "No, no, you stay here in house, stay and rest in three days." I responded, "How to rest Madam, more pain inside but now you see Madam my body not walk, I don't know how to walk now."

It was after her accident, as she lay in bed in severe pain, that Elanie decided to abscond. She could not help but think that she was likely going to die if she did not. Prior to her accident, Elanie had requested a transfer of employment, only to be berated by her recruitment agency. She had asked for the transfer not only because of her onerous work duties but also because her employer hit her every time she made a mistake. Elanie was also not adequately fed and, as she put it, treated "like an animal." Attempting to use the channels legally available to her only added to her misery, as Elanie's employer, upon learning of her transfer request, stopped paying her wages out of fear that if the request was granted, he would lose the fee he had paid the agency.[9]

"My employers treat me like an animal" is an observation that is not unique to Elanie: it was frequently mentioned by other runaways as well. Women were not only called *kalb*, which means dog but is also a derogatory term, but they were also treated and fed like dogs. Being inadequately fed was a condition shared by more than half of the interviewees who had absconded. Many had been fed only once a day, including Arlene, who complained, "In the morning, I am already out of food. Then, for lunch, I only eat at 3 o'clock in the afternoon. Bread only. Then at night, I don't have anything to eat." Others had their food rationed, including Mary Jane, whose employer disciplined her to the point that she was terrified of touching any food in the kitchen without her employer's permission. She explained, "Whenever the food inside the refrigerator is gone, she will accuse us of stealing it." Others were restricted to leftovers. Some migrant domestic workers initially coped with food deprivation by stealing food, for instance by hiding a piece of *kubos* (pita bread) in their pocket or sticking an apple or orange in their underarm. Others tried to reason with their employers, only to face moral deprivation. As Mariam noted, "I stayed with them for too long to the extent that I tried to win their trust, but I was always at fault . . . they looked at me as their slave. They never cared."

Elanie is one of many interviewees who claimed not only to have been made to work like a machine but also to have been treated like an animal. She described being deprived of food:[10]

> What's painful to me is that I work but I am not fed. I do the cooking, all of the work, what they feed me is leftovers—chicken bones—that is what they let me eat. Even when there is left over in the pot—there's still something inside—they won't let you eat it. They put it in the fridge and lock the fridge.[11] For one year, I didn't get to eat rice. All I ate was *tamar*,[12] dates, and water. That's it. That's why when I came here [to the migrant shelter] I was so pale and it seemed like I was losing my mind. I really didn't have—no strength in my body.

The person who denied Elanie access to food was the Emirati grandmother who managed the household. But others were also complicit in Elanie's deprivation, including the grandmother's son—Elanie's official sponsor—who did not believe her complaints of inadequate food provisions.[13]

Severe physical abuse as well as sexual harassment or assault also compel domestic workers to escape. This was the case for almost a quarter of the interviewees who had fled servitude. Some had been nearly beaten to death. This includes Veronica, who, after more than 14 years of working in the same household, was beaten to a pulp and lacerated with an *agal*[14] by her sponsor's nephew. What compounded the injury of Veronica's near-death experience was her sponsor's request that she not file charges against her nephew and attempts to appease Veronica by claiming that she was "like family." Sheryl, after being beaten daily for four months by her female employer, escaped by jumping out of a second-story window, causing her to break her back. JoAnn, who was tortured and locked in the apartment by her sadistic employers, finally managed to flee after more than a year of abuse when the house keys were accidentally left on the table in the middle of one afternoon.[15]

Physically abused domestic workers tend not to fight back. None of those I met in the UAE had done so. This included Veronica, who had passively taken the beating by her employer's nephew. When asked why they refused to fight back physically, they explained that they could not afford to do so. Fighting back could potentially result in their arrest and imprisonment. As Genlin, who was also repeatedly beaten by her female employer, explained:

> I can't [fight back] because I might be the one charged. If your employer is a local and you fight back, tendency is they will twist the story especially if they sustain bruises. . . . When we had our PDOS [pre-departure orientation seminars] and OWWA orientation, we were told not to fight back with our employers. When she slapped me, I could easily fight back but I was thinking of the consequences that if I fight back, I might end up in jail so I just decided to leave.

Despite not having been paid by her employer for several months, Genlin absconded. She also avoided seeking assistance from her recruitment agency, as her experiences with them when she first arrived in the UAE six months earlier had not been positive.[16]

Finally, some abscond to escape situations of forced labor. In the UAE as well as in other Arab states, employers will sometimes force domestic workers to work beyond the duration of their contract. They do this in order to delay or avoid having to pay the agency fee for the placement of a new domestic worker in their home. For this same reason, employers often refuse to allow domestic workers to terminate their employment before the end of their contract, resulting in a situation of "forced labor" in the eyes of the domestic worker but a "breach of contract" from the perspective of both the employer and recruitment agency. Employers have been known to charge domestic workers the cost of the placement fee as a condition of release from their employment. This was the case for a handful of interviewees who had been charged upwards of 10,000 dirhams (US$2,778) for their release. One domestic worker who found herself unable to quit was Alma, a single mother:

> I had no choice but to run away. If you can't stand the work, you're not going to commit suicide at your place of employment. Me, I don't want this, but there is no choice. You're about to fall at work. Then they're ordering you around. And, they lecture you every day. Your brain won't be able to take that. Plus, you're exhausted, rest deprived . . . I couldn't take it. Then, my agency, that's another one. They were really pushing me over there. I wasn't allowed to—I said, I am going home even if I have to buy my own ticket. They refused. They wouldn't let me go home. My agency won't let me go home. I said, even if I had to buy my own ticket. I've been there a month, right? I've already gotten my salary. I said, "I'm going home. I can't stand my work." "No." That's why I thought about getting out.

Although Alma tried to terminate her employment within the trial period of three months,[17] during which time either the employer or the domestic worker is supposed to be able to request a transfer, Alma's agency refused to cooperate, forcing her to abscond.

In summary, domestic workers run away to escape conditions of overwork, inadequate food provisions, harassment or abuse, or forced labor. Contrary to the claim made by staff at the recruitment agencies I visited in Dubai, domestic workers do not abscond because they are unwilling to work. They also do not abscond to avoid subpar working conditions. In their own words, they abscond because they are made to work "like a machine," treated "like an animal," or both. Notably, absconders rarely face only one form of abuse. Being seen "like a machine" usually means being overworked, denied a day off, and paid inadequately. Being treated "like an animal" means that they are not only inadequately fed but that they are also likely to be kicked "like a dog."

The Catharsis of Escape

In the early hours of one Friday morning, Geraldine, a frail, petite 45-year-old woman from Dumaguete, woke up determined to flee. A first-time migrant worker, Geraldine had been working for a wealthy Indian family residing in one of the high-rise condominiums in Dubai Marina. While her employers never beat her, they put her life at risk in other ways. First, they overworked her; second, they refused to feed her adequately; and third, they insisted on locking her in their 27th-floor condominium whenever they left the house, leaving her to fear that she might die if a fire broke out in the building. I met Geraldine at the Philippine consulate in Dubai, where she was waiting to be repatriated back to the Philippines, determined never to go abroad again.

Geraldine claimed that she would likely have died if she had not run away. At times made to work 18 hours a day, she suffered from fatigue. Airing her grievances, Geraldine explained:

> The outcome was my injured wrist got aggravated. I broke so many glasses because my arm had no strength. My back—because of all the laundry I had to do followed by me having to hold a glass of water—I got *pasma*. The stress on my back was a lot. I could not move my neck. To look back, I had to move my entire body. I could barely get up from bed in the morning. I think my max sleeping time was 5 hours. And my food was not enough. I just ate what I could eat because their food was unbearably spicy. And you cannot understand the smell and taste. What I would just do is make rice and I would eat that with tomatoes and cucumbers which I would marinate in lemon and salt. That would be my meal.

Pasma, a physical ailment of trembling hands and sweaty palms induced by strenuous manual labor, is a "folk illness" in the Philippines that is frequently mentioned by domestic workers in the UAE. Geraldine decided to flee after her employers refused to give her the rest she so needed to rid her body of *pasma*.

Never having had a day off in her seven months in the UAE, Geraldine sought help from other Filipino domestic workers in the building, those she occasionally met in the hallways and elevator. When she told them of her ordeal, they did not doubt or question her. Instead, they insisted on helping her. Though they had been fortunate to have "good employers," they were well aware of the ease with which an employer, including their own, could mistreat domestic workers. Without giving it a second thought, two of them decided to help Geraldine, prearranging a taxi ride for her that would pick her up from her building at 4 o'clock in the morning to be taken to the consulate. Terrified that her employers would be awakened by her noise, Geraldine fled without much thought, leaving the condominium wearing no shoes but not caring as she ran down the hallway to the elevator and across the lobby to her two friends and the taxi parked just outside the building.

Geraldine's escape to the Philippine consulate in Dubai went more smoothly than those of others in the same predicament. The door-to-door service she received is rare among runaways. Most others had to endure more harrowing experiences. Other interviewees had escaped by jumping from second-floor balconies, scaling walls that enclosed the gated villa of an employer's home, fleeing in the middle of the night and walking miles without knowing where they were going, jumping from moving vehicles, riding taxis without a cent in their pocket, sleeping overnight on park benches or in airport toilet stalls, or even slowly plotting their escape only to be reported by a co-worker who was afraid of being left alone. Escaping usually resulted in such physical injury that women at migrant shelters often asked me to bring them back extra-strength pain relievers the next time I visited.

Escaping is cathartic, and respondents frequently shared the experience through uncontrollable tears. Not one interviewee had fled by merely walking out; instead, like Geraldine, all had had to develop intricate escape plans. While most relied on the assistance of friends, some had no friends to call on. Some did not even have access to a mobile phone nor any money in their possession. Still, they managed to run away. Domestic workers abscond in response to the cumulative effects of abuse. Absconding is not a choice that they make lightly, as it puts them at risk of detention and deportation and also exposes them to the wrath of both their employers and recruitment agencies. As we have seen, domestic workers in the UAE cannot quit their job or transfer employers without the permission of their current employer, who has to "release" them from their contract.[18] Yet employers do not always willingly extend permission, forcing those who are severely abused to abscond.

Another difficulty that workers face in absconding is the fact that it is illegal for anyone to assist them, as that would technically constitute harboring a fugitive.[19] In the UAE, assisting an absconding domestic worker can result in a penalty of 6 months of incarceration and a fine of 10,000 to 100,000 dirhams (US$2,778 to 27,778).[20] And yet, despite this policy, both friends and strangers assist domestic workers in distress. Lala, for instance, a 35-year-old unauthorized domestic worker, had been illegally placed by her recruitment agency in a household that had been barred by the UAE government from hiring domestic workers, due to past cases of abuse. Not long after arriving in this household, Lala experienced regular beatings from her Emirati employer, a single mother of three. Lala was overworked, required to hand-wash the entire laundry, inadequately fed, and after more than two months had yet to be paid her salary. Lala could not help but fear for her life, frequently wondering, "What if my employer kills me?" It was only upon the urging of other domestic workers—who worked for relatives of Lala's employer—that she gathered the courage to escape. These other domestic workers secretly gave Lala 100 dirhams (US$28), which she used to get to the airport but without giving much thought to her next steps. Recalling the trauma of her escape nearly five years earlier, she recounted:

> [With the 100 dirhams (US$28)], I went to the airport like a crazy person. Taxi, no choice like I am going home. I am crying and then I approached the Filipinos. They were scared because they're afraid they'll also get caught if they adopt [help] me. Then, somebody took pity and gave me 40 dirhams (US$11), "Go to Dubai."

Following the instructions of the Filipino who gave her 40 dirhams—again, someone taking a risk, making themselves culpable of "harboring a fugitive"— Lala took the bus from the airport in Abu Dhabi to the one in Dubai. She continued:

> And I kept on crying. You're like staring into space, not realizing you've ridden [the bus], because it's your first time to be outside. You don't know what the rules are, that you should . . . so then I was able to go to Dubai, going around and around. . . . Then, I didn't get to eat all day that time, and I was at the airport

in Dubai, looking like a fool waiting for nothing. Then, I slept in the restroom. When they were cleaning, the Filipina cleaning person asked, she felt sorry. She felt sorry for me. She adopted [helped] me.

Taking pity on Lala, the cleaning lady took her to the working-class migrant neighborhood of Satwa, where she introduced her to other unauthorized Filipino migrant workers and where Lala has now worked and lived clandestinely for the last five years.

Other absconding domestic workers could likewise not have made it without the help of strangers. In the UAE, there exists a strong sense of camaraderie among *kabayan* (compatriots), as members of the Filipino migrant community are likely to acknowledge one another with a nod, smile, and a greeting of "*kabayan*" when running into one another on the street. As Cecile described it, "You know here you don't feel that you are in a foreign country, because in the mall, in the restaurants, in the stores, everywhere, there are Filipinos. You know even in Greece, when you see another Filipino they don't say hi to you, but here they always do. You feel that you know each other even though you don't. Even the Indians are calling me *kabayan*!! And I say, you're not Filipino!"[21] In the UAE, to not reciprocate a greeting from a *kabayan* would be considered odd and an affront. For this reason, many also feel compelled to assist a *kabayan* in distress. This is the case even when it is illegal to do so. Cecile, for instance, is one of many domestic workers who assist their *kabayan* in running away. As she told it,

> We have a group here, all the Filipinos. We are trying to help those kinds of persons that are running away or are trying to go back to the Philippines and need money. It is not allowed. . . . During Christmas we also help those who run away in the consulate. We have parties and then we give them credits to call home in the Philippines. . . . And also those housemaids that don't go out every Friday, they only have one Friday off a month, so we do things for them and they enjoy it. We encourage them to go out and we play guitar and play games in the park.

As one might expect, it is mostly Filipinos who assist other Filipino domestic workers in distress. Those who have assisted absconding interviewees include Filipinos at the consulate or embassy who have collected money to pay for their taxis, and Filipinos whom they encountered on the street and who helped them in the form of food, money, or shelter for the night. This was the case for JoAnn, for instance, whose physical appearance, including her black eyes, uneven hair, and visible welts made it difficult to deny that she had been physically abused.

The first Filipino she encountered on the street could not help but personally escort her by taxi to the Philippine consulate. Yet it is not only Filipinos who assist domestic workers in distress. Some interviewees had likewise been assisted by South Asian taxi drivers, who let them ride for free or at a discount; neighbors of their employers, who let them take shelter at their home after they witnessed their abuse; domestic workers of their employers' friends and relatives, who gave them money or a cellular phone; and even locals, that is, Emirati, who chose to turn their backs and not report them even though it was clear from looking at them that they were engaging in the criminal act of absconding.

In some cases, domestic workers in dire need of escape turn to social media, specifically Facebook, to plead for help and assistance. Numerous groups exist to provide support to domestic workers on Facebook. Pinoy OFW Tambayan, OFW household service worker, and Filipino Domestic Worker Abuse in Saudi Arabia are just some of the social media groups to which domestic workers in the region can subscribe. These groups provide a necessary social outlet for those without a day off, but also a source of assistance for those in distress. Johnna, an active member of one of these groups, explained:

> We communicate with [domestic workers without a day off] through Facebook. . . . They envy us every time they see our pictures posted in the Facebook. There are some who have never seen the outside of Dubai for 5 years already. . . . We are plenty in the group. If one member encounters a problem, we usually help her to leave her employer. . . . The most common problems are the beatings and physical injuries inflicted on them by their employers. There is also [a group] who comes to rescue them during worst cases. The helpers are told to exert all means to be able to go out of the house. We will go to their place and rescue, our cars would be waiting outside. . . . Yes in Ras Al Khaimah, one of our members was rescued since her employer was really that bad and threatened to kill her. It was even in the news. A team was ready outside to rescue her.

One need not be an active member of a group to turn to Facebook to plead for help. Those who feared for their life would, as a last resort, announce their distress by publicly posting pictures of welts induced by a beating, rashes formed from the pouring of scalding hot water on their skin, and black eyes incurred from repeated punches on their face. They would also post video recordings or speak on Facebook Live, providing a public testimony of their abuse and crying as they begged to be rescued. Some would even say, "I think my employer plans to kill me." They would share their address, describe their residence, and give landmarks that could help identify their whereabouts. If they had one, they would also post their cell phone number in hopes that it could assist in coordinating their rescue. Philippine government officials in the UAE admit to learning of the distress of domestic workers via Facebook. This was the case for Veronica, for instance, who shared pictures of her badly beaten body on Facebook, along with her phone number. In a matter of hours, a government official from the Philippine consulate in Dubai had reached out to her and helped coordinate her escape that evening from her residence in the emirate of Ras Al Khaimah.

Notably absent, in general, from the list of those assisting the abused domestic workers are the labor recruitment agencies. According to the Philippine government, the agencies are supposed to act as advocates for the workers once they are in the country of destination. However, due to their financial interests, there is little incentive for agencies to side with domestic workers in cases of abuse. While some do put aside their financial interests and assist abused domestic workers, more of them are likely not to do so, according to domestic workers. Agencies have been described by interviewees as bullying them into tolerating subpar working conditions, berating them when they request to be reassigned to another employer, and physically harming them when their employer returns them to the agency's office to request a better suited worker.

The Unfreedom of Criminalization

Filipina migrant domestic workers who abscond usually either flee to a Philippine government-run shelter or escape into Dubai's shadow economy. While the domestic workers in the government shelter include some with pending legal cases against their employers,[22] most run to the shelter in hopes of avoiding incarceration for absconding and to process their repatriation to the Philippines. Asked why they chose not to stay in the UAE as unauthorized workers, most expressed discomfort with the uncertainty of "being illegal." First, they would be separated from their family indefinitely. Second, their labor status would be precarious. Third, they would be forced to remain clandestine. And fourth, they would incur a substantial financial penalty of at least 25 dirhams (US$7) a day for every single day they remained in the UAE as an unauthorized migrant.[23] Rather than "becoming illegal," therefore, they would prefer to return to the Philippines and process their re-migration legally, whether to the UAE once again or to another destination. Indeed, almost all the runaways whom I met at government shelters, including those who had experienced extreme brutality and maltreatment, planned to migrate once again, because returning permanently to the unfreedom of poverty they had originally escaped was simply unfathomable.

The unfreedom of poverty in the Philippines is also the reason why domestic workers who chose to stay in Dubai as unauthorized workers refused repatriation. Many are the primary income earners for their extended families and/or single mothers whose children would not be able to continue attending school if their mothers returned to the Philippines. Jenny, a member of the indigenous T'boli, who had previously worked in the KSA, explained:

> Just for me to really achieve my aspirations for my children. That's all there is, really, My dream is just simple—just to finish school, be able to eat every day. That is really all there is. And for my family to be whole again. That's really all. I won't chase after anything more. For me, I just want to see my children happy, that they finish school, that's pretty much it. That they don't go through what I went through.

It was to ensure the survival of their family that unauthorized migrant workers such as Jenny opted to stay in Dubai.

And yet, the price of remaining in Dubai is living with the unfreedom of criminalization, a subject-position that stems from the "legal non-existence" of these migrants.[24] This concept cogently captures the exclusionary subject position of unauthorized migrants who are "physically present and socially active . . . and yet lack legal status."[25] Without legal status, migrants exist in subjugation as they are in constant threat of deportation, confined to low-end jobs, denied basic needs such as health care, and criminalized. In the UAE, unauthorized migrants are defined foremost by their status as criminals, as any association with them can result in prosecution. A zero-tolerance policy looms over their legal status, restricting their access to jobs, various services, and particular spaces. As mentioned earlier, anyone who assists domestic workers in the act of absconding, including hiring them, could be charged a penalty upwards of 100,000 dirhams (US$27,778) and face incarceration of up to six months, followed by deportation.[26] The public is encouraged to participate in the "legal non-existence" of absconders in that individuals who accommodate them—from doctors in hospitals to front-desk clerks in condominiums—can also face penalties.[27]

Unlike runaways in Lebanon, who are concentrated in domestic work but also have access to a variety of other jobs and include cleaners, tailors, nurses, waitresses, salon workers, or factory workers,[28] all but three of the unauthorized migrants in this study are domestic workers with childcare responsibilities.[29]

Those who hire unauthorized migrants, in spite of the legal risks, generally do so in order to avoid paying the annual fee that the UAE government typically charges foreigners who employ domestic workers. While most unauthorized migrant interviewees work for fellow Filipinos[30] who also reside in a working-class migrant neighborhood, some are employed by foreigners from Italy, Pakistan, and Tunisia. The Filipinos who employ unauthorized migrants are usually lower-middle-class, semi-professional workers, for instance administrative assistants or assistant managers, part of a two-income household, and parents who are choosing to raise their preschool children in Dubai. They tend to pay below-market rates, offering salaries less than the 1,500 dirhams (US$417) to which newly hired live-in domestic workers from the Philippines are legally entitled. The interviewees who worked for Filipinos were a mix of live-in and live-out workers and earned anywhere from 600 (US$167) to 1,500 (US$417) dirhams per month, with most salaries ranging from 1,000 (US$278) to 1,200 (US$333) dirhams. They can earn more as live-out domestic workers employed by other foreigners, with monthly salaries ranging from 2,000 (US$555) to 2,500 (US$694) dirhams. While two of the domestic workers had found employers on the Internet, specifically on the website of Nannies Dubai as well as the employment listing website of dubizzle.com, these sites usually cannot yield leads for unauthorized migrants due to their criminal status as absconders. As Mariam explained, "It's difficult. If you don't know anybody, who would help you? Because I looked in dubizzle before, they asked for papers. I looked all over the place." Due to their lack of proper documentation, most could only secure a job through word of mouth within Filipino ethnic enclaves in Dubai.

Being unauthorized is not a status that my interviewees would wish on anyone. When asked if they would prefer to be authorized or unauthorized, all, without hesitation, said they would prefer the former. While this might not be surprising considering the penalties and risks associated with "being illegal," what is surprising is that the response was similar even when the question was reformulated to specifically ask: "Would you rather have papers but work for an employer who's a bad person, or be in your current situation?" All still insisted that they would prefer to be authorized. Some explained that that was because they would then have more stable employment. Others mentioned that their lives would generally improve, pointing out that they would, for example, have access to medical care. Mariam, for instance, noted, "I like having papers better because if I get sick, I can go to the hospital. Right now, if I get sick, I cannot be taken to a hospital." The majority also talked about the ability to see their children in the Philippines, including Cherry, a single mother who has worked in the UAE for nearly six years. She shared, "Me, if I had money,[31] I would like to go home. I really want to go home. I miss my children already. Right now, if I had some money, I will go home. We won't be here [alive] forever." In the most basic sense, they would prefer to be authorized because it would enable them to live without fear. That psychological state is denied to unauthorized migrant workers, including Nada, who pointed out: "With papers, you are not scared of everything. You're really scared of your previous employer. You're also scared of the police."

Contrary to claims that describe illegality as a state of liberation from the legality of indenture,[32] illegality and the subject-position of criminality that it engenders in fact generate a specific type of unfreedom. As in the case of the "legally nonexistent" Salvadorans observed by Susan Coutin in the United States, an unauthorized status yields precarious labor conditions, substandard housing, the denial of basic needs including medical care, and a life lived in fear.[33] Unauthorized migrants live a stress-filled life that is financially, geographically, and socially constrained. According to my interviewees, working in the informal economy as unauthorized laborers has not been ideal. First, because most of them are live-out workers, their earnings are de facto less than those of their live-in counterparts, who do not have to pay for housing. Second, as unauthorized migrants, they have limited bargaining power. Employers hold almost all of the power in setting the terms of their employment. They can just decide to pay less than the rate initially agreed upon, as experienced by Mishra, who shared, "They decrease my salary I took as a part time . . . I was really mad and I went home very late . . . because they knew I don't have papers so I can't complain."

Unlike what others have observed,[34] my finding was that unauthorized migrant domestic workers in Dubai did not receive higher salaries than their authorized counterparts. On the contrary, their criminalization hampered their ability to freely participate in the labor market. Employers often offer wages that are less than market rate because they are aware that unauthorized migrants have no leverage to bargain for better work conditions. As Nada exclaimed, "Even if it were 800 (US$222), we'll take it! At least, you have a job instead of just hanging around like I do now." Mishra concurred: "If they say just 1,000 (US$278), it's OK with us because it's better than not having a job or money to pay for the house." Finally, unauthorized workers suffer from the inconsistency of their income. Unlike their authorized counterparts whose employers are legally obligated to continue to pay them even when they are out of town, unauthorized domestic workers labor under the condition of "no work, no pay." Mariam explained: "Here's the problem: When they go on vacation, I won't have a job. I don't know where I'm going to get money to pay for the house." During the time of our interview, Cherry, for example, had been without a salary for 45 days; her Filipino employers did not see the need to pay her while their family vacationed in the Philippines. She complained, "It is so hard . . . I have nothing to buy food with . . . I am late with the [rent] payment for now."[35]

A significant challenge faced by unauthorized migrants is their limited access to medical care due both to their lack of health insurance and to their segregation from spaces requiring identification. Identification is required for hospitals as well as condominium buildings, hotels (if they wish to check in), and alcohol shops. For this reason, they can be, and have been, denied access to the hospital. Nada, for example, has been suffering from the slow deterioration of her vision due to a cataract, but was denied treatment when she went to a hospital to get her eyes checked after they started hurting. She recalled, "The doctor said no, that there needs to be a working permit. He said he couldn't do it."

Health care is a need that the interviewees often had in the back of their minds. When asked what they would do if they got sick, all voiced a similarly emphatic response that they were unable to afford to get sick. "I cannot get sick" or "We do not get sick" were the common responses. The problem, however, is that they do get sick, which was the case for Ruth, who chose not to seek medical treatment after she lost more than 30 pounds in less than a month, not long before our interview. Unbeknownst to her, she had actually developed terminal cancer. She passed away three months after our interview, never having been able to see the house that she was having built in the Philippines and that she was proudly showing pictures of when we first met. Someone like Ruth could have theoretically visited a clinic serving migrants in a working-class neighborhood, but doing so would have been cost-prohibitive. In these clinics, a consultation can cost upwards of 100 dirhams (us$28), which is a significant portion of the monthly earnings of someone like Ruth, while a blood test costs at least 55 dirhams (us$15). Mishra, for instance, visited a clinic after fearing that she had developed breast cancer. Finding out that the lump in her breast was benign cost her 500 dirhams (us$139). Dental visits, which domestic workers would only seek in cases of emergency, can cost even more. Mary Ann, who had to have a root canal, paid 1,000 dirhams (us$278) for the procedure.

One of the other worries for unauthorized migrant domestic workers is housing, which is their largest monthly expense in Dubai. Most reside in "villas" in the working-class migrant communities of Satwa, Karama, or Deira. Villas in these neighborhoods are enclosed compounds with usually no more than four units each, facing an outdoor courtyard. The units, old and not updated, have long been abandoned by local Emirati. Each unit in the villa is usually just one large room without a toilet or kitchen. The kitchen is often an additional box-shaped room that is not large enough to hold a refrigerator, which then has to be kept outdoors. There is usually only one toilet in the entire villa. The units in the villas I entered were approximately 250 square feet in size, rectangular in shape, and would each house 4 to 5 bunkbeds, accommodating at least 10 individuals per room if not more, as some choose to share a bunk to save money in rent. Unauthorized migrant domestic workers usually rent a "bed-space" of one bunk, which would cost them approximately 450 dirhams (US$125) per month for a top bunk or 550 dirhams (US$153) per month for a lower bunk.[36] Those who share, which is not unknown in the community, would pay only half. In addition to their rent, they must also cover a portion of the Dubai Electricity and Water Authority costs as well as the Internet, which together usually come to 100 dirhams (US$28) per month. Housing accounts for more than half the monthly expenses of most unauthorized domestic workers, with the rest of their money going to food, for which they usually allocate no more than 300 dirhams (US$83) per month, and to remittances to family in the Philippines. As they are unable to secure their own housing without proper documents, unauthorized migrants are beholden for their room or bed-space to an authorized migrant who is able to carry a lease and from whom they can rent. Due to the high cost of housing in Dubai, the latter do not usually make too much of a profit from the rental of bed-spaces in villas, but do have the guarantee of having their own monthly rent covered, at the very least.[37]

The villas and apartments occupied by unauthorized migrants are usually crowded facilities. How they navigate the shared use of their housing was initially difficult for me to grasp, but I later learned that they accomplished this through time management of their occupancy. This is described in my field notes from May 31, 2014:

> Mishra lives in a two-bedroom apartment with 10 other individuals. Her room had 3 bunk beds—four of which were occupied by one person and another by a married couple. Another bunk was used for storage space. . . . Quite small, the open space in her bedroom could not accommodate a yoga mat. The place was quite crowded. The door to her bedroom did not open completely as behind it was a stack of large tubs, which I assume are used for storage.

She told me that her roommates had good jobs in offices; some of them, she said, were engineers. I was surprised, asking her why they would live there considering that they are likely to have some sort of housing allowance. She told me that they might be pocketing that money in order to have more to send to the Philippines.

I visited on a Friday afternoon. Mishra's roommates were mostly there, as it was a day off. Most were asleep. She was starting to cook dinner at 5 pm. She told me that the others had been using the kitchen for most of the morning and she had taken a nap earlier to give them space.

Particularly striking in the kitchen were the two rows of rice cookers. There were a total of ten of them, stacked on two shelves. The other shelves were stuffed with plastic grocery bags. In the bags were the cooking supplies of various residents— nonperishable foods, a tong, a spatula, and other such things. The bags allowed them to separate their things from those of others.

In the villa, the policy is "kanya, kanya lang." Meaning, "to each their own." No one shared. So, along with the ten rice cookers, there were about ten bottles of dish soap. Mishra told me that she and Nada each had a cup, and that they had an extra cup for guests such as myself. Likewise, they had one plate each, and one fork and one spoon. They shared one frying pan, one rice cooker, one small pot. The rest of the roommates each had their own.

The apartment was definitely crowded. The only place to "get together" or to welcome guests was the kitchen, which was as small as a pantry. Flies were swarming the kitchen, which was separated from the air conditioning in the house. There were three plastic stools that are usually stacked under the table. With the three of us each occupying a stool, there was no space left in the kitchen, not even to stand. At some point, a man peeped through the glass of the door to the kitchen, but he opted not to come in as he could see how crowded it was.

Even though it was crowded, however, my unauthorized migrant interviewees spent most of their time in their residences, and specifically on their bunks. This is not only where they slept but also where they would watch television programs on their tablets or mobile phones, read the daily news, communicate with family in the Philippines, and chat with friends. Yet their use of personal space was constrained, as they had to accommodate the schedules of roommates, some of whom worked night shifts. This forced them to constrain their actions even when in their bunks. Still, they maximized their time there because the bunk represented the safest space for them in Dubai; it is where they felt that they were the least likely to be under threat of detention and deportation.

Like the unauthorized migrants in Israel,[38] unauthorized migrant domestic workers in the UAE live in fear of arrest. Raids of villas in their neighborhoods are frequent. Stories of individuals randomly stopped by the Criminal Investigation Department (CID) often circulate among unauthorized domestic workers. "Do you know so-and-so, she was stopped at the corner last night," is a conversation one often overhears in Satwa.

Interviewees managed the threat posed by the CID in numerous ways. Some avoided trains and only took buses, because the CID supposedly never checks the migrant status of passengers on the latter. Some never took public transportation at all, sticking primarily to their neighborhoods in hopes of blending in with other Filipinos. Along with trying to blend in with other co-ethnics, they also tried to minimize attention to their unauthorized status by trying to appear middle-class in dress. Mishra explained:

> It is important that when you go out to work part time, you need to dress up like I do, like you're going to the office. It's like, you'd think like you're going to the office so they won't look jobless. . . . My friend, she's working without papers, every day she brings her laptop. She had a laptop, you'd think she were a manager. But she was decked out in jewelry. She said she wore those plastic jewelry just so she could accessorize.

Finally, they self-segregate and geographically contain their movements. They minimize their time outside their work and home. Some, for example, have never entered a mall. This includes Alma, who told me: "I haven't been to the malls here. I have been outside for one year [meaning that she had been a runaway for one year]. I haven't." To shop for clothes, Alma only visits rummage sales in her neighborhood, where she can pick up T-shirts for 1 dirham (US$0.27) and dresses for 5 to 10 dirhams (US$1.39 to 2.78). Others, in more extreme cases, never leave their apartment. They arrange, for instance, to do babysitting at home, asking parents to drop off and pick up their children from their residence. One woman who prefers not to leave her apartment is Nada: "I don't go downstairs, I am really scared." It was actually only with me that Nada finally felt comfortable enough to venture into a restaurant in her neighborhood, as she felt protected by the middle-class status projected by my appearance. Unfortunately, unauthorized migrants are not necessarily even safe in their own accommodations; Nada's apartment was eventually raided by the CID within a year after we first met in Dubai, and she was sent back to the Philippines.[39]

To Love Unfreely

Those who escape servitude tend to have a limited network of friends to whom they can turn for support. Of those who opt to stay indefinitely as unauthorized workers, many choose not to disclose their legal status to other Filipinos, even including their housemates, who often know better than to ask them about it. The more people that know of their legal status, the greater the risk of someone reporting their presence to the CID, which is not an unknown occurrence in the community. Indeed, many of the unauthorized migrant domestic workers whom I met in Dubai have since been deported, with two having been caught in a raid at their home. For unauthorized migrants, pursuing a romantic relationship is a more common strategy for securing support than relying on an expansive network of friends. Yet doing so means that they once again exceed the terms of the *kafala*, as the pursuit of romantic relationships is perceived as *haram*, meaning strictly forbidden.

Because sex outside of marriage is prohibited not only for domestic workers but for the population at large, romance is generally disallowed by employers. Less than a handful of the domestic workers I met in the UAE were permitted by their employers to pursue romantic relationships. Most employers bar any form of sexual relations, even for married women whose husbands also reside in the UAE. One employer in this study had even installed security cameras at her home after learning that the husband of her domestic worker had secured a job in a factory in the UAE. She feared that he would secretly visit his wife, her domestic worker, at night after she had declined her domestic worker's request for him to move in with her.[40] According to the employer, she was worried about the safety of her family because the husband was a stranger to them—the intimacy and familiarity that they had unavoidably developed with their domestic worker of many years not extending to her husband.

Yet domestic workers who have escaped servitude still find ways to pursue love and romance. Those who are still working under servitude have less flexibility to meet potential lovers, though some resort to long-distance romances via Internet dating. Domestic workers pursue romantic relationships with Western European men online, locally based South Asian men, and, finally, locally based Filipino men.[41] The romantic pursuits of domestic workers tend not to be devoid of financial motivations. Those who escape servitude turn to romance for the protection and stability it can potentially offer them. Securing a *jowa*, meaning a boyfriend or girlfriend in Filipino street language, usually means acquiring more stable housing, as a *jowa* can either subsidize or cover the cost of a bed-space or allow them to move in with them in the *jowa*'s living space.⁴² The latter was the case for Ruth, who, before passing from cancer, lived with her *jowa*, a married Filipino man whose wife lived in the Philippines. After absconding, Ruth primarily earned a living by selling cooked foods to Filipino vendors at the wholesale shopping center Dragon Mart. Ruth's *jowa* offered her protection from possible arrest by driving her to and from their home, provided stability by giving her free housing, and minimized her expenses to their daily food. Among the absconders I met in Dubai, Ruth was not alone in turning to Filipino and South Asian men to be their *jowa*. Those with a *jowa* usually received financial assistance, ranging from having basic expenses subsidized, such as payment for their Dubai Electricity and Water Authority bill or cellular phone data plan, to having their housing costs covered in full.

Yet relying on a *jowa* remains risky for domestic workers. The lesser risk is being stopped and interrogated by police when seen in public with a member of the opposite sex. This happened to Mary Ann and her Indian *jowa*, who were noticed for holding hands in public. Pregnancy is the greater risk, as it results in deportation. The authorized domestic worker Arlena, after being impregnated by her Pakistani *jowa*, quit her job and returned to the Philippines before her pregnancy began to show in order to avoid incarceration in the UAE. Her forced return to the Philippines, however, meant that she lost her income. Unauthorized domestic workers who get pregnant have it worse, as it is not as easy for them to leave the country. They must surrender to the authorities, who could enforce the 25 dirham (US$7) daily charge for unauthorized workers in the UAE and incarcerate them for their crime of absconding as well as for the crime of having a child out of wedlock. Mishra, Nada, and Mariam are just three of the unauthorized women I met who were eventually incarcerated prior to their deportation.

Finally, dependence on a *jowa* can leave women vulnerable to abuse. Since escaping servitude, the 29-year-old unauthorized worker Arlene, for example, has relied on her *jowa*, a much older and married professional Filipino man, to send her children in the Philippines 3,000 dirhams (US$833) per month. In exchange, she is barred from working or from leaving her bed-space without his permission. Arlene limits her interactions with others, particularly other men, as her *jowa* has more than once become violent, exploding in a jealous rage. Indonesian domestic workers who escape servitude seem to be even more vulnerable to abuse. Without the cushion of a robust ethnic community, they tend to depend primarily on Bangladeshi lovers for support. This has resulted in cases of human trafficking. Court dockets released from the Dubai Criminal Court regularly report on Bangladeshi men luring absconding domestic workers, often from Indonesia, into prostitution.[43] In contrast, such reports have not been made with reference to absconding Filipino domestic workers.

Conclusion

Migrant domestic workers confront a multitude of forms of unfreedom. They migrate in response to the unfreedom of their poverty in the Philippines only to confront the unfreedom of servitude in the UAE and, as established in this chapter, the unfreedom of criminalization for those who choose to escape the unfreedom of servitude. The embodiment of their migration as a series of unfreedoms, or scales of unfreedom, suggests the limited choices of domestic workers, or how the decisions they make are perpetually carried out under "compulsion by necessity." It also speaks to their limited negotiating power. Migration as a series of unfreedoms ensures countries such as the UAE a supply of affordable labor, starting with how the unfreedom of poverty pushes individuals to tolerate the unfreedom of servitude. Yet servitude means that even as authorized migrants, domestic workers are without the ability to freely participate in the local labor market and negotiate and leverage for better working conditions. Escaping servitude does not make them fare any better, as doing so results in their criminalization.

CHAPTER 5

Mobility Pathways and the Unfreedom of Poverty

IN 1995, AT THE AGE OF 16, Neneng found herself widowed with two children, a 6-month-old and a 3-year-old. Residing in a remote area of what is known as the Autonomous Region in Muslim Mindanao in the southern Philippines, she was without wage employment opportunities. This was due not only to her low level of educational attainment—she had only completed six years of elementary school—but also to the lack of jobs in her rural community. Neneng then decided to pursue migrant domestic work in the UAE, as it seemed to be her most feasible means of survival. Although she was not yet 25, the minimum age required by the Philippine government for migrant domestic workers as of 1994,[1] Neneng bypassed government scrutiny and managed to depart the Philippines by using the services of a "fixer," i.e., an informal recruiter, who provided her with an altered passport. In the UAE, Neneng worked in three different households from 1996 to 2003.

Yet Neneng's migration to the UAE was short-lived, curtailed by conflicts she encountered with her third employer, who chose not only to deport her from the UAE but also to impose a one-year ban on her reentry. In the Philippines, Neneng found herself once again without job options. Still in need of wages to support her children and unable to afford to stay in the Philippines for too long, she decided to pursue migration once again, this time securing employment as a domestic worker in the KSA, and arrived in Riyadh within six months of her deportation from the UAE. In the KSA, Neneng worked for one family from 2003 to 2011. She enjoyed her job in the KSA. It gave her the opportunity to travel, as she frequently accompanied her female employer to Paris and St. Tropez, where she experienced the pleasures of staying in her own room in luxury hotels. However, conflicts with a co-worker increasingly made her work untenable, forcing her to decide to "retire" and return to the Philippines. Yet, after two years and a failed business, she once again sought domestic work outside the country and in 2013, at the age of 33, reentered the UAE on a domestic worker visa. Not long after arriving in the UAE, Neneng found herself working in a household where, compared to the one in Riyadh, she was not treated adequately. Instead of returning to the Philippines and risking the imposition of another ban on her reentry to the UAE, however, Neneng then decided to abscond and join the ranks of the criminalized workers toiling in the country's shadow economy.

Women such as Neneng pursue migration to overcome the unfreedom of an impoverished life in the Philippines. The question remains whether or not they succeed: whether succumbing to the unfreedom of servitude enables them to rise above poverty. I address this question by tracing and examining the mobility pathways of migrant domestic workers, meaning the courses of action they undertake to secure economic security. "Mobility pathways" refer not only to migratory practices and processes but also to shifts in employment and in legal and social status. Neneng's journey offers a window onto the multiple mobility pathways that are constituted in the migration of domestic workers. First, it points to their multi-country migration. Second, it demonstrates their cross-national restriction to domestic work. Lastly, it illustrates their long-term dependence on labor migration and the unlikelihood that they will ever reach their ultimate goal, which is to amass the financial resources needed to open and operate a small business in the Philippines. As discussed extensively in the introduction, domestic workers in the UAE pursue migration in order to survive, i.e., feed their family. Yet they aspire to eventually do this in the proximity of their family. It is for this reason that they wish to return permanently, or "for good," to the Philippines.

Filipino migrant domestic workers engage in three salient types of mobility pathway: temporary return migration, serial labor migration,[2] and staggered temporary labor migration. First, there are those who try to resettle in the Philippines. They do not always do so willingly, as some return due to deportation or an unplanned pregnancy. For many, their return to the Philippines is merely temporary, making them nothing but temporary return migrants. This is because they are unlikely to secure a steady income, which eventually forces them to re-migrate out of the Philippines. Many then become serial labor migrants. Of the three types of mobility pathway, serial labor migration is the most common, referring to itinerant multi-country labor migration. In this scenario, migrant domestic workers currently in the UAE would have previously worked in another country and are also likely to later pursue migration to yet another country. Indeed, some domestic workers whom I met in the UAE have since relocated to other countries, including Jordan and the KSA. Finally, some just stay in the UAE. They comprise the staggered temporary labor migrants. The mobility pathway of staggered temporary labor migration refers to the prolonged migration of temporary migrants in one destination. Their migration is, however, not likely to be continuous but instead staggered because, reflecting the temporary nature of their residency, securing a new labor contract requires that they must exit the country to mark the end of their old contract and beginning of the new one.

Temporary Return Migration

As the ultimate goal of migrant domestic workers is to return to their country of origin, it should be no surprise that a sizable number of those working in the UAE have at some point attempted to resettle back home. Those who have attempted to return to the Philippines are the ones who have managed to build a home and save sufficient funds to operate a business. While the Philippine government has instituted robust programs to facilitate the return of OFWs, that is Overseas Filipino Workers, back into the economy and society, migrant domestic workers in the UAE admit to only minimally participating in these programs.[3]

While my research design does not allow for the inclusion of those who successfully returned and secured a viable means of livelihood in the Philippines, a sizable number of my interviewees[4] have at one point returned for a prolonged period to the Philippines, with many of those[5] eventually departing once again as either a "serial labor migrant"[6] or a "staggered migrant."[7] Supporting this observation is the survey I conducted of 199 return migrants in one province in the Philippines, in which 95 percent of the respondents expressed their intention to go back abroad, with 44 percent citing the lack of available jobs as the motivating factor.[8] There is a high likelihood that return migrants, meaning individuals attempting to resettle in the Philippines, will opt to pursue migration once again due to the challenge of maintaining a viable livelihood in the undeveloped economies in their rural regions of origin, where access to wage employment, including in agriculture, remains scarce, or even in urban areas, where they would be restricted to unskilled work in the informal economy. As many complain, "one earns abroad and spends in the Philippines."

Josie, who was 45 years old at the time of our interview, had worked in the KSA, Malaysia, and Hong Kong prior to the UAE. Before pursuing domestic work in the UAE, she had attempted to open a "buy and sell" business in the Philippines, but could not sustain it. Instead, she saw the dwindling of the savings she had amassed from earning US$550 a month in Hong Kong for more than six years. As she complained, "I decided to go home and I would stay 'for good.' I was 40 years old. But you know the problem in the Philippines. You just spend and spend and do not bring any in. My savings got depleted before I knew it. So, I wanted to go back abroad."

The businesses that most returning migrant domestic workers attempt to start are small in scale and limited in scope, due to the returning migrants' small budgets, and are unlikely to thrive due to the saturation of the markets that they enter. This was true not only for Josie but also for Mishra. Deported after 10 years in the UAE, Mishra decided not to return to her southern rural community on Basilan Island, due to the absence of economic opportunities, and instead opted to settle in the closest urban area, which is Zamboanga City. Upon her return, she purchased a wooden house for 28,000 pesos (US$540) near the water, in an area surrounded by members of the Sama Dilaut, an economically displaced indigenous community otherwise known as Badjao, or "Sea Gypsies," and opened a *sari-sari* store (sundry store) selling water, charcoal, and rice, specifically targeted to her Sama Dilaut neighbors.

Yet Mishra's business was not sustainable. It cost her almost US$2,000 to establish, and she saw very little return from her investment.[9] As most households in the community do not have direct access to clean water, Mishra intended for water to be the primary product sold at her store. To secure her access to water, she installed pipes and a pump, for which she paid 35,000 pesos (US$677), and, as she had been without electricity, purchased a generator for 12,000 pesos (US$231) and a water-storage tank for 2,000 pesos (US$39).

Mishra could not have expected to earn much, as the market rate for water in Zamboanga City is only 4 pesos a gallon (US$0.08), or 1 peso for a liter (US$0.02): she could not have expected to generate enough profit to cover the recommended minimum daily wage of 296 pesos, or US$5.80, in Zamboanga City.[10] During her first few months, Mishra earned 70 pesos (US$1.36) a day from selling water. She augmented her earnings by also selling rice at 20 pesos (US$0.39) a cup, allowing her to earn 30 pesos (US$0.58) for every kilo of rice that she purchased in the market for 70 pesos (US$1.36). She also earned 20 pesos (US$0.39) for selling a sack of charcoal at 5 pesos (US$0.10) a bag. With her goal being only to feed her children three meals a day, Mishra generated sufficient profits from her store to survive on a day-to-day basis. Yet, not long after she opened her store, a neighbor also decided to open a water-supply business, leading to a decline in Mishra's profits and an over-saturation of the market for water in her neighborhood. Limited in her funds, Mishra could not diversify her products to counter her dwindling earnings. But the downward spiral of her business did not stop there, as not long afterwards, a fire broke out in her neighborhood and wiped out her customer base: many of her Sima Dilaut customers were left homeless and relocated elsewhere. Forced to rely on her brother, who is a hospital worker in the KSA, Mishra then sold her house by the water at a loss and moved in with her brother's family. Not surprisingly, Mishra then prepared to venture abroad again. After less than two years in the Philippines, Mishra has once more secured a job as a migrant domestic worker. This time she will be migrating to Oman, where she has agreed to a salary of approximately US$300 a month, far less than the recommended wage of US400.

It is not only in sustaining a business in the Philippines that return migrants struggle; they also face difficulty in finding jobs that could earn them sufficient wages. The latter is illustrated by the case of Junna, who had previously worked in Hong Kong. Barely eking out a living as a laundrywoman in Manila, Junna could only afford to migrate to Hong Kong via a salary-deduction scheme. As she explained, "I found an agency that did not cost anything. You just had to go to a seminar. But the placement to go to Hong Kong is 120,000 pesos [US$2,850]. When you go there, they will take 10,000 [pesos] monthly [US$238] from your salary of 18,000 [pesos] [US$428]." But before she could cover the cost of her migration, Junna was terminated, and then deported as a result, because she could not find another employer to sponsor her residency prior to the end of the 14-day grace period given to domestic workers who lose their jobs in Hong Kong. After returning to the Philippines, Junna struggled to survive on her wages as a laundrywoman; her daily earnings of 200 pesos (US$4) could not cover her monthly expenses as a single mother, including not only food for her children but also the cost of utilities and rent (3000 pesos, or US$58). It was for this reason that she decided to migrate once again, reaching the UAE in 2011.

In other cases, the remigration of return migrants is made inevitable by the absence of any cushion they might have against emergencies such as the unforeseen illness of a family member or a natural disaster that hits their community. Manuella encountered both. After more than a decade of working in Lebanon, Manuella had amassed sufficient earnings to build a home with a partial cement structure in the Philippines, with enough funds left over to start a small *carinderia* (food stall) business in front of her house. She proudly shared:

> In the span of three years, I was able to fix our house. It is not that complete but the bamboo floor was cemented. So if a hurricane comes, it will maybe the roof will only be removed. And we already have the electricity and water line under my name. . . . Before we don't have a line, we get our water in the well. We don't have lights before, *kingki* [gas lamp] yeah, and also when I am doing my assignments in accounting of course there is a due date, if there is a storm, then *kingki* will die and then I have to put it on again, that is life.

From her earnings in Lebanon, then, Manuella had managed to install electricity and running water in her home as well as invest in cement flooring. But her return to the Philippines was short-lived, as her father contracted cancer soon afterwards, leading to her accumulation of 60,000 pesos (US$3,122) in debt. Around the same time, a typhoon hit their community, blowing the roof off her home. Many other return migrants, like Manuella, are forced to pursue migration if a family member falls ill or a natural disaster such as an earthquake or typhoon hits their community, because they are unlikely to have substantial savings or to have been able to afford home insurance.

This is a reality not lost on employers. Recognizing how unaccounted expenses often prevent his domestic worker from ever saving money, one Lebanese employer observed:

> Yeah, the poor lady sends everything. Every few months she has a disaster and she asks for salary ahead of time and sends it to her family. So, I had to pay her ahead of time and sometimes just help her as well with extra money. . . . She has nothing [after 6 years]. Everything she sends ahead of time. OK, her sister is studying at a university and her mom got sick and [then the] accident [happened]. She had her house washed away. Don't know one or two times now in 6 years. I don't know how this will carry on. I am not sure.

Return migration is not a feasible mobility pathway for many. Upon their return to the Philippines, they are still likely to confront economic precarity, as they face an unstable labor market where they are limited to low-wage employment as unskilled and contingent workers, or alternatively, face difficulty in identifying a sustainable business. The businesses that the government suggests as successful options are usually *babuyan* (pig farms), *carinderia* (food stalls), or *sari sari* stores (sundry stores), all of which are vulnerable to competition and liable to failure.

In addition to "buy and sell" businesses and *sari-sari* stores, other failed businesses of the domestic workers I interviewed include an Internet shop, a *babuyan* (pig farm), and beauty parlor. What adds to the likelihood of failure for return migrant domestic workers is the absence of protection against unforeseen expenses. And further aggravating their vulnerability are the minimal government benefits and protections in their undeveloped regions, where medical services are scarce, deforestation intensifies the effects of natural disasters including flooding, and economies remain stagnant. In other words, the conditions that initially prompted their migration remain in place and encourage their remigration.

Serial Labor Migration

The ideal mobility pathway for a migrant domestic worker is to secure uninterrupted employment where they can remain in one country with a "good employer," one who does not physically harm, overwork, underpay, or underfeed them, as this not only guarantees their access to a continuous income but also minimizes the costs of their migration. In this scenario, the employer would give them regular raises and send them to the Philippines for annual or biennial paid vacations. This mobility pathway, one of "segmented assimilation"[11] into domestic work, is, however, a rare enough achievement that accomplishing it can even earn one a feature in *Gulf News,* one of the largest English-language circulating newspapers in the UAE.

This was the case for Aurelia Villarta, whose return migration to the Philippines after working in one household for nearly 30 years was celebrated in the media.[12] Arriving in the UAE in 1991, Aurelia, with no children of her own, worked continuously for one Greek family, acting as a second mother to the now-adult sons of the family whom she helped raise from the time they were three months and 3 years old, respectively. At the age of 71, and having exceeded the maximum age of 65 for migrant domestic workers in the UAE, Aurelia was eventually forced to retire and return to the Philippines in 2019. What made Aurelia's story merit media attention was its exceptionalism. Of my 85 interviewees, only 10 had worked in the UAE for more than a decade.

Unlike Aurelia, most migrant domestic workers find that the precarious conditions of their temporary residence may mean the interruption of their labor migration by forces beyond their control. This then instigates their return to the Philippines, followed by their likely remigration to another destination. This scenario, that of serial labor migration, is the most common mobility pathway among domestic workers. Of my 85 interviewees, 41 could be categorized as serial labor migrants, having worked in more than one destination in the course of their migration. Serial labor migration refers to the "multi-country, itinerant labor migration patterns of temporary low-skilled migrant workers."[13] This mobility pathway is distinct from "stepwise international migration," meaning a multi-country upward-trajectory migratory scheme undertaken by domestic workers who begin in a lower-cost destination such as Singapore and end up in the higher-cost destinations of, first, Hong Kong and, ultimately, Canada, where they can settle permanently.[14] Serial labor migrants have less control over their mobility pathway than do stepwise international migrants. They are less likely to aspire to and practice a multinational stepwise ascension across the migration tiers. They find that various structural factors, including the possibility of deportation, limited financial capital, and a low level of educational attainment prevent them from following a linear, progressivist trajectory of stepwise migration. These structural forces place ceilings on their mobility options and in most cases prevent their entry to the highest-tier destination of Canada.[15]

Various forces account for the interruption of the "segmented assimilation" of migrant domestic workers in one country in such a way as to prompt their multinational migration as serial labor migrants.[16] For some interviewees, it was the outbreak of war or uprisings that interrupted their labor migration. This was the case for Jovie, a single mother of two teenage children, who saw firsthand the bombing of buildings during the war in Lebanon. She recalled fleeing to the Philippine embassy, where officials assisted her and other displaced nationals, transporting them by bus from Beirut to Damascus and eventually by plane to Manila. But the trauma of war did not deter her from pursuing migration once again, as soon after returning to the Philippines she worked on processing her outmigration, ending up initially in Kuwait, where she worked for two years. and then eventually landing in the UAE. As she recalled, "I went home and then I stayed in the Philippines for three months. Then I applied to an agency. . . . [The war] was nothing to me. I just could not stay in the Philippines."

In other cases, conflicts with employers lead not just to the termination of a worker's contract but also to deportation, resulting in the interruption of that worker's labor migration. In most countries of destination, employers face no penalty if they choose to process a domestic worker's deportation. Among my interviewees, some had been deported for the most minor of infractions, including posting "sexy" pictures on Facebook, lightly spanking a child who had hit them, or working too slowly. Illustrating their despotic power, employers can even force the deportation of a domestic worker as retaliation for the worker's decision not to renew their contract. This had occurred to at least two of my interviewees.

Because deportation does not eliminate the dependency of migrant domestic workers on their earnings from labor migration, it should not be a surprise that the vast majority of those who run away from abusive labor conditions and await repatriation at the Philippine embassy or consulate intend to pursue labor migration once again. This was the case for Maricar. Due to her experience of abuse, domestic work was not a job that she would recommend. As she emphatically stated, "For me don't come here if you will just work as maids. If you have the brain, talent and skills, why work as maids here? They treat you like animals here, like a pig, like a dog." But her negative experience did not deter her from wishing to migrate once again. When asked if she planned to pursue migrant domestic work in another country after her repatriation to the Philippines, she responded, "If given the chance, why not?" Likewise, 36-year-old Rose, who had absconded from an employer who had treated her as an emotional punching bag, planned to process her migration soon after she was repatriated to the Philippines. Explaining why, she commented: "I want to make things right for my son then I'll work abroad again for my son's future."

It is not always "bad" experiences such as war or workplace abuse that interrupt the settlement of domestic workers in one country, prompting their *serial labor migration*. In some cases, it is a lack of investment in their job that discourages migrant domestic workers from renewing their contract and accordingly encourages their pursuit of labor migration elsewhere. This was the case for many interviewees, including Manuella, who wondered if she would find a less racist employer in a country other than Lebanon, where an employer had forced her to use lice remover when first entering their home. Jocelyn, after working for more than 6 years in one household in Jordan, no longer wished to stay after being denied a salary increase. With her salary stagnating at US$200 per month, she decided to pursue migration elsewhere in hopes of finding an employer who would compensate her with the minimum monthly wage of US$400 recommended by the Philippine government. She also wanted a different experience. As she reported, "I went home. They wanted me to come back. But I changed my mind. Then she told me to give them my contact number in case they needed me. Before I came here [UAE], they called me and asked me to go back there. But I wanted to experience something different." What allowed Jocelyn the option of migrating elsewhere was the robust migration infrastructure in the Philippines and the hundreds of agencies she could turn to to assist her in securing a job in one of the more than seventy countries across the globe where Filipino domestic workers are employed.[17] Interestingly, after two years in the UAE, Jocelyn ultimately decided to return to Jordan, because she realized that her former employers had treated her relatively well despite her low earnings.

While Filipino migrant domestic workers have a wide range of choices of destinations, those who are in the UAE have mainly circulated across Arab states. Common countries of previous employment include Bahrain, Kuwait, Lebanon, Jordan, the KSA, and Qatar, though a sizable number have also been employed in Hong Kong, Israel, Malaysia, Taiwan, and Singapore. They remain concentrated in the region for a variety of reasons. First, many do not meet the minimal educational qualifications to migrate elsewhere. With most only having finished the sixth grade, they do not have the high school degree required in most other destinations nor of course the college degree required in Canada. Second, they wish to minimize the cost of migration. This is the case for example with Jing, a domestic worker in her thirties, who considered migrating to Hong Kong or Taiwan after she had completed a two-year contract in Kuwait. But she was deterred by the hefty placement fees she would have been saddled with if she migrated to either destination. It was for this reason that she settled on the destination of the UAE, where she has since renewed her contract to work in the same household more than once.

In many cases, serial labor migration is prompted by unpredictable interruptions to the labor migration of domestic workers, whether because of war, job termination, or state deportation. Adding to the unpredictability of their situation is their inability to select their specific country of destination, as this is largely determined by the available "job order" at a government-accredited recruitment agency. Indeed, serial labor migration is a result of the minimal control that domestic workers have over their migration process, indicating that this mobility pathway is a reflection of the precarity of their labor migration.[18]

Staggered Temporary Labor Migration

Maximizing their labor market opportunities in one destination country offers migrant domestic workers the most promising mobility pathway. Staying in one country allows them to minimize their migration costs, as it enables them to avoid recruitment agency fees and shorten their period of unemployment between jobs. Yet staying in one country, even with consistent employment, still requires temporary migrant workers to exit and reenter, because their legal residence is contingent on their exit upon the termination of their contract and reentry with a visa that corresponds to their new contract. The inability of migrant domestic workers to stay continuously as permanent legal residents leads to their staggered temporary labor migration. As is the case for the "staggered [Asian] migrants" who enter, exit, and reenter Australia on a variety of visas on their pathway to permanent residence, the process of obtaining legal residency for migrant domestic workers who seek long-term temporary residence in the UAE requires that they maintain labor contracts for a variety of temporary durations, which entails their regular exit from and reentry into the country.[19]

Representing a smaller group than serial labor migrants, staggered temporary labor migrants are those who have solely worked in the UAE.[20] Indicating the precarity of their legal residence, the staggered temporary labor migration of domestic workers is contingent on the cooperation of their employer-sponsor and their willingness to "release" as opposed to "cancel" their visa. As mentioned in earlier chapters, releasing them means allowing them to seek and secure another sponsor upon the termination of their employment, while canceling means not allowing them to do so, resulting in their deportation from the country. Haydee, a 51-year-old domestic worker who had worked for more than two decades in the UAE, tolerated what she considered subpar labor conditions because she feared the cancellation of her visa. She explained:

> I really want to [quit], I want a higher salary. But I don't want to move out with them until they release me. I don't want that they cancel my papers. They're very selfish. They would never release you instead they will just cancel your employment. I will just wait for them to release me so I can also look for another employer.

To secure her "release," Haydee is waiting to complete her two-year contract. Then, she plans to obtain a job in another household. Haydee is not alone. To avoid cancellation and deportation, domestic workers are unlikely to quit prior to the end of their contract, which in some cases means that they have to tolerate less-than-ideal conditions.

This was the case for 29-year-old Roda, for example, who also tolerated poor working conditions so as not to risk her "cancellation." During her first three years as a domestic worker, she earned well below minimum wage and significantly less than a family friend of hers, who earned a monthly salary of 2,500 dirhams (US$694). Every six months or so, Roda saw an incremental increase in her salary, which started at 700 dirhams (US$194) and eventually topped out at 1,200 dirhams (US$333). Her friend, who had prior experience working as a domestic worker in the KSA and Singapore, advised Roda not to tolerate her subpar labor conditions: "She taught me to become brave. How, they will just step on you and you will not answer you need to answer back if you know your rights. So she said do not be scared as long as you are right, you fight." However, as a first-time migrant worker, it was difficult for Roda to heed her friend's advice to "fight," and instead she found herself tolerating the absence of a day off for three years, lack of access to a cellular phone or Internet,[21] inadequate food, and even the initial withholding of her salary, as her employers insisted on being the ones to send money to her family in the Philippines. Though she was tempted to abscond, Roda did not do so, as her employers were withholding her passport and she did not want to become an unauthorized worker in the UAE. Tolerating subpar labor conditions does not always guarantee one's eventual release, but in Roda's case her patience and perseverance paid off. She admits, however, that she had to go to extreme lengths to ensure her release, at some point relying on black magic to gain her employers' trust.

Domestic workers are compelled to tolerate subpar labor conditions in hopes of being "released" due to their relation of asymmetric interdependency with employers under the *kafala*. This is the case despite claims by employers that they would never act on their despotic power and refuse a domestic worker's request for an early "release," because that would be inhumane. Mary Ann, 29 years old, for example, reported: "[My employers] told me that they will let me go if I do not want to renew with them. They said they cannot do anything about it. They cannot force me. They will let me go and look for another."

Domestic workers wish to be released because remaining in the UAE as staggered temporary labor migrants can potentially enable them to command a higher salary. Hiring locally lets employers bypass agency fees because the UAE government does not require their use, allowing the employers to pass along the savings to the domestic worker. For this reason, local hires tend to have an entry rate in excess of 2,000 dirhams (US$555), as compared to the minimum wage of 1,500 dirhams (US$417). Prior to the termination of their contract, domestic workers who secure a "release" from their sponsor can search for a new employer, which they have been known to do through referrals by their old employer, the website dubizzle.com, or job bulletins at local supermarkets.

Those who are not able to find a new employer in time have the option of leaving by car for a neighboring country such as Oman or, as they did in the past prior to the escalation of tensions between Iran and the UAE, taking a 45-minute airplane ride to the free-trade zone of Kish Island in Iran. They can then reenter the UAE on a 30-day visit visa through the sponsorship of a friend, usually another Filipino migrant worker, during which time they can again attempt to secure employment. If successful, they must then re-exit the country yet again on their visit visa, and finally reenter on their employment visa. In some cases, domestic workers must leave without yet having any guarantee of employment because they have failed to secure a job or to complete the processing of their employment visa prior to the expiration of their visit visa. Those who are awaiting their employment visa usually exit to a neighboring country but risk not being able to reenter the UAE. It is not unknown for Filipino migrant workers to wait in limbo for their employment visas to the UAE in various transit cities: during the time of my research, the Philippine ambassador to the UAE, Grace Princesa, visited Kish Island in order to verify the validity of claims about "trapped" Filipinos, and was surprised to find them to be true.

Migrant domestic workers who complete multiple labor contracts in the UAE tend to earn more than newcomers. Those who work continuously for one household tend to earn the highest monthly incomes, as employers sometimes reward those who choose to renew their labor contracts. Jing, for instance, opted to stay with her employers despite not having a day off, and as a reward for her loyalty saw her monthly salary triple, increasing from 800 (US$222) to 2,400 dirhams (US$667). Likewise, 26-year-old Johnna, who worked for one household for more than five years in the UAE, also saw her salary steadily increase, from an initial rate of 1,000 (US$278) to 1,200 (US$333), 1,400 (US$389), and then 1,500 dirhams (US$417).

Yet domestic workers cannot always rely on being continuously employed, as the majority of employers are foreigners who are only temporarily based in the UAE. Upon the departure of their employers from the UAE, domestic workers will not only see an end to their employment but possibly also a disruption in the upward trajectory of their salary and other employment benefits they have earned out of loyalty to one household. While they will still, as staggered temporary labor migrants, likely earn more than newcomers from the Philippines, they are not always able to secure work that pays above the minimum wage. When moving from one job to the next, domestic workers actually cannot expect to see a gradual increase in their salary or improvement in their workplace conditions, despite their labor experience and expertise.

Instead, staggered temporary labor migrants who stay employed in the UAE but for a variety of households often see, upon the termination of their contract, a mismatch in the upward and downward trajectories of their labor conditions.

Many, for instance, will see a decline in salary. This was the case for Haydee, whose monthly salary declined from 1,500 (US$417) to 1,300 (US$361) dirhams a month when she switched jobs for the third time since arriving in the UAE, nearly two decades earlier. Likewise, 44-year-old Lei, who initially entered the UAE on a visit visa and found her jobs locally with British families on dubbizle. com, saw her monthly salary decline, from 4,000 dirhams (US$1,111) with her first employer to 3,000 dirhams (US$833) with her second employer. Lits, a 54-year-old who has changed employers numerous times in the past decade, claimed that she does not hesitate to ask for a release whenever she is no longer satisfied at work. As she noted, "If I am not happy with any sponsor, I would ask for a release and find someone else." Yet changing jobs has led to a decline in her monthly salary, which is currently 1,300 dirhams (US$361), and much less than her earlier salary of 2,000 dirhams (US$555).

Others, in contrast, see an improvement in their job conditions from one employer to the next. Cecille, who was employed for four years by the same Greek family, where she earned a monthly income of 1,700 dirhams (US$472), found that her work conditions improved when she switched jobs and secured employment with an Australian family that paid her 2,500 dirhams (US$694) per month. Yet sometimes a salary increase comes with its own set of burdens. This was the case for 31-year-old Divina, who initially worked for a young Emirati couple with school-aged children. Only earning 700 dirhams (US$194) per month, Divina requested and secured her release at the end of her two-year contract. She landed in the household of a Canadian family that more than doubled her monthly salary, to 1,800 dirhams (US$500), but the price for this was an intensified workload. While she had worked for no more than 8 hours a day for the Emirati family, for the Canadian family she had to work nearly nonstop from 6 am to 10 pm, and also saw her weekly day off reduced, from a full day to only 10 am to 6 pm on Friday.

These variations across households in salary and conditions indicate the absence of labor standards in domestic work. As domestic workers move from one job to the next, the inconsistencies in labor standards also establish the absence of any guaranteed reward for their labor experience. This in turn disincentives many from staying in the UAE upon the termination of their labor contract. At the same time, it invites them to pursue other types of employment, for instance front-stage jobs. Unlike in other destinations, such as Singapore, domestic workers in the UAE are not barred from securing other types of jobs. Yet, perhaps due to their low level of educational attainment, domestic workers on the whole are unlikely to seek higher-status employment. Those who do include younger workers and those with a higher level of education. My interviewees included some who later transitioned to working as counter help in a fast-food establishment, as a supermarket clerk, as teaching assistants in classrooms with autistic children, as a cabdriver, and as a waiter. It is even more unlikely for other ethnic groups of domestic workers to secure other types of employment. Filipinos are distinguished from other groups by their better command of the English language, which opens up a wider range of jobs to them.

Although it is possible, the transition from domestic work to another occupation presents a challenging feat, one that requires resources. In some cases, employers assist in the transition. The aforementioned Johnna, for example, was being encouraged by her employers to pursue classes in a technical school so as to acquire the skills necessary to eventually secure a higher-paying job. Likewise, 29-year-old Rosa, who previously worked in Jordan, is now a supermarket clerk, which is a job she obtained with the assistance of her Emirati employers. Roda is another one of the few domestic workers who transitioned to front-stage employment; she now works as a waiter in a popular American restaurant chain. However, it was not easy for Roda, because her former employer did not encourage her to seek other work. Instead, Roda first had to secure her "release" by convincing her employer to allow her to work elsewhere. Unsure that her employer would give her permission, she resorted to lying, telling the employer that she planned to return to the Philippines to pursue her education. Soon after being released, however, she opted to forgo the plane ticket that her employer had purchased for her to return to the Philippines, instead purchasing her own ticket for Kish Island, where she waited for her visa from the restaurant that had agreed to hire her. The visa did not come as soon as she thought it would, and Roda found herself waiting on Kish Island for nearly a month, but even though she sometimes thought the visa would never arrive, it eventually did (and Roda noted that not all of the Filipinos she met on Kish Island were as fortunate). One of the things that made it possible for Roda to afford the cost of her occupational transition was an aunt in California, who loaned her US$1,000 to cover her expenses while waiting for her visa.[22]

Conclusion

The labor migration of domestic workers consists of a constellation of mobility pathways, which need not but often do exceed the territorial boundaries of nation-states and comprise temporally and geographically diverse cross-border movements. These pathways indicate the shortcomings not only of the "method-ological nationalism"[23] of assimilation and segmented assimilation narratives[24] but also of transnationalism,[25] calling as they do for the need to account for the rising multinational migrations[26] of temporary labor migrants. The mobility pathways of serial labor migration, staggered temporary labor migration, and temporary return migration define the migrant adaptation of domestic workers.

Tracing and identifying these three pathways provides insights into the labor migration of domestic workers. First, it points to their "immobility" due to poverty and their continued dependence on labor migration.[27] It indicates that even those who accumulate sufficient savings to open a business in their country of origin will likely eventually fail in that business, resulting in the temporary duration of their return migration. As illustrated by the case of Aurelia Villarta, it is likely that migrant domestic workers will not see an end to their labor migration until they are forced to retire in old age. While the design of this study does not permit the consideration of those who do accumulate sufficient savings to allow for their earlier retirement in their country of origin, it does establish that there are a number of migrant domestic workers who have tried to "retire" in the Philippines but have failed, finding themselves having to pursue migration once again. This suggests that, for domestic workers, migration often means the reproduction of the poverty that initially propelled their migration, dispelling the notion of migration as a path to inevitable economic mobility and security.

Second, the mobility pathways of domestic workers also point to their lack of security, as these pathways often emerge in response to unexpected events, including the sudden departure of their employers from the UAE, placement in an abusive household, or deportation for sometimes the most minor of infractions. It is for this reason that mobility pathways are not always planned but also consist of unplanned trajectories. The formation of multinational mobility pathways indicates that the precarious conditions of both the labor and the migration of domestic workers make it unlikely for domestic workers to stay continuously employed in one country.

Third, upon the termination of their labor contract, migrant domestic workers see little incentive to stay in one country unless they wish to renew their contract and stay employed with the same employer. Those who choose to end their contract and seek a new job locally are not guaranteed to see an improvement in their labor conditions or any recognition of their experience. The inconsistency and absence of labor standards in their occupation means that domestic workers can experience either an upward or downward trajectory in their employment standards as they move from one job to the next.

Finally, mobility pathways reflect the contours of the various structural impediments that define the labor and migration of domestic workers, including the exclusionary terms of their membership in various host societies, their relation of unequal dependency with employers, and the absence of standards in domestic work. Illustrating the efforts of domestic workers to seek consistent employment and sources of income across various countries, mobility pathways reflect their resilient responses to the structural impediments that derail their consistent migrant employment and ultimate goal of return migration to the Philippines.

The Moral Project of Unfree Labor

UNFREE DOES NOT IN ANY WAY DENY the vulnerabilities to which the *kafala* exposes migrant domestic workers. However, it disagrees with claims that this system results in their universal abuse, which is a view advanced by various rights advocacy agencies and organizations, including Human Rights Watch, Free the Slaves, and the U.S. Office to Monitor and Combat Trafficking in Persons. Calling attention to the mistreatment of migrant domestic workers in the UAE has been a long-standing moral imperative for these organizations, as well as for scholars of the region.[1] In some cases, advocates punctuate this moral imperative with the strategic elicitation of moral panic in their awareness campaigns. This is the case, for instance, in the writings of the provocateur Kevin Bales, who insists on categorically identifying migrant domestic workers as "modern-day slaves."

According to the Global Slavery Index, there are 40.3 million individuals subjected to slavery in the 21st century.[2] Slavery, defined by Bales as "the complete control of a person for economic exploitation by violence or the threat of violence," is said to be manifested in three forms in the modern-day world: chattel slavery, debt slavery, and contract slavery.[3] Chattel slavery, referring to the ownership of a person and their descendants, is how we most commonly imagine enslavement. Debt slavery, or debt bondage, in contrast, is the use of a person's labor as security for payment of a debt. Contract slavery, finally, refers to the contractual binding of workers so as to subject them to slave-like conditions in which they are denied freedom of movement and not adequately compensated for their labor. According to Bales, this last is "the most rapidly growing form of slavery,"[4] and he considers it to apply to migrant domestic workers in the UAE.

As Cornell and Bales assert, "Women come to the UAE from India, Sri Lanka, Bangladesh, Indonesia, Ethiopia, and the Philippines for domestic work, and, similarly, many find themselves locked up with their wages withheld."[5]

Indeed, not only Bales, but other scholars as well, suggest that the restrictions of the *kafala* system, coupled with the absence of labor protection, constitute systemic abuse.[6] A *New York Times* opinion editorial takes a similarly outraged stand:

> From Lebanon to Saudi Arabia, many employers view domestic workers, the vast majority of whom are women, as servants who do not deserve the freedom to leave the house or even the right to rest.
>
> A recent report from the International Labor Organization says that "while many employer-domestic worker relationships are positive" in the Middle East, "continuing and credible allegations of abuse and fraudulent behavior continue to plague the sector." Human Rights Watch has documented hundreds of incidents of mistreatment.[7]

In the case of the UAE, minimal protection is said to result in such "poor working conditions" that it pushes domestic workers into absconding to the supposedly better option and more autonomous occupation of sex work.[8] The anthropologist Pardis Mahdavi notes: "What my fieldwork revealed, however, was a group of women looking for a way *out* of the oppression they experienced in domestic work and *in* to the relative autonomy of sex work" (emphasis in the original).[9] But sex work was not an occupation that was sought by the domestic workers I interviewed for this study: they mentioned that the clientele they would attract, namely low-wage Bangladeshi laborers, would usually pay no more than 30 dirhams or US$8 a trick. In the sex-work hierarchy of the UAE, domestic workers would likely fall to the bottom due to their lack of resources to invest in their body and appearance, including make-up and clothes.[10] Regardless, seeking to identify the redemption of domestic workers in some other occupation, whether that be sex work or something else, might be misguided just because each type of low-wage employment carries its own set of challenges and struggles.

There is no question that abuse of domestic workers occurs in the region, as it does elsewhere, but there is an unmistakable Orientalism undergirding the dominant discourse of domestic worker abuse that is narrated by Western scholars of the situation in the UAE.[11] The discourse of abuse projects the notion of the Arab world as backwards, uncivilized, and dangerous. Indeed, what is missing from these abuse narratives is the fact that a large number of employers, particularly in a country such as the UAE where the vast majority of the labor force is made up of foreigners, are from the West. If abuse is understood to mean the infliction of physical brutality, emotional assault, and mental torture, this book shows that, while some domestic workers are subjected to the most sadistic of employers, others, likewise, are assigned to more considerate ones. The likelihood is greater, in fact, that domestic workers will encounter considerate employers than sadistic ones. This book thus diverges sharply from previous studies on domestic workers in the region, because it cannot be described as a documentation and illustration of the abuses they face upon migration. Unlike other studies, this book does not merely acknowledge the existence of positive experiences among domestic workers and then sweep them under the rug because they inconveniently complicate the story of exploitation that one wishes to project of the region.[12]

Rather than providing a documentation of abuse, this book illustrates the absence of labor standards in domestic work. This absence results in the emergence of three cultures of domestic work across households in the UAE, as we have seen: cultures of dehumanization, infantilization, and recognition of the humanity of domestic workers. As described extensively in chapters 1 and 3, these three cultures are expressed through various labor conditions, including domestic workers' access to communication, day off, workload, salary, accommodation, and food consumption. Domestic workers accordingly find that they can be placed with employers who recognize their right to communicate freely with friends and family; employers who infantilize them, only allowing them to do so at particular times; or employers who dehumanize them, denying them any access to communication with the outside world. Similarly, with regards to workload, they can have employers who recognize their expertise as domestic workers and allow them to determine how and when they should do their work; who infantilize them, insisting that they, the employers, know best how domestic work should be done; or, lastly, who dehumanize them, imposing an impossible workload that requires more than 21 hours of work every single day. Finally, and best illustrating the cultural variations in domestic work, there is food consumption: there are employers who dehumanize domestic workers by feeding them no more than once a day; those who infantilize domestic workers by feeding them adequately but not acknowledging that they might perhaps have their own food preferences; and, finally, those who recognize their humanity by giving them access to the foods they wish to eat, including the Filipino food that they often much prefer over the food fancied by their employers.

What is the significance of finding variations in labor conditions for domestic workers across households? In addition to confirming the absence of labor standards in the occupation, it questions the reduction of our understanding of their labor to the structures that determine them. Scholars have repeatedly assumed that the *kafala* system singularly determines the conditions of domestic work in the UAE. Underlying the narratives of abuse is an assumption that the majority of employers will act on the despotic power granted to them by the *kafala* in order to maximize the labor of domestic workers. This assumption is repeatedly asserted despite the fact that it is common knowledge in labor studies that coercive practices are ineffective, while the creation of consent is an effective means of maximizing production.[13] I propose that the reason this observation is ignored, and the reason why there is minimal questioning of the repeated claims of rampant abuse of domestic workers, can be found in deep-seated Orientalist assumptions and beliefs about the region. I do, however, cautiously recognize that a domestic worker is more likely to be killed by their employer in Arab states than in other known destinations, which speaks to the much weaker laws for protecting the rights of domestic workers and the overall lesser recognition of their humanity. And yet, while this is indeed the case, and employers do indeed commit egregious offenses, we need to acknowledge that extreme acts of brutality, such as those described in chapter 4, are the exceptions and not the norm among employers in the region.

The absence of standards in domestic work also suggests that employers react to their arbitrary authority in a multitude of ways. While some maximize their ability to coercively extract labor, others minimize it so as to create consent. Morals help explain variations in employer behavior, suggesting that unfree labor—which is the status of these workers, as they are bound to their employers—is a morally mediated experience. This confirms that morals do intersect with markets, in this case labor markets, to result in varying conditions of domestic labor across households.[14] This likewise substantiates that domestic work is a "moralized [labor] market," and (labor) markets as "intensely moralized, and moralizing, entities" explain the emergence of distinct cultures of domestic work across households in the UAE.[15]

Finally, the absence of labor standards points to the constitution of domestic workers as unfree laborers. The diversity of their labor conditions across households speaks to the arbitrary authority of employers, which is an authority that allows them to indiscriminately dominate domestic workers. Following a republican definition of freedom, domestic workers are made unfree by their susceptibility to arbitrary authority and domination.[16] To not be allowed to quit their jobs without the consent of their employers, to be rendered criminal for absconding from abusive employers, and to be without the freedom to depart the country without the permission of their employers all increase the stranglehold of employers over domestic workers, their ability to dominate the workers, rendering the domestic workers unfree by assigning to the employers the power to constrain the workers' actions. Without question, being unfree renders them susceptible to horrific treatment in the workplace.

The fact that the absence of employment standards in domestic work can result in the most brutal treatment of domestic workers is of rightful concern to various stakeholders, including human rights advocates, sending states, receiving states, employers, and workers. A constellation of stakeholders has accordingly made it their moral imperative to foreground the unfree status of domestic workers and address the vulnerabilities wrought by their unfreedom. They include the online site migrant-rights.org and the U.S. Department of State Office to Monitor and Combat Trafficking in Persons, via its *Trafficking in Persons Report*, which, similarly to Human Rights Watch, puts its efforts into awareness campaigns. Other stakeholders attempt to enact change via legislation. As described in chapter 1, domestic workers in the region saw concrete change after the passage of the 2011 ILO Convention on Decent Work for Domestic Workers, as most destinations have since enacted labor protection laws that include the provision of a weekly rest day, a maximum number of hours of work per day, and even sick days. Still, these destinations resist fully acknowledging domestic workers as independent laborers and insist on keeping domestic workers bound as dependents of their employer under the *kafala* system. This sends mixed signals to employers about how to manage their domestic workers, as they are prompted by the law to give and simultaneously to deny domestic workers more flexibility via a day off: while the new federal law enacted in the UAE in 2017, for example, encourages the provision of a day off, the *kafala* maintains the liability of employers for crimes committed by domestic workers, including out-of-wedlock pregnancy, thereby in fact discouraging the provision of a day off. This contradiction leaves employers torn, with some repressing their fear of the possible pregnancy of their domestic workers and allowing a day off anyway, others limiting them to chaperoned excursions, and yet others acting on their fear and categorically denying the day off.

Even before the passage of the 2011 ILO Convention on Decent Work for Domestic Workers, the Philippine government worked towards protecting domestic workers from the vulnerabilities wrought by their unfree status. It would be inaccurate to claim that the Philippine government fails to offer protection to migrant workers, viewing them as mere commodities that it places into an assembly line of workers for export.[17] As described extensively in chapter 2, the Philippines maintains a robust migrant protection program centered around the establishment of aspirational labor standards that it then seeks to enforce with the assistance of recruitment agencies and migrant domestic workers. Yet, to what extent can the Philippines in fact protect its migrant workers?

The limits of its protective abilities are perhaps best illustrated by the constant warnings extended in its compulsory pre-departure orientation seminars to domestic workers bound for Arab states of the likelihood that they will be raped. And yet, even though the Philippine government cannot protect domestic workers from rape, it does not prevent them from migrating to a position where they will be vulnerable to rape. The fact that the seminars make a point of alarming prospective migrants with rape stories provides insights into the protectionist culture of the Philippines as being, in fact, one of moral absolution. In other words, the sharing of rape stories strategically enables the Philippine government to morally absolve itself of the harms of migration, as it transfers culpability, in the process, onto the migrant worker who still chooses to depart the country despite knowing of the risks.

How do we mitigate the susceptibility of unfree migrant domestic workers to abuse and domination? Various advocates for their freedom have long insisted that the abolition of the *kafala* would render domestic workers free.[18] Yet this solution is based on an impossible liberal ideal of freedom, which is to live a life free of restraint. Such a solution also fails to consider the continuum of unfreedom that constitutes the existence of domestic workers in the UAE. As illustrated in this book, migrant domestic workers see the unfreedom of servitude in the UAE as a better option than the unfreedom of poverty in the Philippines. However, the unfreedom of servitude rarely in fact liberates them from the unfreedom of poverty. Moreover, escaping the unfreedom of servitude, of "legal servitude," does not provide them with "free illegality,"[19] as illegality instead paves their way to the unfreedom of criminalization. This continuum of unfreedom—poverty, servitude, criminalization—poses the challenge of identifying ways to mitigate their susceptibility to domination. How do we counter and suppress the ability of the employers to dominate these domestic workers?

Guiding us in the accomplishment of this goal is the political theorist Philip Pettit, who argues that formal mechanisms such as legislation must act as forces of "antipower" and must be put in place to reduce the susceptibility of the unfree and vulnerable to domination.[20] In the case of domestic workers, the informal nature of their occupation limits their ability to rely on formal instruments such as the law. *Unfree*, extending Pettit's discussion, illustrates the forces of "antipower" that operate informally through the moral mediation of domestic work. It establishes the use of morals as a tool of resistance. Migrant domestic workers engage in what Zelizer calls "relational work" by employing acts of moral claims-making to redefine their employer's perception of them as a domestic worker and improve their labor conditions.[21] Even those who are most severely abused demonstrate their refusal to passively acquiesce to their mistreatment in the workplace, insisting that they use morals and "fight if right." And, as a last resort, they abscond. This is not to say that an unfortunate few will not meet their demise. The passing in 2019 of the domestic worker who jumped from the third floor to flee the abuse of her Syrian and Egyptian employers, who had insisted on keeping her locked inside their apartment in Dubai, reminds us of this stark reality.[22]

When are domestic workers "right," and how do they know they are "right?" As described in chapter 3, domestic workers learn "what is right" from one another,[23] from past experience, and, finally and perhaps most significantly, from the Philippine government's mandatory seminars. In these seminars, the Philippine government ensures that each prospective migrant worker departs the country fully informed of their basic rights, including the aspirational labor standards of a monthly minimum wage of US$400, access to three meals per day, free work clothing and toiletries, and eight hours of rest per day. It is important for domestic workers to know "what is right" because this knowledge functions as the moral toolkit that they in turn use to negotiate for better working conditions. Morals, that is the knowledge of "what is right," likewise provide the justification for absconding from the direst of workplaces.

While *Unfree* calls attention to the limited utility of setting our sights on the abolition of the *kafala* as a solution to the abuse of migrant domestic workers, it does not deny that eradicating the *kafala* system would reduce the vulnerabilities of the migrant domestic workers. However, what I have tried to point out here is that, because of the difficulty of enforcing the law, due to the private setting and informal nature of the occupation of domestic work,[24] our solutions for ensuring the fair treatment of domestic workers must exceed the law. The challenge is to guarantee the implementation of a fair, albeit informal, "law of the household workplace."[25] In other words, the informal nature of the occupation requires not only formal but also informal mechanisms for ensuring the fair treatment of domestic workers. In this regard, *Unfree* identifies the need to impose moral pressure on those who have been given the arbitrary authority to recognize the humanity of domestic workers, illustrating the need to recognize domestic work as a morally mediated experience and calling for the recognition of morality as a force that mitigates, neutralizes, or aggravates—in other words, shapes—the vulnerabilities engendered by unfreedom.

Acknowledgments

I am deeply grateful to the migrant domestic workers who shared with me their time and stories. They made this book possible. I also wish to thank those who played a pivotal role in helping me meet them. In Dubai, these include the Philippine ambassador at the time of my research, Grace Relucio Princesa; the Philippine labor attaché at the time of my research, Delmer Cruz; Froilan Malit; and Ryan Pescade.

The research for this book started not long after I arrived at the University of Southern California, which extended support in a variety of ways, including through an Advancing the Humanities and Social Sciences Grant from the Provost's Office. This allowed me to do the pilot study necessary to demonstrate the feasibility of the project to external funders, including the National Science Foundation (SES-1346750) and the Social Sciences and Humanities Research Council of Canada (File No: 895-2012-1021, PI: Ito Peng). This book has been enriched by the research assistance provided by undergraduate and graduate students at USC, including Tamara Cesaretti, Min Haeng Cho, Yu Kang Fan, Stevie Gibbs, Jennifer Glaeser, Irene Hu, Hannah James, Minwoo Jung, Krittiya Kantachote, Kyunghwan Lee, Cathleen McCaffery, Vanessa Nahigian, Lucero Noyola, Matthew Ripley, Karina Santellano, and Alakea Woods. This book has also benefited from conversations with my colleagues Nina Eliasoph, Jen Hook, and Paul Lichterman. I also want to thank the staff of the sociology department for their support, including Amber Thomas Hanford, Melissa Hernandez Beatty, Lisa Losorelli, and Stachelle Overland.

The initial analyzing of data for this project took place in 2015–2016 at the Institute for Advanced Study in Princeton and the Institute on Globalization and the Human Condition at McMaster University in Canada. At the Institute for Advanced Study, I benefited from the intellectual community assembled by Didier Fassin and the scholarly exchanges I had with Alice Goffman, Todd Hamilton, Enze Han, and Monica Kim. At McMaster University, I was welcomed by the late Don Goellnicht, who unfortunately passed in 2019. The ideas in this book have gone through many iterations. For helping me think through them, I must thank colleagues who read and commented generously on versions of the material: Eileen Boris, Emmanuel David, Maria Hwang, Pei Chia Lan, John O'Brien, Yasmin Ortiga, Smitha Radhakrishnan, and Rachel Silvey. I am also grateful to Abigail Andrews, Ann Orloff, and Poulami Roychowdhury for inviting me to participate in their Gender and Power working group.

I had the opportunity to share and refine the arguments of the book with many audiences, including at Brown, Bryn Mawr, Harvard, Humboldt University, Indiana University, McGill, McMaster, Nanyang Technological University, National Sun Yat-sen University, National Taiwan University, National University of Singapore, Northwestern, the Ohio State University, Pennsylvania State, Princeton, Simon Fraser, Singapore Management University, Sussex University, University of Alberta, University of California–Berkeley, University of California–Irvine, University of Colorado Boulder, University of Kyoto, University of Houston, University of Oregon, University of Pennsylvania, University of Southern California, University of Toronto, University of Victoria, Utrecht University, Vrije Universiteit, Waseda, and Yale. I am grateful to those who gave me critical feedback at these lectures, including Walden Bello, Barry Eidlin, Gary Alan Fine, Lamia Karim, Laavanya Kathiravelu, Yasmin Ortiga, Eileen Otis, Aliya Rao, Josh Seim, and Viviana Zelizer.

Earlier versions of some chapters have appeared elsewhere: materials from chapter 1 appear in "The Moral Conundrum of the Day Off," *Turkish Policy Quarterly* (2019); chapter 5 was previously published in *Journal of Ethnic and Migration Studies* (2020); and materials from chapter 2 appear in the chapter "Monitoring International Labor Precarity: The State Management of Migrant Domestic Workers" in *Deepening Divides: How Territorial Borders and Social Boundaries Delineate Our World*, ed. Didier Fassin (London: Pluto Books, 2020) as well as in an article I co-authored with Rachel Silvey, "The Precarity of Migrant Domestic Work," *South Atlantic Quarterly* (2018).

Many friendships sustained me through the writing of this book, some of which took place at yoga writing retreats in Bali, Indonesia and Las Vegas, New Mexico. This book was made much better by this experience that I shared with Maylei Blackwell, Carolyn Choi, Emmanuel David, Kimberly Hoang, Maria

Hwang, Julia Meszaros, Dina Okamoto (and her partner Chris), Eileen Otis, Aliya Rao, and Robert Vargas. I must also thank my yoga teacher, Arvind Arya Sharma. His classes helped clear my mind so that I could develop the ideas and arguments in this book. Another person I must also really thank is my collaborator, Rachel Silvey. This book draws from our larger comparative study on Filipino and Indonesian domestic workers in the UAE and Singapore. Many of the ideas in this book have benefited tremendously from our intellectual exchanges over the past decade. Finally, I wish to extend a huge thanks to my family. My sisters, Celine Shimizu, Cerissa Piamonte, Juno Parreñas, and Frankie McNeil, have provided constant support through our daily group chats. And I could not have written this book without the companionship of my globe-traveling dogs, Gugma and Pangga, and my husband, Ben Rosenberg, who has been an amazing parent to our daughter, Malaya.

Methodology
An Ethnography of Subjectification[1]

Unfree is a book not about domestic work but about unfreedom and the experience of unfreedom. It is an ethnographic study that documents and analyzes the experiences and constitution of Filipino migrant domestic workers in the UAE as unfree subjects. It seeks to explain how differences in experience emerge from the governance and disciplining of domestic workers as unfree laborers. By foregrounding the status of domestic workers as unfree persons, this ethnographic study refuses to provide a merely empiricist account of their experiences but instead builds a theoretical foundation in its insistence on producing an ethnography that is attuned to migrant domestic workers' process of subjectification as unfree persons.[2]

This book seeks to document and examine not only how domestic workers experience labor migration but also how they are constituted and accordingly experience labor migration as unfree persons. In other words, its analytical focus is on explaining processes of becoming persons rather than describing processed persons. It fits what Michael Burawoy describes as structural ethnography, which "seeks out the macro conditions of micro processes."[3] Though it is centered on people, this methodological approach cannot be categorized as a "substantialist ethnography" because it focuses not on places, bounded or categorized groups, processed people, or cultural homogeneity but instead on the process of subject-formation, meaning how persons are disciplined and constituted as particular subjects and how they in turn negotiate this process, including by resisting it.[4]

An ethnography of the subjectification of domestic workers as unfree persons exceeds what Matthew Desmond identifies as "relational ethnography," in that it does not give "ontological primacy . . . to configurations of relations" and moves beyond describing the struggles and co-dependencies of two or more actors or agencies who occupy different positions within a shared social space.[5] In this case, the transactions involved are those between employers and employees. Capturing the process of subjectification means conducting a study that is neither merely place-bound, i.e., limited to the workplace, nor primarily relational, i.e., defined by the struggles and interdependencies of employers and employees. The study must instead provide a multi-scalar and multi-temporal approach that describes and examines how domestic workers are constituted and governed as unfree persons throughout the migration process.

Capturing the subjectification of domestic workers as unfree laborers requires an account of how various stakeholders govern their unfreedom and how they accordingly respond to their governance. In the case of domestic workers in the UAE, stakeholders include the sending and receiving states, recruitment agencies, migrant rights advocates including intergovernmental organizations and NGOs, employers, and domestic workers. By focusing on processes of subjectification, this study aims to achieve a protagonist-driven ethnography[6] that refuses to give equal bearing to various stakeholders. In other words, this is an ethnography of the experiences of domestic workers and not of those who benefit from their unfreedom—employers, children and/or other dependents, government officials, or migrant recruiters. Key to the success of this study was capturing the perspectives and experiences of domestic workers, which I must admit was not an easy endeavor.

Gathering data for this study came with many challenges. First, capturing the sequence of experiences that constitute the migration process required that I conduct research in both the Philippines and the UAE. Second, ensuring the inclusion of the broadest range of stakeholders required a bird's-eye view. Some were easy to identify—domestic workers, employers, recruitment agencies, and sending and receiving states—but others, such as advocacy groups, were not, due to the absence of civic groups in the UAE. Third, accessing the migrant domestic workers was made difficult by their isolation, as many never have a day off. And fourth, conducting interviews with government representatives in the receiving state of the UAE was an elusive goal. These challenges posed tremendous roadblocks that I did, however, eventually overcome.

Unfree asks: What are the experiences of unfree labor? How do various stakeholders recognize and attend to the status of domestic workers as unfree workers? These questions, which I raised in order to capture the processes of subjectification, required the design of a multi-scalar and multi-sited ethnography,[7] which in turn entailed the use of multiple methods: interviews with key stakeholders, including domestic workers, employers, government officials, migrant recruiters, activists including NGO representatives, and skills-training officers; participant observation of the recruitment, labor migration, and labor of domestic workers; content analysis of the laws of sending and receiving countries, binational memoranda of understanding, newspaper articles on domestic workers, and reports by migrant rights advocates; and, lastly, surveys of outgoing and returning migrants.

Feasibility

On first hearing of my research, colleagues often doubted its feasibility. Reviewers of my grant applications even warned against funding this study due to the unlikelihood of its feasibility. I was aware of this risk, but the relative absence of studies on this largest group of migrant domestic workers made it a risk that I wished to pursue. The question of feasibility is raised not only by the clandestine nature of domestic work but also by the challenge of doing research in the UAE. In 2018, after I had completed my field work, Matthew Hedges, a British doctoral student studying the UAE's foreign and domestic security strategies, was arrested on suspicion of spying on behalf of the British government. He was sentenced to life in prison but was eventually pardoned after being incarcerated for more than six months.[8] In 2019, Laavanya Kathiravelu, the author of *Migrant Dubai: Low Wage Workers and the Construction of a Global City*, was denied entry to Dubai.[9] Surprised to learn that the UAE government even knew about her academic work, she had no choice but to purchase the next ticket available for a return flight to Singapore. While I was doing my research, Andrew Ross, a professor at New York University, was blocked from boarding a plane to Abu Dhabi.[10] And prior to starting my field research, I had also heard of the decision by the UAE to ban the book *Dubai: The Vulnerability of Success*, which was critical of what the author Christopher Davidson calls the "rentier pathology" between the monarchy and its non-taxpaying citizens.[11] I also knew about the ordeal of the sociologist Syed Ali, whose research on foreign professionals led to his being detained and interrogated for 13 hours by Dubai authorities near the end of his field research. They wanted to know about his research, his curiosity about the lives of locals and non-locals, and his funding sources. They later confiscated and erased his computer's hard drive.[12]

I did not want any of this to happen to me, which is why I decided to go to the ministry of the interior soon after I first arrived in the UAE and introduce myself to anyone who would meet with me, to let them know about my study. I figured that it would be better to be deported at the beginning and not near the end of my field research, as I would then at least avoid wasting resources on a study that I was unlikely to be able to finish. At the government office, I was told that I had to make the request in writing. Following their instructions, I returned with a formal letter requesting an audience, only to be told that the letter had to be in Arabic. As instructed, I went to a translation service and returned with a one-page letter in Arabic describing my research project and providing my local address and phone number. I waited for anyone from the government to reach out to me, but no one ever did.

In the middle of my research, during my third visit to the UAE, a high-ranking government official did eventually reach out to me. He requested a meeting to learn more about my research, which he had learned about not from the ministry of the interior but from a family friend, who had expressed an interest in pursuing a PhD in sociology under my supervision. She had thought it would be a good idea to put us in touch with one another, to help me gain some insight on local perspectives on domestic work. In the lobby of the Shangri-la Hotel, I first found myself interrogated for about ten minutes, but it did not take long for the meeting to turn from an interrogation into an informal conversation lasting more than two hours. This was because the official told me that he did not disagree with my main finding that employers either dehumanize, infantilize, or recognize their domestic workers. After realizing that I was not going to relay a one-dimensional story of dehumanization, he then willingly shared information with me about domestic workers, but only off the record. With the exception of this one meeting, I did not have any other dealings with the UAE government.

Navigating a Hard-to-Reach Population

I had the opportunity to share some of my preliminary findings at various lectures, conferences, and symposia. One of these events was particularly striking for me in that it made me realize that others would be questioning not only the feasibility of this study but also the representativeness of the domestic workers whom I interviewed. The event in question was a symposium on domestic work. After my lecture, a respected senior colleague said to me, "I want to extend to you some sisterly advice. It is important that you clarify that your findings are limited by your use of convenience sampling."

But in fact I did *not* use convenience sampling. This study, defying assumptions that research on domestic workers in the UAE is not possible because the domestic workers are so inaccessible, draws from an unparalleled set of data that I gathered during nonconsecutive periods between 2013 and 2017. The study relies mainly on interviews conducted with 85 Filipina domestic workers in the UAE. Reflecting a diverse and as representative a sample as possible, the interviewees included authorized and unauthorized migrants; domestic workers with and without a day off; and workers whose employers were Emirati, other Arabs, Iranians, Westerners, South Asians, and Filipinos. All of the interviewees gave their consent to participate in the research.

Most of the interviews with domestic workers (82 of 85) were digitally recorded. They were one hour to three hours in length and focused on the workers' migration patterns, work experience, leisure activities, and family relationships. The interviews also covered basic demographic information about the migrants, including age, marital status, number of children, time spent working abroad, and previous countries of employment. Specific questions on the migration process included a) navigation of government bureaucracy, including their use of recruitment agencies; b) past migration experiences; c) the choice of UAE as a migration destination; d) future migration plans; and e) migration goals. Questions about their labor experiences sought to capture their daily routine throughout the week as well as their views on employer-employee relations and the quality of their employment. Those with previous experience in other households, including in other countries, were asked to describe and identify similarities and differences in their experiences.

Those research participants who had faced severe abuse, including physical, sexual, and mental abuse, were treated sensitively. For instance, I did not prod interviewees to share their worst experiences. They themselves chose to divulge such information. In interviews, they would ask me, "would you like to know what happened to me?" or tell me, "you would not believe what happened to me," after which they would proceed to share stories that were, I must admit, challenging to hear. I did not feel equipped to handle hearing about the viciousness of some of their experiences, and at times I could not help but think that domestic worker migration to this region should be altogether banned. I did ask interviewees to share their motivation for participating in my study. I learned that it was personally important for them, particularly for those who had had the worst experiences, that their story be made known to the public. While I had intended to capture a holistic picture of their labor and migration, the brutality of some of these experiences made it a challenge to ask questions about leisure activities, especially considering that even those who had not run away had also often had subpar labor conditions. While my inquiries into leisure activities were minimal, I did still ask about their activities during their days off or during their breaks.

I located and observed interviewees in five primary sites in Dubai: the Philippine government migrant shelter for runaways;[13] food courts in three different malls that were known hubs for domestic workers who had days off; parks in a middle- and upper-class neighborhood; supermarkets; and a Filipino migrant neighborhood known to shelter undocumented workers. I also visited the migrant shelter run by the Philippine government in Abu Dhabi. I identified these locations with the help of front-stage Filipino workers, who, quite noticeably, staffed almost all of the businesses I patronized in Dubai, including restaurants, hotels, and various retail outlets. Front-stage workers were inclined to help me because they recognized me as a *kabayan*, a compatriot, and it is a common practice among Filipino migrants to help compatriots settle in Dubai.

It was not easy to ensure that I captured a diversity of experiences. Of the various constituencies of domestic workers, the easiest to identify were those located in migrant shelters, as their presence in these facilities, which are primarily located within embassies or consulates, is common knowledge. However, oversampling from the shelters would give a skewed picture of labor conditions in the UAE, overemphasizing the worst-case scenarios, as those were the experiences of the runaways who are to be found in these locations. I thus consciously avoided gathering interviews from any one particular location. Nor did I rely on snowball sampling, except in seeking to locate unauthorized migrant workers. While the migrant domestic workers in the shelters were the most convenient to access, it was the unauthorized migrant domestic workers who were the least convenient. In the UAE, unauthorized migrant workers are rendered criminals because the act of absconding, that is terminating their employment without the permission of their employer, is considered a crime. This is the case even if the worker is fleeing an abusive situation. Once they abscond, migrant workers are technically violating the terms of their visa and are considered to be overstaying in the UAE. Due to this criminalization, therefore, gaining the trust of the unauthorized workers was a major obstacle. Many feared that I would report them to local authorities. This visceral fear was clearly manifested in some of my interviews, when an interviewee would literally shake uncontrollably in fear of my possible motivations. When this occurred, I would offer to end the interview, but they usually insisted that we continue. They often did so as a kind of gamble, betting on the possibility that I might potentially be able to extend emergency assistance to them if they ever needed it. This in fact turned out to be the case, as I later assisted a handful of unauthorized workers who had been caught in a raid by the police. I was able to help them by covering the cost of the shipment of their personal belongings and plane tickets back to the Philippines after their arrest and detention.

What was also challenging was gaining access to domestic workers who had no day off. While those who were granted a day off were relatively easy to locate, in food courts or places of worship, on Fridays, that was not the case for those who did not have a day off. I eventually learned, however, that domestic workers who do not have a day off are not always isolated in private spaces but are in fact often hidden in plain sight. When I approached domestic workers in parks and supermarkets, I learned that many of them had no day off. I managed to include them in the study by employing incremental interviews to accommodate their schedule. For instance, I conducted a series of interviews with unsupervised dog walkers at 6 am, childminders caring for children at a public park between 4 and 6 pm, and grocery shoppers in the late mornings. Taken together, these interviews yielded me access to those without a day off.

While migrant domestic workers are considered a hard-to-reach population, almost all those I approached agreed to participate in this study. This includes unauthorized migrant workers, most of whom I interviewed at their homes. Most wanted to share not only their wretched stories of abuse but also their triumphant stories of resistance and escape. Many participated in the research because, as Melanie, a 32-year-old first-timer from the Philippines, explained, "It is important that the world know about the plight of migrant domestic workers." These interviews with domestic workers conducted in the UAE captured their experiences both past and present. To account for the future and their mobility or lack thereof, I then used Facebook to follow those who later left the UAE and returned to the Philippines.[14] Some chose not to renew their contracts, while others were deported. And finally, to enhance my understanding of return migration, I conducted a survey, with the assistance of the store manager, of 199 return migrants who visited the only appliance store in an impoverished province in central Philippines.

Most of the interviews were conducted in either Filipino or Tag-lish (i.e., a combination of Filipino [Tagalog] and English), with eighteen carried out by undergraduate students in English. The interviews were fully transcribed, and those in Filipino and Tag-lish were then translated into English. The inconsistencies in the English grammar of the domestic workers cited in this study are a result of my decision not to fully translate the Tag-lish interviews and not to correct the grammar of those interviewed by the undergraduate students in English.

Sequential Ethnography

To capture the experience of labor migration and attend to the various stakeholders that determine this experience, this study also offers what could be called a sequential ethnography. It does so by accounting for the experiences of domestic workers at each step of the migration process, at their procurement of a recruitment agency, selection of a migration training center, participation in a mandatory pre-departure seminar, departure from the Philippines, arrival in the UAE, and entrance into domestic work. I capture most of this experience via interviews with domestic workers, but enhance this data using interviews with other stakeholders and participant observation conducted at the institutions and sites that domestic workers must engage with or visit at each step in the migration process. These include the training facilities, recruitment agencies, and mandatory pre-departure seminars.

Not enough of the scholarship on migration provides a sequential perspective, as most instead give a snapshot of the migrant or immigrant experience. Yet an ethnography of the subjectification of migrant domestic workers as unfree persons requires that we capture their experience across the different steps of the migration process as they unfold over time. At each step, one must document the experiences of migrants through their subjectification by policies and programs that constitute them as unfree persons or manage their constitution as unfree persons. In other words, we need to account for their governance across time and space, including the pre-migration recruitment stage, the pre-migration labor-processing stage, and the post-migration labor stage. Our analysis must also consider how they are governed, not only by governments but also by migrant institutions, such as recruitment agencies, and by employers.

Another scholar who uses a sequential approach is the anthropologist Olivia Killias, who traces the steps undertaken by Indonesian domestic workers from their rural village in Java to a training center in Jakarta and, finally, to the migrant destination of Malaysia.[15] While she also documents and examines the sending state governance of migrant domestic workers, my analysis takes us one step further by also accounting for how their governance shapes experiences in the country of destination. Killias, in contrast, admits to having faced difficulty in gaining access to domestic workers once they had arrived in the receiving country for the reason that they "work[ed] behind closed doors."[16] My employment of sequential ethnography is admittedly limited by the absence of accounts of village life prior to migration, as I did not conduct participant observation in their rural areas of origin. The wide geographic range of these areas, along with the fact that many of my informants originate from provinces that are designated "Level 4: Do Not Travel" or "Level 3: Reconsider Travel" by the U.S. Department of State, made this an unfeasible endeavor.[17] Migrant domestic workers from Indonesia, in contrast, come primarily from one province, namely West Java.[18] However, the absence of observations of village life should not take anything away from my analysis of migrant governance and its impacts on migrant labor experiences.

In my employment of sequential ethnography, I look at the subjectification of migrant domestic workers in both the Philippines and the UAE. The key institutions in the emigration process are recruitment agencies, skills-training facilities, and the state. To capture the emigration process, I conducted interviews with ten owners and managers of government-licensed recruitment agencies that deploy domestic workers to Arab states, as well as three illegal recruiters. Interviewees were asked about the process of obtaining an employer for domestic workers and fulfilling their migration requirements, including a police clearance, skills-training certification, medical certification, and completion of mandatory government-run seminars. To obtain a holistic understanding of the skills-training certification, I then conducted interviews with teachers as well as participant observation of classes at three different government-accredited facilities.

To understand the government logic behind the implementation of various emigration programs, I have drawn from content analysis of government policies and programs as well as interviews with Philippine government officials. I learned about various government programs from these interviews. The interviews with government officials focused on issues concerning migrant domestic workers in Arab states and sought to identify government strategies for addressing their common problems as unfree workers, which include illegal recruitment,[19] contract substitution,[20] and workplace violence. A broad picture was obtained by conducting interviews with officials in different units of the government offices that manage Philippine migration. To have a framework of comparison, I also interviewed five Bangladeshi government officials in the UAE.

Then, to capture how the Philippine state prepares domestic workers to become unfree workers, in 2015 and 2016 I conducted 90 hours of participant observation in Manila of compulsory seminars for prospective migrant domestic workers bound for Arab states. These seminars are administered by OWWA. I supplemented that observation by conducting a survey of 84 domestic workers bound for Arab states. To have a framework of comparison, I also supplemented this data with 16 hours of participant observation of two different seminars for domestic workers bound for Singapore, as they constitute another large group of migrant domestic workers from the Philippines.

To account for their governance as unfree workers in the receiving state, I examined the management of domestic worker migration by the state, recruitment agencies, and employers. To understand state policies and programs, I relied on government documents, including memoranda released on domestic workers. I also drew from interviews with domestic workers and their descriptions of their dealings with the state, including their process of entry and exit and, for those who were incarcerated, their conditions of imprisonment and deportation. I examined the response of migrant advocacy groups to the state governance of domestic workers through a close examination of their reports. I also interviewed individuals connected with migrant-rights.org[21] and a writer for Human Rights Watch. I met regularly with members of the UAE chapter of the activist organization Migrante International, which is the largest advocacy group for Filipino migrant workers across the globe. To have a better grasp of the migration recruitment process from the perspective of the receiving state, I conducted interviews with staff at five recruitment agencies.[22]

As they play a pivotal role in the disciplining of domestic workers, my research team completed interviews with 35 employers in the UAE. Representing a wide range of nationalities, they included Emirati, other Arab, Iranian, Western, and South Asian employers. Visits to the households of the employers, including local Emirati, where I could observe interactions between employers and domestic workers, enhanced the information obtained from interviews.[23] While I personally interviewed a handful of employers, I strategically relied on a white female research assistant to identify and conduct interviews with most of the employers, as I assumed that my shared racial identity with the majority group of domestic workers in the UAE, who are from the Philippines, would inevitably cause employers to be less truthful about their sentiments about domestic workers.[24] In contrast, my research assistant was someone they might easily be able to imagine as a potential fellow employer, someone with whom they could be more truthful in sharing their standards of employment and means of disciplining domestic workers. Still, a possible limitation in interviewing employers was the likelihood that they would withhold embarrassing information, such as about their violent outbursts or unfair working conditions. Yet, to my surprise, employers had no qualms sharing some practices that might be seen as inhumane, such as denying domestic workers a day off, grumbling about the workers' food consumption, or requiring "7-star service" from workers whom they paid no more than US$400 per month.

What deeply enhanced my interviews with employers were my informal interactions with them, including with local Emirati whom I met in various ways, from merely standing in hotel lobbies to introductions by foreign diplomats. I was later welcomed into their homes and hosted for lavish meals. On one occasion, my research assistant and I had the experience of dining with an Emirati who insisted on ordering the entire menu of more than twenty dishes so that we might try a vast array of local cuisine. We learned firsthand that his daily practices far exceeded conspicuous consumption, instead constituting excessive consumption. On another occasion, I had the opportunity to see how an Emirati could break the law without reproach or consequences, as I rode as a passenger in a luxury vehicle that intentionally occupied two lanes of Sheikh Zayed Road, the main road in Dubai, with the driver knowing no one would stop him because his two-digit license plate established not only his wealth but also, and more significantly, his identity as an Emirati. The presence of my undergraduate students also helped with my access to the community, as some local employers were interested in helping them to learn about Emirati history and culture. We were given a private evening tour of Dubai's Al Fahidi Historical District, also known as Al Bastakiya, and invited to join a large group, representing two generations, of Emirati men at a private teahouse in the district. We soon learned that the men around us, watching football on flat-screen TVs or casually chatting outside this nondescript teahouse, included quite high-ranking government officials. In these informal spaces, I had the opportunity to have plenty of conversations with locals about the treatment of domestic workers in the UAE.[25]

Finally, I captured public discourse about domestic workers. First, I drew from local media reports in order to have a context for understanding how various stakeholders, including employers and recruitment agencies, represent their relations with domestic workers. I conducted content analysis of all newsprint reports from 2013–2014 on "domestic workers" and "maids" published in two of the largest English-language newspapers in the UAE: *Khaleed Times* and *The National*. Second, I sought to identify the rights discourses advanced by various advocacy groups, including intergovernmental agencies such as the ILO, international advocacy groups such as Human Rights Watch, regional NGOs such as migrant-rights.org, and Philippine-based groups such as Migrante International. Last, I turned to support groups formed by domestic workers on the social media outlet of Facebook that I identified through research participants. Most of these groups are closed, but some, such as OFW household service worker, are public. While public groups usually share a variety of news announcements about domestic workers (e.g. reports on death sentences in the region, changes in policies), closed groups are spaces where testimonies of abuse are shared via videos or pictures. In these closed groups, domestic workers also seek advice on how to handle a difficult employer or urgently ask to be rescued from abusive households.

In summary, the data collected provides a holistic and sequential perspective of the governance as well as the experiences of migrant domestic workers towards their constitution as unfree persons. This study documents the unfolding of the migrant experience for Filipino domestic workers in the UAE, from the process of their recruitment in the Philippines to their subjection to the arbitrary authority of employers in the UAE. Its analysis draws from the perspective of multiple stakeholders, including domestic workers, employers, migrant rights advocates, recruitment agency staff, and government representatives. Drawing from this data, *Unfree* offers a robust study of the hard-to-reach population of migrant domestic workers in Arab states, a group that is highly vulnerable to human trafficking, and advances our understanding of unfreedom in the 21st century.

Notes on Human Trafficking, Forced Labor, and Slavery

The dominant discourse has reduced our understanding of the experiences of migrant domestic workers in Arab states to human trafficking, forced labor, or slavery. It is, admittedly, difficult to argue against the applicability of these categories to their experiences. Take the case of human trafficking, for instance. Trafficking consists of a three-part process involving a particular act, means, and purpose: the act of recruitment, transport or receipt; the means of some form of fraud, force, or coercion; and the purpose of exploitation.[1] What makes migrant domestic workers in the region into trafficked persons is the common experience of "contract substitution," which refers to the practice of employers ignoring the terms and conditions of employment stipulated in the original contract they had agreed upon with domestic workers in the country of origin. Upon arrival in the country of destination, domestic workers are then given a different contract, stipulating worse conditions of employment.

In the UAE, it is common practice for migrant domestic workers to receive lower wages than the amount stipulated in the original contract. Nearly all of my interviewees experienced contract substitution. Take for example the case of Junna, who reported, "I actually agreed to 1,500 dirhams (US$417). It was not until we arrived here that we learned our salary is only 1,000 (US$278). It is because we signed the contract that said our salary will be 1,500 (US$417). They just told us otherwise once we were here. But because you are already here, you could not really complain." Marjie, who shared Junna's predicament, complained: "The first problem is the salary you earn is different from what you agreed to in the contract that you signed in the Philippines. I agreed to a contract of 1,500 dirhams (u s $ 417) a month in the Philippines and learned once here that I was only going to receive 850 dirhams (u s $ 236) a month." Contract substitution constitutes human trafficking because it involves the deception, i.e., being lied to about one's salary, and exploitation, i.e., receiving a wage less than the stipulated minimum wage of u s $ 400, of the migrant domestic workers.

In other cases, contract substitution might involve being assigned to an occupation other than what was agreed upon prior to migration. Among my interviewees, those who had been duped into domestic work included a college-educated teacher who had been misled to believe she would be a private tutor; a certified massage therapist who was assigned not to a spa, as she had been made to believe, but to the private home of an infirm, elderly man; and an experienced sales clerk who had thought she was going to be working as a salesperson in a mall rather than as a domestic worker. All of these cases constitute trafficking because they involve the transport of a person by fraudulent means that then results in their exploitation, specifically their forced labor due to their inability to transfer jobs.

Domestic workers in the region are vulnerable to forced labor, which occurs when employers prevent them from terminating their employment.[2] As described in the introductory chapter, this was the case for Joy, whose employer held her against her will and did not allow her to return to the Philippines at the end of her two-year contract. Whenever she expressed a desire to leave, they would find ways of coercing her to stay, such as having her accompany them on a vacation in Europe. Joy's experience is not unique, and I heard such stories repeatedly while in the field. Employers do this, refuse to let their workers go, in order to avoid the higher cost of hiring a new domestic worker as opposed to renewing the existing contract. One could also argue that the *kafala,* because it requires employers to "release" as opposed to "cancel" the contract of a domestic work in order for the latter to be able to secure a new job elsewhere and avoid deportation, invites the forced labor of domestic workers. Indeed, as we see with the case of Haydee in chapter 5, many tolerate subpar labor conditions for fear of being canceled by their employers, which would force them to leave the country.

"Modern-day slavery" is another concept applied to the situation of migrant domestic workers in the region.[3] It is said that the *kafala* subjects domestic workers to "contract slavery" in that it binds them to their sponsor.[4] This in itself is seen as exploitation. However, I disagree with this conception of slavery, which is premised on the control of one person by another person. Instead, I adhere to the definition advanced in the Slavery Convention of 1926, which views slavery as "the status or condition of a person over whom any of all of the powers attaching to the right of ownership are also exercised."[5] The key condition in this definition is not "control" but "right of ownership," which many would argue does not necessarily apply to migrant contract workers.

Though the experiences of migrant domestic workers in the UAE validate claims of the widespread existence of "human trafficking," "forced labor," and "modern-day slavery," I hesitate to utilize these conceptions of unfreedom for a few reasons. First, they suggest a universal experience of rampant abuse, which is an inaccurate portrayal. Second, they assume that all employers are bad actors. And lastly, there is limited utility in universalizing the experiences of migrant domestic workers to the picture of extreme abuse projected by the social constructions of "human trafficking" and "modern-day slavery," as these constructions fail to provide us with productive solutions to the problems confronting migrant domestic workers. Both "human trafficking" and "modern-day slavery" are politically charged concepts with a one-size-fits-all solution of "rescue, rehabilitation, and reintegration," and these concepts do not necessarily account for the nuances in the experiences of migrant domestic workers and the different needs that may arise from the varying forms of subjugation they confront in the course of their labor migration. "Rescuing" them would result in their removal from their workplace, a solution that would likely be welcomed by those who face extreme abuse, but rejected by those who do not.

Notes

Introduction: What Is Unfree Labor?

1. During the time of my research, one US dollar was approximately 3.6 dirhams.

2. See, for example, Human Rights Watch 2014; Mahdavi 2011. For a more nuanced perspective, see Sabban 2012.

3. Interviews with domestic workers were conducted in Filipino, English, or Tag-lish (a combination of the two). Throughout the book, there will be inconsistencies in the English of research participants. I have chosen not to correct the grammar or wording of those who spoke in English or Tag-lish. Interviews in English were conducted by undergraduate students from the University of Southern California who accompanied me for one month in Dubai.

4. I solicited interviews at the Philippine consulate with the assistance of the labor attaché at the time, Delmer Cruz, who informed the women sheltering at the consulate about my research. He requested volunteers and arranged for interviews to take place in a private room at the consulate. I did not directly compensate research participants. However, I showed my appreciation by purchasing Filipino pastries sold by vendors outside the facilities and giving them to the women at the shelter. I also donated rice and cooking oil to the shelter.

5. I asked research participants at the migrant shelter to tell me why they had run away, and then I asked them to compare their situation with those of others who were also sheltering there. Frequently, I did not even have to ask, as they often volunteered this information at the beginning of the interview, which they would usually start by asking me if I wished to know what had happened to them.

6. In Islamic law, a *diya* refers to the financial compensation extended to victims or their family in cases of murder, bodily harm, or property damage.

7. Since JoAnn's harrowing escape and brief stay in the shelter, she has returned to the Philippines to be with her son. A single mother, JoAnn hopes to eventually join her boyfriend Adrian in Maryland. The challenge, however, is Adrian's undocumented status in the United States: he is a migrant worker from Mexico. JoAnn met Adrian through Yahoo Chat and communicated with him before she migrated to Dubai. Prior to her migration,

he had regularly sent her money. She continued to sneak in ways to communicate with Adrian once she was in Dubai, and it was he who emboldened her to escape.

8. Bryant 2013.

9. See for example Bahrain 2012; Kingdom of Saudi Arabia 2013; Kuwait 2015; and United Arab Emirates 2017.

10. Longva 1999.

11. See *United States v. Kozminski,* 487 U.S. 931, 943–44 (1988). In this ruling, the Supreme Court of the United States determined servitude to be identical to the deprivation of free will.

12. Estimate obtained from the website of a migrant advocacy group in the region, migrant-rights.org. See https://www.migrant-rights.org/statistic/domesticworkers/. Accessed December 25, 2018.

13. United Arab Emirates 2017.

14. Pettit 1996.

15. Even the scholars who underscore the abuse of migrant workers in the region admit to observing extreme variability in the experiences of migrant workers under the stringent conditions of the *kafala*. Mahdavi (2011), for instance, acknowledges that some domestic workers maintain "strong ties with families who provide good accommodations and regular time off," while others face "abusive situations" (142). Likewise, Gardner (2010) observes of migrants in Bahrain that the governance of workers under the *kafala* system depends largely on the sponsor, with some accommodating and invested in protecting workers and others taking advantage of their power and abusing workers. However, they have chosen to ignore these differences in advancing the argument that the *kafala* system is nothing but a form of structural violence. Those who write about domestic workers see the *kafala* as akin to human trafficking, forced labor, or slavery. The existing scholarship generally implies the near universal abuse of migrant domestic workers in the region. See also Jureidini and Moukarbel 2004; Jureidini 2010; Pande 2013; Fernandez 2014.

16. See Appendix A for an extended discussion of the methodology.

17. Official numbers are unavailable. Of 750,000 estimated domestic workers in the UAE, it has been said that approximately 200,000 are from the Philippines. See news report by Dajani (2017).

18. Ahmad 2017; Gardner 2010.

19. For Israel, see Brown 2019 and Liebelt 2011; for Malaysia, see Chin 1998; for Lebanon, see Fernandez 2013; Jureidini 2010; and Pande 2013; and for the UAE, see Mahdavi 2011 and Sabban 2012.

20. Anderson 2000; Jureidini and Moukarbel 2004; Fernandez 2013; Lan 2007; Mahdavi 2011.

21. For examples of scholarship that follow a Marxist understanding of freedom, see Constable 2007; O'Connell Davidson 2010; Pratt 2012; and Fernandez 2014.

22. For examples of analysis that follow a liberal framework, see Anderson 2000; Jureidini and Moukarbel 2004; Lan 2007; and Mahdavi 2011.

23. As Polanyi elaborates, "Freedom's utter frustration in fascism is, indeed, the

inevitable result of the liberal philosophy, which claims that power and compulsion are evil, that freedom demands their absence from a human community. No such thing is possible; in a complex society this becomes apparent." (2001: 265–66).

24. Pettit 1996 and 2002.

25. Marx 1987.

26. Mill (2001 [1859]) insists on the individual right to autonomy, which he argues should only be constrained by its potential harm to others. Individuals have the basic rights to "liberty of thought" (16) or "freedom of opinion" (24); "liberty of tastes and pursuits" (16); and the "freedom to unite" (16). He expands: "As soon as any part of a person's conduct affects prejudicially the interests of others, society has jurisdiction over it, and the question whether the general welfare will or will not be promoted by interfering with it, becomes open to discussion. But there is no room for entertaining any such question when a person's conduct affects the interests of no persons besides himself, or needs not affect them unless they like (all the persons concerned being of full age, and the ordinary amount of understanding). In all such cases, there should be perfect freedom, legal and social, to do the action and stand the consequences" (69–70). See also Guyer and Wood 1992.

27. Nozick 2013 (1974).

28. Berlin 1969.

29. See Fernandez 2014; Fudge and Strauss 2014.

30. Harvey 1989.

31. O'Connell Davidson 2010: 250.

32. Xiang and Lindquist 2014.

33. Fernandez 2014; Fudge and Strauss 2014.

34. Silvey and Parreñas 2020.

35. Fernandez 2014.

36. Ibid.

37. An example of this argument is the observation by the geographer Geraldine Pratt (2012) that the two-year live-in requirement historically imposed in Canada pressures domestic workers to accept less-than-ideal working conditions.

38. See Anderson 2000; Lan 2007; Mahdavi 2011; Pande 2013.

39. Pettit 1996: 595–96.

40. See Pande 2013.

41. Anderson 2000.

42. Among those who advance this argument in their analysis of domestic workers in Arab states are Jureidini and Moukarbel 2004, Mahdavi 2011, and Pande 2013. See Appendix B.

43. This argument is advanced by Pei Chia Lan (2007), writing on domestic workers in Taiwan, and Pardis Mahdavi, writing on domestic workers in Dubai (2011). As Mahdavi observes, "many women who migrate into the formal sphere of domestic or care work in the UAE experience frustration and turn to the informal economy for higher wages and increased mobility" (2011: 129). Amrita Pande (2013), writing on domestic workers in Lebanon, somewhat agrees with this argument but brings some nuance to her analysis,

seeing legality and illegality as resulting in various sets of vulnerabilities. However, she still finds that not being bound to a sponsor is likely to result in the improvement of labor conditions.

44. Blackett 2019; Fish 2017.

45. See Human Rights Watch 2014.

46. Jureidini 2010; Mahdavi 2011; Pande 2013.

47. Nozick 2013 (1974).

48. Berlin 1969.

49. According to Christman (1991), "The conception of positive freedom that emerges, then, is a subjectivist, internalist notion, and one which adequately captures the core idea of self-government (and its value) without including untoward (external) value conditions" (359).

50. See Mahmood 2004. I also advocated for a positive liberty approach in my analysis of migrant hostesses in Japan (Parreñas 2011).

51. Christman 1991.

52. Michel Foucault (1997) also offers a formulation of freedom that considers its constitution in the context of relations of power. For Foucault, relations of power are contingent on the freedom of subjects. As he notes, "It should also be noted that power relations are possible only insofar as the subjects are free. If one of them were completely at the other's disposal and became his thing, an object on which he could wreak boundless and limitless violence, there wouldn't be any relations of power" (292). If we are to apply Foucault's formulation of freedom to domestic workers in the UAE, we would recognize that in the context of the "state of domination" that is the *kafala* system, migrant domestic workers would still be free, albeit with an "extremely limited margin of freedom" (292), as they still retain the ability to employ everyday strategies to defuse domination. Various studies have documented these everyday strategies, including for instance the subversive act of working at a slower pace. See Constable 2007 (for a discussion of domestic workers in Hong Kong) and Lan 2006 (for a discussion of domestic workers in Taiwan). Domestic workers in both destinations confront legal systems similar to the *kafala*. See also the discussion in chapter 3, footnote 47.

53. See Pettit 1996. Also adhering to a republican understanding of freedom are Karl Polanyi (2001) and Quentin Skinner (1997).

54. Pettit 1996: 586.

55. Ibid., 576.

56. See Nozick 2013 (1974).

57. Polanyi (2001) identifies this illegibility when he observes: "If regulation is the only means of spreading and strengthening freedom in a complex society, and yet to make use of this means is contrary to freedom per se, then such a society cannot be free" (266). For Polanyi, freedom can only be attained via regulation that minimizes the economic forces of self-interest that characterize the market economy. This suggests that Polanyi himself is demanding a reformulation of freedom that shifts from a liberal framework towards a republican understanding more fitting with Pettit's formulation.

58. As Pettit notes of antipower, "I mean the sort of intervention designed to empower

certain people—to give them equality in basic capabilities—and thereby to guard them against various forms of subjugation, various forms of vulnerability. Such empowering is mainly assured via welfare-state initiatives" (1996: 591). This goal notably agrees with those of Polanyi, who saw the need to counter the forces of the market economy via heightened regulation for the purpose of the "strengthening of the rights of the individual in society" (2001: 264).

59. Employers, for instance, are now more likely to extend a day off to domestic workers, due to the inclusion of a mandatory weekly rest day in the recently passed domestic worker law.

60. Pettit 1996.

61. Ibid., 591.

62. Bakan and Stasiulis 1997 and 2003.

63. Pettit 1996: 592.

64. For a discussion of the absence of civil society in the UAE, see Mahdavi 2011. Pettit elaborates: "Think of the protection, regulation, and empowerment that are effectively mounted, at least in certain circumstances, by trade unions, consumer movements, prisoners' rights organizations, environmental movements, women's groups, civil liberties associations, and even competitive market forces. And think of the impact of the standing cultural and community practices that make it possible for young offenders to be constructively rebuked within their own milieu, for people in a minority status to be able to rely on informal social sanctions against those who ridicule them, for women in domestic distress to be helped and supported by their friends in the neighborhood, and so on" (1996: 592).

65. Blackett 2019: 48.

66. Responding to a question about the accuracy of the report of rampant abuse of domestic workers in the UAE released by Human Rights Watch, Maureen disagreed with the report but presumed that certain groups are more likely than others to be abusive: "Somebody recently said there's 300 and something different nationalities in Dubai. I think there is probably more than that. And I, at the risk of sounding a bit racist, I think there are cultural aspects, like, in some cultures, having a maid is like having a slave . . . I don't know which groups of people would be guilty . . . maids that have worked for me, as well as friends of maids that have worked for me, that say that's why they like to work for Western people. Not that all Western people treat their maids, you know, well, because I have witnessed the opposite."

I should note that the vast majority of employers disagreed with the report and dismissed it as biased, saying that it shared only negative stories and overlooked the positive ones. Employers also insisted that it was construction workers and not domestic workers who were most likely to face abuse.

67. Pettit 1996.

68. Fourcade and Healy 2007.

69. As noted above, almost all the employers interviewed for this study defensively argued against accusations of rampant abuse in the region (see Human Rights Watch 2014). As Nilo, an Indian employer, put it: "we never abuse, we never touch her you know."

While employers would of course be likely to contest a stereotypical depiction of them as abusive, many of them did not deny acting on their power over domestic workers, with some admitting to using "really abusive language," others divulging the inconsistency of their domestic worker's day off, and yet others disclosing that they restricted the access of domestic workers to food in their household despite not providing them with a food allowance. Yet, overall, employers were likely to recognize the basic human rights of domestic workers, whether it is the right to have access to communication with family, rest adequately, or receive sufficient food.

70. See Jureidini and Moukarbel 2004; Jureidini 2010; Mahdavi 2011; Pande 2013.

71. Mahdavi (2011), for example, insists that power inequalities prevent domestic workers in Dubai from directly questioning the authority of employers.

72. Following the original definition of "structural violence" advanced by Johann Galtung (1969), the *kafala* system is seen as harmful to individuals to the extent that it denies them their basic human needs. See Gardner 2010; Mahdavi 2011.

73. Scott 1985: 30; Scott 1990.

74. Scott 1985: 30.

75. Granovetter 1985; Bandelj 2020.

76. An exception is Irwin and Bottero 2000.

77. Braverman 1998.

78. Hondagneu-Sotelo 2001.

79. Romero 2002.

80. In the literature on domestic workers, the few discussions of the effects of social relations on employment conditions focus on how employers indirectly or via subversive means create or blur boundaries (Ray and Qayum 2009; Lan 2006) and how domestic workers attempt to do the same (Lan 2006; Romero 2002), with a salient question being whether the constitution of domestic workers as "one of the family" blurs their status as employees and thereby allows for the extraction of uncompensated labor (Rollins 1985; Romero 2002).

81. The observation of varying labor conditions across households diverges from the literature on domestic work, which insists on a pervasive culture of employment within particular historical periods. Based primarily in the United States, the literature establishes a historical teleology in employer-employee relations. In the early 20th century, it is said that distance defined employer-employee relations, as a stark division of labor marked the relationship between domestic workers and employers; the relegation of physically onerous and demeaning household labor, i.e., the dirty work, to the former allowed the latter to embrace their domesticity (Palmer 1991). By the late 20th century, distance had given way to the cultivation of personal relationships in the household. This cultural shift blurred the status of the domestic worker as an employee and paved the way for employers to make demands that exceeded the contractual obligation of the worker (Romero 2002). How employers cultivate personal relationships has shifted over time, from "benevolent maternalism" (Rollins 1985) in the late 20th century to "instrumental personalism" (Hondagneu-Sotelo 2001) in the early 21st. "Benevolent maternalism" foregrounds the "superordinate-subordinate relationship" in domestic work through acts of maternal

protection that, in their provision, degrade the worker (Rollins 1985). An example would be the treatment of the domestic worker as childlike and ill-informed on how to do their job. In contrast, "instrumental personalism," or "strategic intimacy," refers to the cultivation of personal relationships for the purpose of generating the loyalty and commitment of the worker to the job (Hondagneu-Sotelo 2001). Personalism is used to instrumentally manufacture consent. This historical teleology resonates with but does not quite fit the culture of employment for domestic workers in the UAE, where employers maintain a wide range of employment standards: some maintain distance, as is said to have happened in the early-20th-century United States; some cultivate "benevolent maternalism," as is described for the late-20th-century United States; and lastly, some prefer "personalism," as is supposed to occur in contemporary U.S. society. Indeed, distance defines the relationship in households that *dehumanize* domestic workers; benevolent maternalism captures the dynamics between employers and domestic workers in households that *infantilize* domestic workers; and finally, one can say that employers who *recognize* the personhood of domestic workers practice instrumental personalism.

82. Jureidini 2010; Mahdavi 2011; Pande 2013.

83. Zelizer 2012a: 149. Key to unpacking relational work is seeing how participants perceive and negotiate "the meanings of relations, transactions, and media including their moral valuation, combined with constant negotiation, modification, and contestation of those meanings" (Zelizer 2012b). Economic sociology, particularly in its discussions of relational work, provides us with tools to understand the engagement of domestic workers in direct negotiation with employers. Scholars of relational work identify and examine varied mutual constitutions of social relations and economic activities, including the earmarking of money (Zelizer 2005), negotiating morally problematic exchanges (Zelizer 2005; Lainer-Vos 2013), and, most significant for us here, using social relations to accomplish economic exchanges (Chan 2009; Hoang 2018). Chan (2009) shows how Chinese life insurance agents manage the taboo around their new financial product by drawing from pre-existing family or friendship ties. Hoang (2018) identifies the various relational strategies that market actors use to manage risky investments. Investors work around the market by obfuscating bribes through bundling and brokerage, but also by developing long-term relations via gift-giving. These various discussions establish that relational work is *work* (Bandelj 2012). Despite this, labor scholars have not used the concept of relational work to understand employer-employee relations. Yet doing so allows us to further our understanding of labor negotiations in action, specifically beyond collective bargaining and subversive acts (Fish 2017; Blackett 2019).

84. Scott 1985; Bakan and Stasiulis 1997; Anderson 2000; Mahdavi 2011.

85. Bandelj (2012) notes that "power is . . . part and parcel of relational work, whether it is apparent in blunt physical force that one can exert over the other in a relation, or conveyed through subtle linguistic expressions that give away the asymmetry between the participants in relational work" (180).

86. Zelizer 2007: 160.

87. While domestic workers become privy to these standards during the pre-departure orientation seminars mandated by the Philippine government, employers learn about

them from media reports, legislation, international conventions, and the direct negotiation of domestic workers.

88. Fourcade and Healy 2007.

89. Pettit 1996.

90. Human Rights Watch 2014.

91. See Appendix A for a more extensive discussion of the methodology.

92. See Constable (2007) for the characteristics of domestic workers in Hong Kong and Parreñas (2015) for a description of domestic workers in Italy.

93. Interviewees ranged in age from 21 to 64 years old, with the majority in their 30s. Muslim interviewees had usually given birth to their first child by the age of 14.

94. Department of Labor and Employment 2020.

95. Of 85 interviewees, only five had attained some years of college.

96. It is only Arab states that do not have a minimum education requirement. In fact, I have encountered illiterate domestic workers. Most other destinations require the completion of high school. This is the case, for example, in Hong Kong and Singapore. See Parreñas 2017.

97. International Organization for Migration 2015.

98. Studies focus instead on transnational mothering in the Global North (Francisco-Menchavez 2018; Madianou and Miller 2012; Parreñas 2015; Pratt 2012); migrant domestic workers in other destinations including for example Hong Kong (Constable 2007), Taiwan (Lan 2006), and Israel (Liebelt 2011); and migrants and their children in Canada or the United States (for example Pido 2017; Pratt 2012; Ocampo 2016).

Chapter 1: Legal Infantilization and the Unfreedom of Servitude

1. Gabriel 2018.

2. Rey 2018.

3. As Qattan states, "I have the right as a *kafeel* to keep my employee's passport, and I am responsible for paying a deposit of up to KD1,500 (US$4,900)."

4. See Article 12 in Kuwait 2015. Previously, employers could hold the passport if granted permission by the domestic worker.

5. See Article 22 in Kuwait 2015.

6. Qattan had to temporarily suspend the comments on her Instagram page due to the onslaught of criticism she received from Filipino netizens.

7. Newbould 2018.

8. See July 23, 2018 posting on the Instagram page of Sondos Al Qattan. Available at https://www.instagram.com/sondos_aq/?hl=en. Accessed December 30, 2020.

9. As Qattan defiantly posted in her follow-up statement on Instagram, "As far as the four-day-a month off days, the condition differs from a household worker compared to a business worker. In comparison, many household employers don't allow the worker any off-days if the contract specifies a certain number of off-days."

10. Wasmi 2018.

11. For reactions from other social media influencers, including in the UAE, see Debusmann 2018a and 2018b.

12. Qattan dismissed criticisms directed at her as "foreign media campaigns" against not only her but "Islam, the hijab, and Kuwait." See Debusmann 2018b.

13. International Labour Organization 2015a.

14. Diop, Johnston, and Le 2018.

15. International Labour Organization 2015b.

16. Ibid.

17. Ibid.

18. Ibid. See also Parreñas, Silvey, Hwang, and Choi 2019.

19. Ahmad 2017.

20. Fernandez 2013; Mahdavi 2011.

21. Numbers available at the website of the advocacy group Migrant-Rights.org, at https://www.migrant-rights.org/. Accessed April 9, 2019.

22. Parreñas 2017. Granted, other foreigners in Arab states, including second-generation migrants born in the country, likewise do not qualify for permanent residency. For a discussion of the second generation in the UAE, see Vora 2013. In 2019, the UAE began to offer what is called a "Golden Visa," which offers long-term residence to exceptional persons, including wealthy investors and talented individuals. See the announcement, available at https://u.ae/en/information-and-services/visa-and-emirates-id/residence-visa/long-term-residence-visas-in-the-uae. Accessed April 20, 2021.

23. See Israel government manual, available at https://mfa.gov.il/MFA/ConsularServices/Documents/ForeignWorkers2013.pdf. Accessed November 17, 2020. See Taiwan Ministry of Labor website, available at https://www.wda.gov.tw/en/NewsFAQ.aspx?n=2 6470E539B6FA395&sms=0FCDB188C74F69A0. Accessed November 17, 2020.

24. Kakande 2015: 9.

25. Jureidini 2010; Mahdavi 2011; Pande 2013.

26. Yeoh and Huang 1998.

27. Stenum 2011.

28. Pratt 2012.

29. Liebelt 2011.

30. Lan 2007.

31. Constable 2007.

32. Parreñas 2015.

33. International Labour Organization 2017.

34. The first to revisit the *kafala* was Bahrain, which introduced legislation allowing foreign workers to change employment without needing to secure the permission of their sponsor (Diop, Johnston, and Le 2018). Other countries followed suit. For example, in Qatar, most migrant workers can now leave the country without an exit permit, but workers excluded from the labor law, such as domestic workers, are not covered in this reform (Qatar Law No. 13 of 2018).

35. In 2009, Jordan included domestic workers under its labor law; earlier, in 2003, it had established a Unified Standard Contract. In Jordan, labor protections for domestic workers include a maximum of 10 hours of work per day, a minimum of 8 continuous hours of rest per day, a weekly rest day, and regular salary payments. Jordan offers the

most progressive rules and regulations for domestic workers in the region, as it remains the only country that has incorporated them under its national labor law. While Lebanon excludes domestic workers from its labor law, it did establish a modicum of employment standards through the implementation of a Standard Unified Contract in 2009. While this standard contract neither stipulates a minimum wage nor grants an annual leave to domestic workers, it does guarantee them 8 continuous hours of rest per day, a day off consisting of 24 continuous hours per week, and the right to communicate with family (International Labour Organization 2012).

36. The domestic worker law in the KSA, for instance, leaves it to the discretion of the employer to determine "the kind of work to be performed by the domestic worker," "the amount of money the employer undertakes to pay the domestic worker," and the "rights and obligations of both parties" (Article 4 in Kingdom of Saudi Arabia 2013). Similarly, Kuwait does not establish a minimum wage but instead merely requires employers "to pay the agreed wage . . . at the end of every month" (Article 7 in Kuwait 2015). Kuwait likewise fails to extend minimum labor standards, at most barring employers from assigning "dangerous work" (Article 10 in Kuwait 2015). In contrast, Qatar has established 10 maximum hours of work per day, but likewise has not established a minimum wage (Section 12 in Qatar 2017). In the case of Bahrain, domestic workers are granted the right to a standard labor contract but it is left to the discretion of employers to determine the terms of the contract (Bahrain 2012). As Human Rights Watch's critique of this arrangement notes, "the new law does not set maximum daily and weekly work hours for domestic workers or mandate that employers give them weekly days off or overtime pay" (2012: 10).

37. United Arab Emirates 2017.

38. In 2012, for example, the Philippines banned the migration of domestic workers to the KSA, after the latter refused to increase the monthly minimum wage of Filipino domestic workers from US$200 to $400. The ban was lifted within six months, after the KSA agreed to the minimum wage hike. In February 2018, the Philippines likewise imposed a total ban on the deployment of all overseas Filipino workers to Kuwait. This came in response to what the Philippines perceived as the lack of action on the part of Kuwait over the killing of the domestic worker Joanna Demafelis, whose body was found in a freezer in an abandoned apartment in February 2018. It is believed that the body had been there since November 2016. The ban was not lifted until the signing of a memorandum of understanding between Kuwait and the Philippines in May 2018.

39. The supposed ban on domestic workers from the Philippines did not severely impact their presence in the UAE. They remain the largest group of domestic workers in the country and, numbering an estimated 200,000 to 300,000, the largest constituency of the 1 million Filipino migrant workers in the country.

40. This new agreement stipulates the standards set forth in Federal Law No. 10 of 2017, including the provision of a weekly rest day, 12 hours of daily rest of which 8 must be continuous, 30 days of annual paid holiday, round-trip airfare, decent accommodations, and medical insurance. The contract also requires the retention by the worker of their identity documents, including their passports.

41. While limiting the number of Tadbeer Centres, the UAE government does not

intend to replace privately-owned recruitment agencies but over time plans to have a more pivotal role in the hiring of domestic workers. Tadbeer Centres facilitate the migration of domestic workers from key sending countries including Ethiopia, India, Indonesia, and the Philippines. Tadbeer Centres offer four employment pathways for domestic workers: 1) direct hiring from the country of origin; 2) transitional hiring in which one initially works on a six-month temporary contract under the sponsorship of the government before transitioning to a more permanent contract; 3) a temporary hiring scheme with a two-year employment cap; and 4) a flexible hourly, daily, or weekly hiring arrangement for multiple families. In these various scenarios, either the government or the employer holds the sponsorship of the domestic worker.

42. Fernandez 2013; Chang 2018; Silvey and Parreñas 2020.

43. In the case of the Philippines, recruitment agencies facilitate job placements by ensuring that migrant workers meet their employment prerequisites, including any necessary skills training and medical clearances; by verifying the viability and suitability of employment opportunities; and by protecting the workers against unscrupulous employers.

44. See press release described in Cherian 2018.

45. Bakan and Stasiulis 1997 and 2003.

46. Ramos 2019.

47. For a news report and the image of Ruelo tied to the tree, see Panaligan 2019.

48. Cases of infanticide and murder could involve women who have illegal abortions at their employer's home. Women resort to this because out-of-wedlock pregnancy would land them in prison and lead to their eventual deportation. For Indonesian women, having children outside of marriage also means they would be highly stigmatized in their communities (Constable 2014). According to an interviewee who had spent a significant amount of time in prison, many of the incarcerated Indonesian women had had abortions. This is not only illegal in the UAE but also strongly condemned. The interviewee claimed that the guards inflicted severe corporal punishment on women who had had an abortion: not long after the arrival of such an inmate, this interviewee would hear the sounds of loud beatings, followed by wails of pain. She claimed that the Filipinas in prison, by contrast, had generally not had abortions. Instead, most were middle-class women who were incarcerated for failing to pay their debts. Unlike other Filipina interviewees, who had spent limited amounts of time in prison before being deported to the Philippines, this interviewee ended up staying for months because, since she was pregnant, the guards advised her to stay longer to ensure that the state would cover her medical costs as well as other needs of the child.

49. Kanna 2011.

50. The KSA grants domestic workers "one weekly rest day" (Kingdom of Saudi Arabia 2013). Kuwait requires "a paid weekly break" for domestic workers (Kuwait 2015). Qatar grants domestic workers the right to a "paid weekly rest holiday" (Qatar 2017). In Bahrain, however, employers are still not required to grant domestic workers a weekly day off or rest day (Bahrain 2012).

51. Pande 2013: 436. See also Mahdavi 2011; Jureidini and Moukarbel 2004.

52. While employers are technically liable for crimes committed by domestic workers,

incarceration for these crimes is unlikely. None of the employers participating in this study had encountered such an occurrence. If a domestic worker is impregnated, an employer can initially be suspected of being the father, which happened to one interviewee. However, a paternity test cleared him relatively quickly.

53. This is considered an offense because of the financial loss incurred by the employer, who has invested in the residency permit, work permit, and travel expenses of the domestic worker.

54. Mahdavi 2011; Pande 2012; Parreñas, Kantachote, and Silvey 2020.

55. Christman 1991.

56. Human Rights Watch 2014.

57. Employers have also been known to file false absconding cases against domestic workers who file labor abuse cases against them.

Chapter 2: Managing Vulnerable Migrants

1. Medenilla 2019.

2. Ibid.

3. Hapal 2017.

4. While most scholars have ignored this question, Gardner (2012) argues that it is not that migrants in Arab states are ignoring these risks but that they are instead unaware of them. This is however unlikely to be the case for domestic workers from the Philippines.

5. Guevarra 2009; Rodriguez 2010.

6. Guevarra 2009; Rafael 2000.

7. Ortiga 2018.

8. Guevarra 2009; Rodriguez 2010.

9. Fourcade and Healy 2007.

10. Guevarra 2009.

11. See Parreñas 2018. In the end, the subservience of migrant domestic workers to the arbitrary authority of employers limits the extent of their empowerment and allows the risks engendered by this authority to continue.

12. National Economic and Development Authority 2017. See Table 1.7 Stock Estimate of Overseas Filipinos by World Region, Country, Nature of Stay and Land-based and Sea-based Workers, 2013.

13. Philippines Statistics Authority 2018. Table 2.3, Distribution of Overseas Contract Workers by Place of Work and Sex 2018.

14. Battistella 1992.

15. "Elementary occupations" refer to jobs consisting of simple and routine tasks including janitorial work, product sorting, freight handling, and cleaning homes.

16. Philippines Statistics Authority 2018. Table 1.4, Distribution of Overseas Filipino Workers by Major Occupation Group, Sex and Area: 2018.

17. National Economic and Development Authority 2017. See Table 1.12 Overseas Filipino Workers, Census of Population and Housing by Philippine Region, Age Group and Sex, 2010.

18. Ibid.

19. Fiestada et al. 2018; Philippines Statistics Authority 2015.

20. Dajani 2017.

21. See Map 1.

22. Getting access to electricity through a neighbor would involve an illegally installed cord. The neighbor would usually charge 100 pesos or US$2 per month per item (e.g. electric fan) for the use of their electricity.

23. Portes and Rumbaut 2006.

24. The estimate of households without electricity in the Philippines is from the World Bank (2018).

25. Likewise reflecting their poverty are their skills-training classes. Based on participant observation and interviews at three different skills-training facilities, I learned that much of this training focused on developing basic cooking and cleaning skills, exposing domestic workers to electric appliances such as rice cookers, toasters, and washing machines, and teaching them how to set a table.

26. I observed mandatory government seminars for domestic workers bound for Arab states as well as Singapore. These seminars are conducted separately according to the country or region of destination. The government seminar for domestic workers bound for Singapore does not include instructions on how to board an airplane.

27. Chang 2018; Fernandez 2011; Rodriguez 2010; Tyner 2009.

28. Testaverde, Moroz, Hollweg, and Schmillen 2017.

29. This includes Ethiopia, Indonesia, and Sri Lanka. See Tyner 2009; Rodriguez 2010.

30. This is supposedly done to ensure the welfare of overseas workers and prevent their illegal recruitment, deployment to nonexistent jobs, or placement with unscrupulous employers (Hwang 2017).

31. Ibid.

32. Domestic workers must acquire training in four core skill sets, namely housecleaning, laundry and ironing, preparing hot and cold meals, and serving food and beverages. Training facilities are not closely monitored by the government, resulting in a wide disparity in standards as well as in the fees charged by the training centers, which ranged from US$0 to $322 according to the interviewees' reports.

33. Republic of the Philippines 1974.

34. Ibid.

35. In 1977, the government attempted to phase out the private sector, that is recruitment agencies, from the emigration process, but in 1978 it took a 180-degree turn and relinquished most of the recruiting efforts to the private sector.

36. Republic of the Philippines 1995.

37. As stated in Section 2c of the Republic Act No. 8042, otherwise known as the Migrant Workers and Filipino Overseas Act of 1995, "the State *does not promote* overseas employment as a means to sustain economic growth and achieve national development" (*emphasis added*). Instead of promoting migration, the state is said to do no more than monitor and oversee the outmigration of its workers for the purpose of protection. As the act continues, "The existence of the overseas employment program rests solely on the

assurance that the dignity and fundamental human rights and freedoms of the Filipino citizens shall not, at any time, be compromised or violated."

38. Shenon 1995.

39. Republic of the Philippines 1995; Republic of the Philippines 2009.

40. Rodriguez 2010.

41. Tyner 2009.

42. Guevarra 2009; Rodriguez 2010.

43. Republic of the Philippines 2009.

44. Countries deemed dangerous also become ineligible destinations. For instance, a ban on migration to Syria was imposed due to its unstable peace. Noncompliance with the 1995 Migrant Workers Act of the Philippines also results in the barring of migration, as has for instance been the case with Haiti.

45. Protecting migrant workers' rights through government-to-government agreements is a strategy that the Philippine state began pursuing as early as 1968, with the United States. Since then, the Philippines has concluded bilateral agreements with 22 countries including Canada, Norway, Papua New Guinea, and the KSA, as well as occupation-specific bilateral agreements with a wide range of countries that include the KSA for domestic workers and the United Kingdom for nurses. See Mangulabnan and Daquio 2018; Makulec 2014.

46. Battistella, Park, and Asis 2011.

47. This information is based on interviews with government officials in the consulate of Bangladesh in Dubai.

48. In the Philippines, it is POEA and its governing board that can institute a ban.

49. Mangulabnan and Daquio 2018.

50. This story was relayed to me by the former Philippine ambassador to the UAE, Grace Princesa.

51. International Organization for Migration 2003.

52. Asis 2017.

53. Owners of recruitment agencies must be Filipino citizens with a minimum net worth of 200,000 pesos (US$4,000). To open and maintain a recruitment agency requires the filing of 125,000 pesos (US$2,500) worth of bonds every two years and a license that costs 6,000 pesos (US$120). Republic of the Philippines 1995.

54. The Philippines assumes that when workers abscond, meaning run away, it is because of the bad behavior of their employers.

55. For a list of government-certified recruitment agencies, see http://www.poea.gov.ph/cgi-bin/agList.asp?mode=allLB. Accessed November 8, 2018.

56. Employers for instance cannot have a criminal record or past cases of worker abuse.

57. The minimum monthly income that employers need to demonstrate is in fact unclear. While one government website notes that it is 6,000 dirhams, a private information website lists it at 10,000 dirhams. See the UAE government website enumerating the requirements for sponsoring a domestic worker, including the minimum monthly wage at 6,000 dirhams, at http://www.dubai.ae/en/Lists/HowToGuide/DispForm.aspx?ID=45. Accessed July 17, 2019. See a private site, noting the minimum wage to be

10,000 dirhams, at https://www.askexplorer.com/dubai/residents/how-tos/living-in-dubai/domestic-workers/renewing-a-residence-visa-maid#content-section. Accessed July 23, 2019.

58. See Appendix B for a more extensive discussion of human trafficking.

59. For the fees charged by recruitment agencies, employers expect two years of guaranteed service from a domestic worker placed in their home. An employer is therefore unlikely to extend permission to a domestic worker who asks to quit. When employers grant a "release," meaning that they free a domestic worker from their sponsorship without penalty, they are not able to secure a refund from the recruitment agency if the probationary period of three months has passed. Interviewed for a local newspaper article about the lack of rights for employers of domestic workers, one Indian employer, for example, complained of having to forfeit the 15,000 dirhams (US $ 4,167) he had paid an agency for the recruitment of an Indian domestic worker from his native state of Andra Pradesh. See Sankar 2013.

60. Likewise, most other migrant workers pay agencies a fee that exceeds 40 percent of their monthly salary.

61. According to one recruitment agent, prospective migrant domestic workers are burdened with some of the costs of their migration, including the costs of obtaining a passport and processing their medical and police clearance, for the reason that it makes them more invested in keeping their job. Incurring these financial costs is said to increase their tolerance for subpar labor conditions and reduce the likelihood of their quitting for the most minor of infractions. While most interviewees had paid no more than US $ 100 for their job placement in the UAE, others had paid as much as US $ 300. Those who had paid higher fees had likely worked with an unregistered agency.

62. Variations in fees coincide with differences in salary across destinations. For example, Singapore costs less than Hong Kong because one can expect a starting salary of no more than US $ 400 in the former and US $ 550 in the latter. Parreñas 2015.

63. Xiang and Lindquist 2014.

64. In their analysis of the emergence of a migrant infrastructure, Xiang and Lindquist (2014) likewise observe the result of the diminished capabilities of migrant workers to control their labor migration.

65. Silvey and Parreñas 2020.

66. Lan 2006.

67. Constable 2007.

68. Hondagneu-Sotelo 2001; Constable 2007.

69. Chang 2018.

70. See description of pre-departure orientation seminars on the government website. Available at https://www.owwa.gov.ph/index.php/programs-services/education-training. Accessed May 4, 2020.

71. These two additional seminars were instituted in 2007.

72. CPDEP is administered by country or region of destination. The languages taught include Arabic, Cantonese, Hebrew, Italian, and Mandarin.

73. As of April 2014, professional migrants can complete pre-departure orientation

seminars at one of 6 accredited industry associations, 53 land-based recruitment agencies, or 234 sea-based recruitment agencies.

74. Blackett 2019.

75. Chang 2018.

76. Killias 2018.

77. Chang 2018: 707.

78. Fernandez 2011.

79. Jackie's employers refused to let her return to the Philippines and made her work an extra year after the end of her two-year contract. Employers do this to avoid or delay having to pay an agency the fee for placing a new domestic worker in their home.

80. Rodriguez 2010.

81. This reward is clearly a delayed one. The issue of having money to spend while abroad is never raised, as it seems that employers are expected to cover the cost of their food, housing, and other basic needs such as toiletries and clothes. Curiously, the possibility of needing some money for one's weekly day off is also not raised, suggesting that everyone knows or assumes how unlikely it is that they will have one.

82. Cabico 2018.

83. Middle-class professionals, who are concentrated in North America and invest heavily in real estate, are likely a much greater source of foreign remittances (Pido 2017).

84. Encinas 2015; Rafael 2000.

85. Rafael 2000.

86. International Organization for Migration 2003.

87. Parreñas 2018.

Chapter 3: Mobilizing Morality

1. Human Rights Watch 2014. This report is based on interviews with 99 migrant domestic workers in the UAE. The most frequently mentioned forms of abuse are overwork, lack of payment, and restricted freedom of movement (3–4).

2. In the middle of the report, there is a brief admission that some domestic workers do not fare poorly. As it mentions, "some workers said they felt lucky to have good working conditions" (2014: 37), but the report downplays this observation, immediately following it with the counter-perspective that "many, even of these workers, said that they worked or were on call more than 12 hours per day."

3. Mahdavi 2011; Scott 1990.

4. Scott 1995.

5. Mobilizing morality represents a form of "relational work," as domestic workers attempt to revisit the terms of their economic exchange with employers by negotiating the dynamics of their relationship. See Zelizer 2005; Zelizer 2012a.

6. Silvey and Parreñas 2020.

7. Mahdavi 2011; Pande 2013.

8. Mahdavi 2011.

9. Constable 2007; Lan 2006.

10. Romero 2002.

11. Colen 1990: 90.

12. Constable 2007: 185.

13. Chin 1998: 134.

14. Hondagneu-Sotelo 2001: 137.

15. Lan 2006: 235.

16. Dill 1994: 85.

17. Pilots for Emirates Airlines tend to live in the same residential community, allowing domestic workers to meet and enabling them to compare their labor conditions.

18. See the discussion of contract substitution in Appendix B.

19. During the time of my research, domestic workers were able to open what is called a ladies' savings account. At the National Bank of Abu Dhabi, it only required an initial deposit of 1000 dirhams (US$278), had no fees, and did not have a minimum balance requirement.

20. Zelizer 2005.

21. Colen 1995; Constable 2007; Hondagneu-Sotelo 2001; Lan 2006.

22. I had the opportunity to interview Jing regularly because part of her routine was to shop daily for her Emirati employers, whose adherence to a strict gender code means that they never leave the house. She worked for a household of four women, a mother and three adult daughters. Every day at 10 am she would leave with the family's personal driver to go to a branch of the supermarket Spinney's, where she would buy large quantities and varieties of freshly baked bread, bottles of Evian water, and canisters of Glade. Sometimes she would add other items, including chocolate bars or, at one point, Nivea's In-Shower Body Lotion. I learned that this family used at least three canisters of Glade *daily* and that one of the family members washed her face with Evian water. Jing, responding to my question about the large amounts of bread, told me that her employers rarely ate them but liked to have the choice of eating them. Jing often just ended up giving the bread away to workers such as garbage collectors or construction workers outside her employers' home.

23. Hondagneu-Sotelo 2001.

24. James Scott (1990) associates "hidden transcripts" with subordinate and powerless groups. He identifies "hidden transcripts" as the "discourse that takes place 'offstage,' beyond direct observations by powerholders" (4), and distinguishes them from "public transcripts," referring to "the open interaction between subordinates and those who dominate" (2). For domestic workers, "hidden transcripts" have been documented as being formed in various public settings, including buses in Los Angeles (Hondagneu-Sotelo 2001), churches in Lebanon (Pande 2012), and shopping malls and discos in Kuala Lumpur (Chin 1998). According to Scott, there is a sharp divide between the two kinds of "transcripts," as the actions, i.e., "public transcripts," of subordinated groups tend not to reflect their "hidden transcripts" or their critical views of "masters and mistresses" (1990: 18). Morals, and moral norms, arguably also shape public and private discourse. Powerholders, therefore, as we see with the case of employers here, are held to moral standards that result in their also having both "hidden" and "public" transcripts concerning their treatment of domestic workers.

25. This is a dish of vegetables with shrimp paste.

26. Kanna 2011.

27. Indomie is a brand of Indonesian noodles that is popular among Filipino domestic workers.

28. Kemp and Kfir 2016.

29. Becker 1963.

30. Pettit 1996.

31. Fassin 2015.

32. Fish 2017: 44.

33. Ibid., 65.

34. Ibid., 78.

35. Ibid., 78.

36. Ibid., 176.

37. Ibid., 87.

38. Ibid., 90.

39. Human Rights Watch 2012; 2014; 2016.

40. Mahdavi 2011.

41. Employers were familiar with the report by Human Rights Watch. Emirati employers dismissed the report as Orientalist and biased, arguing that Islamic values are in line with the principles of human rights. Non-Emiratis insisted that the report only concerned Emirati employers. When asked about the report, a government official, reflecting the attitude of employers, responded, "if we are so abusive, why do workers keep coming back? Why do they renew their contracts?" Also countering the moral discourse constructed by Human Rights Watch is the more common news coverage of domestic workers as perpetrators of crime (e.g. stealing, abuse of children, public urinating). Local news media regularly report on crimes that are available in court dockets, and crimes committed by domestic workers are more likely to reach the court system than those committed by their employers, as the employers are more likely to file cases against domestic workers than the other way around.

42. Swidler 1986.

43. International Organization for Migration 2003.

44. This is approximately U S $ 194.

45. Irwin and Bottero 2000: 277.

46. Indeed, in parks and food courts, I frequently listened to domestic workers recite to others their plans to engage in acts of moral claims-making, whether in order to gain access to the Internet or to secure a vacation to attend their child's graduation in the Philippines.

47. My observation diverges from other discussions of the everyday resistance of domestic workers. Other studies underscore domestic workers' subversive acts of resistance. It is said that domestic workers insert acts of "chicanery" and "cajolery" into their daily routine (Dill 1994: 50) or "manipulate the rules" of the household (Constable 2007: 175) by, for example, resisting the dress code or rejecting the inadequate foods provided by employers, as Constable describes of domestic workers in Hong Kong, or, as observed by Andall (2000) of domestic workers in Italy, sneaking out at night. Everyday subversions

could also entail the emotional manipulation of employers by using their maternal feelings to generate protection and aid (Ray and Qayum 2009) or engaging in "strategic personalism," that is, using intimacy as a tool to better work conditions (Mendez 1998; Hondagneu-Sotelo 2001). I do not deny that domestic workers engage in subversive acts. I merely show that they also resist in other ways.

48. In 2016, for example, it was reported that a domestic worker from Comoros Islands had been beaten to death by her employer, a 35-year-old Emirati citizen. See http://www.asianews.it/news-en/Murder-of-domestic-worker-highlights-plight-of-foreign-workers-in-the-Emirates-36824.html. Accessed December 23, 2020. In 2013, an Ethiopian domestic worker was said to have been forced to drink bleach, resulting in her death. See https://www.upi.com/Top_News/World-News/2013/06/11/Woman-in-Dubai-allegedly-tortured-maids/64351370970173/?ur3=1&fbclid=IwAR1znYMqW_mNM9d-viy9uiEETXS1Wd3aU8g66NObQwY2p6rfmwlpBMgAubto. Accessed January 1, 2021. Finally, in 2014, a couple was accused of torturing and killing their Ethiopian domestic worker. See Dajani 2014.

Chapter 4: Escaping Servitude for the Unfreedom of Criminalization

1. Ali 2010.

2. Among the 85 Filipina migrant domestic workers interviewed for this study, 37 had absconded, with 15 having entered the shadow economy of Dubai and 22 having sought refuge at the Philippine government-run migrant shelter. Because unauthorized migrant domestic workers were the most challenging to locate, I had to rely on snowball sampling to obtain access to the 15 who participated in my study. Domestic workers in the Philippine government-run migrant shelter, on the other hand, were the most convenient to find, due to their known presence in the facility.

3. Mahdavi 2011; Pande 2013.

4. Lan 2007.

5. O'Connell Davidson 2010.

6. Pande 2013; Fernandez 2014.

7. O'Neill 2011.

8. In 2012, a total of 2,349 domestic workers absconded to the Philippine embassy in Abu Dhabi. The largest group, 25.46 percent, fled due to overwork, followed by 25.71 percent fleeing due to reported mistreatment (e.g. lack of food, no rest), and 16.77 percent claiming nonpayment of salary. Similar figures are not available from the Philippine consulate in Dubai.

9. By the time she escaped, Elanie was owed three months' worth of unpaid wages.

10. Despite her severe case of abuse, Elanie planned to migrate again upon her return to the Philippines. Her past experiences in Jordan and Kuwait had been favorable as she was "treated like family" in those countries, adequately fed, and given access to "all of their things." She was hopeful that she would once again have favorable work conditions.

11. In the UAE, refrigerators with locks are common.

12. *Tamar* is the Arabic word for dates.

13. In contrast, other interviewees shared stories of sympathetic employers, particularly

daughters-in-law who snuck food to domestic workers behind the backs of their older Emirati relatives.

14. An *agal* is a rope used to hold the headscarf of Arab men. It is usually made of goat hair.

15. JoAnn had been so severely battered that it even affected the police officers assigned to her case after she fled to the Philippine consulate. They could not help but offer her money and future employment in their own households.

16. The agency locked her in a room and fed her inadequately for three days before her employer picked her up.

17. This trial period is stipulated in the contract administered by the agency in the Philippines and the UAE. Either the employer or the domestic worker can terminate their contract and request a new employer or domestic worker without penalty during this trial period. This policy is still frowned on by agencies, as it puts them at risk of forfeiting their fees if the domestic worker fails to secure a new employer.

18. A strong disincentive for employers to free domestic workers is the required fee that they have paid to a recruitment agency for the guaranteed two-year placement of a domestic worker in their home.

19. This policy is consistent across countries in the Gulf Cooperation Council. In Kuwait, a Filipino taxi driver was incarcerated for assisting a domestic worker in absconding. See https://www.kwentongofw.net/2018/12/taxi-driver-who-gave-a-taxi-ride-to-an-escaping-filipina-domestic-helper-in-kuwait-imprisoned/?fbclid=IwAR2F_rhjmzrRlXxXXrmM4FZJhbnNjo1DsV5OIQlkMsoOpbo1TdnqoVZXoqo. Accessed December 27, 2018.

20. See Article 29 of UAE Federal Law No. 15 of 2017.

21. Cecile has accompanied her employers on vacation to Greece.

22. Legal cases are most often for back wages.

23. The government regularly extends amnesties to unauthorized workers and forgives the fines of those who "surrender" and exit the country.

24. Coutin 2000.

25. Ibid., 27.

26. See Article 29 of UAE Federal Law No. 15 of 2017.

27. The condominium building where I resided while in the UAE, for instance, required all visitors to show their legal identification. This precluded unauthorized domestic workers from having access to my residence. I learned that this was common policy. It results in unauthorized workers being unable to work as cleaners or babysitters in these types of buildings.

28. Pande 2013: 431.

29. One is a food vendor who gained access to a kitchen she can use to prepare food after she moved in with her boyfriend, a migrant professional. One works in the kitchen of a nightclub. Another is not allowed to work and confined to her room by her *jowa*. Among those employed as domestic workers, one interviewee augments her salary by working informally in a restaurant for 70 dirhams (US$19) on weekend evenings.

30. Nine of my interviewees worked for other Filipinos.

31. In other words, she could operate a small business with the money.

32. See Fernandez 2014; Lan 2007; Mahdavi 2011; Pande 2012.

33. Coutin 2000; Willen 2007; Willen 2014.

34. See Mahdavi 2011 for a discussion of unauthorized work as more materially rewarding. This is an argument advanced by others for unauthorized domestic workers elsewhere as well, thus illustrating that scholarship on domestic work generally abides by a negative liberty framework of freedom. For example, see Lan (2007) for Taiwan and Pande (2013) for Lebanon.

35. I visited Cherry in her home in Sharjah, where she chose to live due to its lower rental rates than Dubai. Cherry lived in an apartment with partitions, meaning an apartment where the bedrooms and living room were divided by makeshift plywood, creating separate boxes occupied by the residents. An Indian migrant was the main renter of the unit, where he had a room and his tenants—all Filipino migrants—had boxed partitions. The unit had 16 residents and one bathroom. I had brought Cherry a bucket of Kentucky Fried Chicken, unaware that she was struggling to find money to feed herself. She told me that she resorted to fishing in the early mornings so that she could have something to eat for the day.

36. Top bunks are cheaper due to the inconvenience of having to climb up to them for access.

37. The risks of renting to unauthorized migrants are relatively low, as many can feign ignorance over their legal status. During raids in migrant neighborhoods, only unauthorized migrants are arrested and incarcerated.

38. Willen 2014.

39. Back in the Philippines, she tried to return to an Arab state to work but faced difficulties because of her eyesight. As I neared the end of writing this book, I heard the unfortunate news of Nada's passing. Her friends tell me that she died of sepsis. Without the financial resources to access adequate medical care in her rural community in Basilan, Nada was not able to seek treatment when she fell ill.

40. The domestic worker lives in separate quarters in the compound. Her husband would not have access to the main house.

41. In the local Filipino community, South Asian boyfriends are often spoken of disparagingly, identified as *itik,* meaning duck, and *pana,* meaning a crossbow. They refer to them as "duck" due to their supposedly poor dancing skills, i.e., it is said that they dance like a duck, and "crossbow" in reference to how Native Americans, i.e., "Indians," historically used a bow and arrow.

42. I rarely encountered same-sex relationships among domestic workers in the UAE: of my 85 (female) interviewees, only one had been engaged in a same-sex relationship. Instead, most pursued relationships with men.

43. For an example of the reported human trafficking of Indonesian domestic workers by Bangladeshi men, see Amir 2018a and Amir 2018b.

Chapter 5: Mobility Pathways and the Unfreedom of Poverty

1. The Philippine government set the minimum age at 25 in 1994, subsequently changing it to 21 in 1998, then to 18 in 2001, then back to 25 in the original 2006 Household

Service Workers Reform Package, before finally setting it at 23 as part of the amendments to the 2006 reform package.

2. See Parreñas, Silvey, Hwang, and Choi 2019.

3. These programs include the provision of loans to assist returning migrants with launching a viable business project via the Overseas Filipino Workers—Enterprise Development and Loan Program (OFW-EDLP), which is run in partnership with private banks such as the Development Bank of the Philippines and Land Bank of the Philippines. Under this program, return migrants who have completed the government's Enhanced Entrepreneurial Development Training qualify for loans of approximately US$6,000 to US$38,000. Return migrants can also participate in the *Balik-Pinas! Balik-Hanapbuhay! Program* (Return to the Philippines! Return to Earning a Living! Program), which is a livelihood support and assistance program that offers technological skills and entrepreneurial training, provides "starter kits and goods," and extends other services to assist return migrants, including distressed migrants who have fled abusive employers, in securing self- or wage employment.

4. If we are to exclude first-time migrants (n=23), then it is a significant count of 17 out of 62 who had attempted to resettle in the Philippines before migrating once again.

5. 12 out of 17 remigrated.

6. Parreñas, Silvey, Hwang, and Choi 2019.

7. Robertson 2019.

8. This survey was conducted in a poor province in the Philippines. The surveys were given to return migrants who made purchases at an appliance store. Participants were limited to return migrants who had been in the Philippines for at least 3 months and were not on vacation. This survey included only land-based workers, excluding seafarers.

9. The father of the child that Mishra had while she was in prison in Dubai helped her to accrue funds for her business.

10. Arcilla 2018.

11. Portes and Zhou 1993.

12. Ponce de Leon 2019.

13. Parreñas, Silvey, Hwang, and Choi 2019: 1230.

14. Paul 2012.

15. The vast majority of domestic workers do not meet the educational qualifications required of domestic workers entering Canada, namely having completed four years of tertiary education.

16. Portes and Zhou 1993.

17. Philippine Overseas Employment Administration 2010.

18. Silvey and Parreñas 2020.

19. The sociologist Shanti Robertson (2019) describes the migration undertaken by prospective Asian migrants on their pathway to permanent residence in Australia as involving a multitude of temporary visas (e.g. student, working holiday, and temporary labor) of varying temporal trajectories. She describes this multinational process leading to permanent residence as "staggered migration," which she defines as "contingent, multi-directional and multi-stage mobility pathways—where the boundaries between temporariness and permanence (as both legal status and subjective state) are increasingly blurry and mutable" (170).

20. Among my interviewees, there were 21 staggered temporary labor migrants.

21. Roda eventually managed to obtain a cellular phone with the assistance of a Filipino garbage man, whom she trusted to buy her one for 150 dirhams (US$42). She recalled: "When I threw the garbage, I saw my countryman. I asked him can you buy me a phone. I gave him 150 dirhams. Then he bought me a sim then it fit so there was no change and I was so happy because it was my first time to hear the voice of my parents. For four months, imagine that, that is when I contact them because they thought what is the news about me, why is she not showing her presence, think of it your parents are really worried. Who is a stupid parent who will not mind their child is not calling. So it was four months when I heard their voices. They were so happy. My mother was crying."

22. Roda was one of the few domestic workers who had some years of college education. What prompted her migration was her father's loss of all of his retirement funds in a pyramid scheme. As the youngest child in the family, and without any family of her own, she felt compelled to seek work abroad to help her parents through retirement. She sought work in an Arab state due to its lower cost than other destinations.

23. Wimmer and Glick Schiller 2002.

24. Portes and Zhou 1993.

25. Kivisto 2001.

26. Paul 2012.

27. Belanger and Silvey 2020.

Conclusion: The Moral Project of Unfree Labor

1. See Jureidini 2010; Mahdavi 2011; Pande 2013.

2. See the organization's website at https://www.globalslaveryindex.org/. Accessed December 30, 2020.

3. Bales 2000: 462.

4. Ibid., 464.

5. Cornell and Bales 2008: 68.

6. Murray 2013; Sonmez, Apostolopoulos, Tran, and Rentrope 2011; Mahdavi 2013.

7. Secorun 2018.

8. Mahdavi 2013: 436.

9. Mahdavi 2011: 127.

10. Hwang 2018; Hoang 2014.

11. Said 1978.

12. See Mahdavi 2011; Human Rights Watch 2014; Secorun 2018.

13. Burawoy 1982.

14. Zelizer 2005.

15. Fourcade and Healy 2007.

16. Pettit 1996.

17. Rodriguez 2010.

18. See for example Pande 2013; Human Rights Watch 2014.

19. Lan 2007.

20. Pettit 1996.

21. Zelizer 2012a.

22. Shouk 2019.

23. Hondagneu-Sotelo 2001.

24. Bakan and Stasiulis 1997.

25. Blackett 2019: 48.

Appendix A: Methodology

1. I previously employed the ethnographic approach of capturing the process of subjectification in *Servants of Globalization,* in which I examined and compared the experiences of domestic workers in Los Angeles and Rome, focusing on how particular dislocations arise from the various institutional processes that define their migration.

2. I draw from Foucault's analysis of the disciplining of subjects and constituting of bodies and populations as subjects. See Foucault 1976; Parreñas 2015; and Saldaña-Portillo 2003.

3. See Burawoy 2017. Burawoy sees structural ethnography as requiring a comparative logic that I take the liberty of extending to include the analysis of differences within in-group experiences.

4. Desmond 2014.

5. Ibid., 554.

6. Cobb and Hoang 2015.

7. Marcus 1998.

8. Parveen and Wintour 2018.

9. Kathiravelu 2015.

10. Redden 2015.

11. Davidson 2009.

12. Ali 2007.

13. Access to these government shelters was provided to me by the ambassador of the Philippines during that time, Grace Princesa.

14. Almost all of the domestic workers interviewed were active users of Facebook.

15. Killias 2018.

16. Ibid. 2018: 151.

17. These provinces are in Mindanao and include Basilan, which is an area known to be dominated by the Jihadist terrorist group Abu Sayyaf. I received plenty of invitations from informants to accompany them to their hometowns, but they were frequently premised with advice that I mitigate the risk of being kidnapped by wearing their clothes *and* hiring private bodyguards.

18. Silvey 2007; Killias 2018.

19. According to the POEA, illegal recruitment refers to "Any act of canvassing, enlisting, contracting, transporting, utilizing, hiring or procuring workers and includes referring, contract services, promising or advertising for employment abroad, whether for profit or not, when undertaken by a non-license or non-holder of authority." See http://www.poea.gov.ph/air/whatisair.html. Accessed May 11, 2020.

20. Contract substitution refers to the practice by employers of refusing to acknowledge the terms of the labor contract signed in the territory of the Philippines and replacing

it with a contract stipulating less-desirable terms of employment once the worker has arrived in the country of destination.

21. Individuals who volunteer for migrant-rights.org wish to remain anonymous due to potential reprisal from governments in the region.

22. I gained access with the assistance of officials at the Philippine consulate in Dubai.

23. My initial entrée to households of Emirati, which is difficult to secure due to the distance between locals and foreigners in the UAE, was facilitated by the Philippine Ambassador to the UAE during that time, Grace Princesa.

24. Victoria Reyes (2020) observes that there are ethnographic toolkits that researchers can strategically draw from to gain field access. These toolkits include social capital and backgrounds, and are both invisible and visible. I agree that backgrounds can be a resource in gaining field access, which was the case in terms of my ability to reach domestic workers, but the same backgrounds can in other cases also hinder field access. This was the case for me with employers. This hindrance would not completely block my access, but it would have required my spending a great deal of time in the spaces inhabited by employers, thereby making me more familiar to potential interviewees, who might then in turn have become more open to participating in my project.

25. Gaining access to locals tended to be a challenge because there seems to be an invisible divide in the UAE separating the worlds of foreigners and locals. The locals whom I encountered were not representative of their population, as they excluded anyone living in poverty or from non-urban areas. They were also likely to be of the privileged class, and specifically people who were interested in introducing their children to American college students from an elite university.

Appendix B: Notes on Human Trafficking, Forced Labor, and Slavery

1. Article 3 of the Protocol to Prevent, Suppress and Punish Trafficking in Persons (United Nations 2000) defines trafficking in persons as the following: "the recruitment, transportation, transfer, harbouring or receipt of persons, by means of the threat or use of force or other forms of coercion, of abduction, of fraud, of deception, of the abuse of power or of a position of vulnerability or of the giving or receiving of payments or benefits to achieve the consent of a person having control over another person, for the purpose of exploitation. Exploitation shall include, at a minimum, the exploitation of the prostitution of others or other forms of sexual exploitation, forced labour or services, slavery or practices similar to slavery, servitude or the removal of organs."

2. According to the ILO Forced Labour Convention (International Labour Organization 1930) (No. 29), forced labor by definition refers to "all work or service which is exacted from any person under the threat of a penalty and for which the person has not offered himself or herself voluntarily."

3. Kevin Bales offers a broad definition of "modern-day slavery" as "the total control of one person [the slave] by another [the slaveholder or slaveholders] for the purpose of economic exploitation." See Bales 1999: 6 and Bales 2004.

4. Bales and Soodalter 2009.

5. United Nations (League of Nations) 1926.

References

Ahmad, Attiya. 2017. *Everyday Conversions: Islam, Domestic Work and South Asian Migrant Women in Kuwait.* Durham, NC: Duke University Press.

Ali, Syed. 2007. "'You Must Come with Us.'" *The Guardian* (November 11). Available at https://www.theguardian.com/lifeandstyle/2007/nov/12/familyandrelationships.firstperson. Accessed January 2, 2021.

———. 2010. *Dubai: Gilded Cage.* New Haven, CT: Yale University Press.

Amir, Salam Al. 2018a. "Human Traffickers Involved in Maid's Death Case to See Out Life Sentences." *The National* (April 21). Available at https://www.thenationalnews.com/uae/human-traffickers-involved-in-maid-s-death-case-to-see-out-life-sentences-1.723478. Accessed December 29, 2020.

———. 2018b. "Traffickers Lure Housemaid into Prostitution before Trying to Sell Her, Dubai Court Hears." *The National* (April 30). Available at https://www.thenationalnews.com/uae/traffickers-lure-housemaid-into-prostitution-before-trying-to-sell-her-dubai-court-hears-1.726072. Accessed December 29, 2020.

Andall, Jacqueline. 2000. *Gender, Migration and Domestic Servitude: The Politics of Black Women in Italy.* Farnham, UK: Ashgate Publishing.

Anderson, Bridget. 2000. *Doing the Dirty Work? The Global Politics of Domestic Labor.* New York, NY: Palgrave Macmillan.

Arcilla, Albert. 2018. "Zamboanga Board Approves P20 Minimum Wage Hike." *Business World* (July 10). Available at https://www.bworldonline.com/zamboanga-board-approves-p20-minimum-wage-hike/. Accessed December 26, 2020.

Asis, Maruja. 2017. "The Philippines: Beyond Labor Migration, Toward Development, and (Possibly) Return." *Migration Policy Institute* (July 12). Available at https://www.migrationpolicy.org/article/philippines-beyond-labor-migration-toward-development-and-possibly-return. Accessed November 5, 2018.

Bahrain. 2012. Law No. 36 of 2012 Promulgating the Labour Law in the Private Sector. Available at https://www.ilo.org/dyn/natlex/docs/MONOGRAPH/91026/105342/F265276925/BHR91026 Eng.pdf. Accessed December 26, 2020.

Bakan, Abigail, and Daiva Stasiulis, eds. 1997. *Not One of the Family: Foreign Domestic Workers in Canada.* Toronto, ON: University of Toronto Press.

———. 2003. *Negotiating Citizenship: Migrant Women in Canada and the Global System*. New York, NY: Palgrave.

Bales, Kevin. 1999. *Disposable People: New Slavery in the Global Economy*. Berkeley, CA: University of California Press.

———. 2000. "Expendable People: Slavery in the Age of Globalization." *Journal of International Affairs* 53(2): 461–84.

———. 2004. "International Labor Standards: Quality of Information and Measures of Progress in Combating Forced Labor." *Comparative Labor Law and Policy* 24(2): 321–64.

Bales, Kevin, and Ron Soodalter. 2009. *The Slave Next Door: Human Trafficking and Slavery in America*. Berkeley, CA: University of California Press.

Bandelj, Nina. 2012. "Relational Work and Economic Sociology." Politics and Society 40(2): 175–201.

———. 2020. "Relational Work in the Economy." *Annual Review of Sociology* 46: 15.1–15.22.

Battistella, Graziano. 1992. *Philippine Labor Migration: Impact and Policy*. Quezon City, Philippines: Scalabrini Migration Center.

Battistella, Graziano, Jung Soo Park, and Maruja M. B. Asis. 2011. Protecting Filipino Transnational Domestic Workers: Government Regulations and their Outcomes. PIDS Discussion Paper Series, No. 2011–12. Makati City, Philippines: Philippine Institute for Development Studies.

Becker, Howard. 1963. *Outsiders: Studies in the Sociology of Deviance*. New York, NY: Free Press.

Belanger, Daniele, and Rachel Silvey. 2020. "An Im/mobility Turn: Power Geometries of Care and Migration." *Journal of Ethnic and Migration Studies* 46(16): 3423–40.

Berlin, Isaiah. 1969. *Four Essays on Liberty*. Oxford, England: Oxford University Press.

Blackett, Adelle. 2019. *Everyday Transgressions: Domestic Workers' Transnational Challenge to International Labor Law*. Ithaca, NY: Cornell University Press.

Braverman, Harry. 1998. *Labor and Monopoly Capital: The Degradation of Work in the Twentieth Century*. New York, NY: Monthly Review Press.

Brown, Rachel. 2019. "Reproducing the National Family: Kinship Claims, Development Discourse and Migrant Caregivers in Palestine/Israel." *Feminist Theory* 20(3): 247–68.

Bryant, Christa Case. 2013. "For Saudi Arabia's Foreign Domestic Workers, Employer's Word Is Virtually Law." *The Christian Science Monitor* (January 11). Available online at https://www.csmonitor.com/World/Middle-East/2013/0111/For-Saudi-Arabia-s-foreign-domestic-workers-employers-word-is-virtually-law. Accessed August 20, 2020.

Burawoy, Michael. 1982. *Manufacturing Consent: Changes in the Labor Process under Monopoly Capitalism*. Chicago, IL: University of Chicago Press.

———. 2017. "On Desmond: The Limits of Spontaneous Sociology." *Theory and Society* 46(4): 261–84.

Cabico, Gaea Katreena. 2018. "Philippines Is 3rd Top Remittance Receiving Country in the World." *The Philippine Star* (April 23). Available at https://www.philstar.com/

business/2018/04/23/1808669/philippines-3rd-top-remittance-receiving-country-world. Accessed December 26, 2020.

Chan, Cherise Shun-ching. 2009. "Invigorating the Content in Social Embeddedness: an Ethnography of Life Insurance Transactions in China." *American Journal of Sociology* 115(3): 712–54.

Chang, Andy Scott. 2018. "Producing the Self-Regulating Subject: Liberal Protection in Indonesia's Migration Infrastructure." *Pacific Affairs* 91(4): 685–716.

Cherian, Dona. 2018. "Tadbeer Centres: Hiring Domestic Workers in the UAE." *Gulf News* (May 16). Available at https://gulfnews.com/lifestyle/community/tadbeer-centres-hiring-domestic-workers-in-the-uae-1.2222253. Accessed December 26, 2020.

Chin, Christine. 1998. *In Service and Servitude: Foreign Female Domestic Workers and the Malaysian "Modernity Project."* New York, NY: Columbia University Press.

Christman, John. 1991. "Liberalism and Individual Positive Freedom." *Ethics* 101(2): 343–59.

Cobb, Jessica, and Kimberly Hoang. 2015. "Protagonist-Driven Urban Ethnography." *City and Community* 14(4): 348–51.

Colen, Shellee. 1990. "'Housekeeping' for the Green Card: West Indian Household Workers, the State, and Stratified Reproduction in New York." In *At Work in Homes: Household Workers in World Perspective*, edited by Roger Sanjek and Shellee Colen, 89–118. Washington, DC: American Ethnological Society Monograph Series, Number 3.

———. 1995. "Like a Mother to Them: Stratified Reproduction and West Indian Childcare Workers and Employers in New York." In *Conceiving the New World Order: The Global Politics of Reproduction*, edited by Faye Ginsburg and Rayna Rapp, 78–102. Berkeley, CA: University of California Press.

Constable, Nicole. 2007 (1997). *Maid to Order in Hong Kong: Stories of Migrant Workers.* 2nd ed. Ithaca, NY: Cornell University Press.

———. 2014. *Born Out of Place: Migrant Mothers and the Politics of International Labor.* Berkeley, CA: University of California Press.

Cornell, Becky, and Kevin Bales. 2008. *Slavery Today: A Groundwork Guide.* Toronto, ON: Groundwood Books.

Coutin, Susan. 2000. *Legalizing Moves: Salvadoran Immigrants' Struggle for U.S. Residency.* Ann Arbor, MI: University of Michigan Press.

Dajani, Haneen. 2014. "Husband and Wife Accused of Torturing and Killing Their Ethiopian Maid, Abu Dhabi Court Hears." *The National* (July 8). Available at https://www.thenationalnews.com/uae/husband-and-wife-accused-of-torturing-and-killing-their-ethiopian-maid-abu-dhabi-court-hears-1.581824. Accessed December 29, 2020.

———. 2017. "Ban on Filipino Domestic Workers Looks Set to Be Lifted as New Agreement with UAE Is Signed." *The National* (September 12). Available at https://www.thenationalnews.com/uae/ban-on-filipino-domestic-workers-looks-set-to-be-lifted-as-new-agreement-with-uae-is-signed-1.627932. Accessed December 30, 2020.

Davidson, Christopher. 2009. *Dubai: The Vulnerability of Success.* Oxford, UK: Oxford University Press.

Debusmann, Bernd, Jr. 2018a. "UAE Vlogger Criticises Sondos Al Qattan over Kuwaiti Domestic Worker Comments." *Arabian Business Industries* (July 25). Available at https://www.arabianbusiness.com/culture-society/401451-uae-vlogger-criticises-kuwaiti-influencer-sondos-al-qattan-over-domestic-worker-comments. Accessed December 28, 2020.

———. 2018b. "Gulf-Based Influencers Condemn Sondos Al Qattan's Domestic Worker Comments." *Arabian Business Industries* (July 29). Available at https://www.arabianbusiness.com/media/401654-gulf-based-influencers-condemn-sondos-al-qattans-domestic-worker-comments. Accessed December 28, 2020.

Department of Labor and Employment (Philippines). 2020. "Region II Cagayan Valley Region, Daily Minimum Wage Rates." Available at https://nwpc.dole.gov.ph/region-andwages/region-ii-cagayan-valley/. Accessed December 26, 2020.

Desmond, Matthew. 2014. "Relational Ethnography." *Theory and Society* 43: 547–79.

Dill, Bonnie Thornton. 1994. *Across the Boundaries of Race and Class: An Exploration of Work and Family among Black Female Domestic Workers.* New York, NY: Garland Publishing.

Diop, Abdoulaye, Trevor Johnston, and Kien Trung Le. 2018. "Migration Policies across the GCC: Challenges in Reforming the *Kafala*." In *Migration to the Gulf: Policies in Sending and Receiving Countries*, edited by Philippe Fargues and Nasra M. Shah, 33–60. Cambridge, UK: Gulf Research Centre.

Encinas-Franco, Jean. 2015. "Overseas Filipino Workers (OFWs) as Heroes: Discursive Origins of the 'Bagong Bayani' in the Era of Labor Export." *Humanities Diliman* 12(2): 56–78.

Fassin, Didier, ed. 2015. *A Companion to Moral Anthropology.* New York, NY: John Wiley & Sons Inc.

Fernandez, Bina. 2011. "Household Help? Ethiopian Women Domestic Workers' Labor Migration to the Gulf Countries." *Asian and Pacific Migration Journal* 20(3–4): 433–57.

———. 2013. "Traffickers, Brokers, Employment Agents, and Social Networks: The Regulation of Intermediaries in the Migration of Ethiopian Domestic Workers to the Middle East." *International Migration Review* 47(4): 814–43.

———. 2014. "Degrees of (Un)Freedom: The Exercise of Agency by Ethiopian Migrant Domestic Workers in Kuwait and Lebanon." In *Migrant Domestic Workers in the Middle East: The Home and the World*, edited by Bina Fernandez, Marina de Regt, and Gregory Currie, 51–74. New York, NY: Palgrave Macmillan.

Fiestada, Justin Oliver, Crystal Joy De La Rosa, and Malou Mangahas. 2018. "Stats on the State of the Region: Hubs of Wealth, Ponds of Poverty." Philippine Center for Investigative Journalism. Available at https://pcij.org/article/1409/stats-on-the-state-of-the-regions-hubs-of-wealth-ponds-of-poverty. Accessed May 4, 2020.

Fish, Jennifer. 2017. *Domestic Workers of the World Unite! A Global Movement for Dignity and Human Rights.* New York, NY: New York University Press.

Foucault, Michel. 1976. *History of Sexuality Volume 1.* New York, NY: Vintage.

———. 1997. "The Ethics of the Concern of the Self as a Practice of Freedom." In *Ethics: Subjectivity and Truth*, edited by Paul Rabinow, 281–301. New York, NY: The New Press.

Fourcade, Marion, and Keiran Healy. 2007. "Moral Views of Market Society." *Annual Review of Sociology* 33: 14.1–14.27.

Francisco-Menchavez, Valerie. 2018. *The Labor of Care: Filipina Migrants and Transnational Families in the Digital Age*. Urbana-Champaign, IL: University of Illinois Press.

Fudge, Judy, and Kendra Strauss. 2014. *Temporary Work, Agencies, and Unfree Labour: Insecurity in the New World of Work*. New York, NY: Routledge.

Gabriel, Elliot. 2018. "Migrant Worker Turned Activist Speaks Out about Gulf Slavery Following Cruel Rant by Kuwaiti Makeup Queen." *Mint Press News* (August 1). Available at https://www.mintpressnews.com/migrant-worker-turned-activist-speaks-out-about-gulf-slavery-following-rant-by-kuwait-makeup-queen/246810/. Accessed December 26, 2020.

Galtung, Johan. 1969. "Violence, Peace and Peace Research." *Journal of Peace Research* 6(3): 167–91.

Gardner, Andrew. 2010. *City of Strangers: Gulf Migration and the Indian Community in Bahrain*. Ithaca, NY: Cornell University Press.

———. 2012. "Why Do They Keep Coming? Labor Migrants in the Gulf States." In *Migrant Labour in the Persian Gulf*, edited by Mehran Kamrava and Zahra Babar, 41–58. New York, NY: Columbia University Press.

Granovetter, Mark. 1985. "Economic Action and Social Structure: The Problem of Embeddedness." *American Journal of Sociology* 91(3): 481–510.

Guevarra, Anna. 2009. *Marketing Dreams, Manufacturing Heroes: The Transnational Labor Brokering of Filipino Workers*. New Brunswick, NJ: Rutgers University Press.

Guyer, Paul, and Alan Wood, eds. 1992. *The Cambridge Edition of the Works of Immanuel Kant*. Cambridge, UK: Cambridge University Press.

Hapal, Don Kevin. 2017. "Timeline: Jennifer Dalquez's Journey to Death Row and Acquittal." *Rappler* (March 31). Available at https://www.rappler.com/nation/165469-ofw-jennifer-dalquez-timeline. Accessed December 26, 2020.

Harvey, David. 1989. *The Condition of Postmodernity*. Oxford, UK: Blackwell Books.

Hoang, Kimberly. 2014. "Competing Technologies of Embodiment: Pan-Asian Modernity and Third World Dependency in Vietnam's Contemporary Sex Industry." *Gender & Society* 28(4): 513–36.

———. 2018. "Risky Investments: How Local and Foreign Investors Finesse Corruption-Rife Emerging Markets." *American Sociological Review* 83(4): 657–85.

Hondagneu-Sotelo, Pierrette. 2001. *Domestica*. Berkeley, CA: University of California Press.

Human Rights Watch. 2012. "For a Better Life: Migrant Worker Abuse in Bahrain and the Government Reform Agenda." New York, NY: Human Rights Watch.

———. 2014. "'I Already Bought You': Abuse and Exploitation of Female Domestic Workers in the United Arab Emirates." New York, NY: Human Rights Watch.

———. 2016. "'I Was Sold': Abuse and Exploitation of Migrant Domestic Workers in Oman." New York, NY: Human Rights Watch.

Hwang, Maria Cecilia. 2017. "Offloaded: Women's Sex Work Migration across the South China Sea and the Gendered Anti-Trafficking Emigration Policy of the Philippines." *Women's Studies Quarterly* 45(1–2): 131–47.

———. 2018. "Gendered Border Regimes and Displacements: The Case of Filipina Sex Workers in Asia." *Signs: Journal of Women in Culture and Society* 43 (3): 515–37.

International Labour Organization (ILO). 1930. Forced Labour Convention (No. 29). Available at https://www.ilo.org/dyn/normlex/en/f?p=NORMLEXPUB:12100:0::NO ::P12100_ILO_CODE:C029. Accessed December 28, 2020.

———. 2011. Domestic Workers Convention (No. 189). Available at https://www.ilo.org/ dyn/normlex/en/f?p=NORMLEXPUB:12100:0::NO::P12100_ILO_CODE:C189. Accessed December 28, 2020.

———. 2012. *Information Guide for Migrant Domestic Workers in Lebanon*. Beirut, Lebanon: ILO.

———. 2015a. "Employer's Perspectives Towards Domestic Workers in Kuwait." Working Paper. Beirut, Lebanon: ILO Regional Office for Arab States.

———. 2015b. *ILO Global Estimates on Migrant Workers, 2015 Report*. Geneva, Switzerland: ILO.

———. 2017. "Employer-Migrant Worker Relationships in the Middle East: Exploring Scope for Internal Labour Market Mobility and Fair Migration." Beirut, Lebanon: ILO Regional Office for Arab States.

International Organization for Migration (IOM). 2003. *Labour Migration in Asia*. Geneva, Switzerland: IOM.

———. 2015. *2015 Global Migration Trends*. Berlin, Germany: Global Migration Data Analysis Centre, IOM.

Irwin, Sarah, and Wendy Bottero. 2000. "Market Returns? Gender and Theories of Change in Employment Relations." *British Journal of Sociology* 51(2): 261–80.

Jureidini, Ray. 2010. "Trafficking and Contract Migrant Workers in the Middle East." *International Migration* 48(4): 142–63.

Jureidini, Ray, and Nayla Moukarbel. 2004. "Female Sri Lankan Domestic Workers in Lebanon: A Case of Contract Slavery?" *Journal of Ethnic and Migration Studies* 30(4): 581–607.

Kakande, Yasin. 2015. *Slave States: The Practice of the Kafala in the Gulf Arab Region*. Alresford, Hampshire, UK: Zero Books.

Kanna, Ahmed. 2011. *Dubai: The City as Corporation*. Minneapolis, MN: University of Minnesota Press.

Kemp, Adriana, and Nelly Kfir. 2016. "Wanted Workers but Unwanted Mothers: Mobilizing Moral Claims on Migrant Care Workers' Families in Israel." *Social Problems* 63(3): 373–94.

Khalaf, Abdulhadi, O. AlShehabi, and A. Hanieh, eds. 2015. *Transit States: Labour, Migration, and Citizenship in the Gulf*. London, UK: Pluto Press.

Killias, Olivia. 2018. *Follow the Maid: Domestic Worker Migration in and from Indonesia.* Copenhagen: Nordic Institute of Asian Studies Press.

Kingdom of Saudi Arabia [KSA]. 2013. Decision 310 of 1434 on Domestic Workers. Available at https://gulfmigration.org/decision-no-310-of-1434-on-domestic-workers/. Accessed December 28, 2020.

Kivisto, Peter. 2001. "Theorizing Transnational Immigration: A Critical Review of Current Efforts." *Ethnic and Racial Studies* 24(4): 549–77.

Kuwait. 2015. Law No. 68 of 2015 on Employment of Domestic Workers. Available at https://www.ilo.org/dyn/natlex/natlex4.detail?p_lang=en&p_isn=101760. Accessed December 28, 2020.

Lainer-Vos, Dani. 2013. "The Practical Organization of Moral Transactions: Gift Giving, Market Exchange, Credit, and the Making of Diaspora Bonds." *Sociological Theory* 31(2): 145–67.

Lan, Pei-Chia. 2006. *Global Cinderellas: Migrant Domestics and Newly Rich Employers in Taiwan.* Durham, NC: Duke University Press.

———. 2007. "Legal Servitude and Free Illegality: Migrant 'Guest' Workers in Taiwan." In *Asian Diasporas: New Formations, New Conceptions,* edited by Rhacel Parreñas and Lok C. D. Siu, 253–77. Stanford, CA: Stanford University Press.

Liebelt, Claudia. 2011. *Caring for the Holy Land: Filipina Domestic Workers in Israel.* New York, NY: Berghahn Books.

Longva, Anh Nga. 1999. *Walls Built on Sand: Migration, Exclusion and Society in Kuwait.* Boulder, CO: Westview Press.

Madianou, Mirca, and Daniel Miller. 2012. *Migration and the New Media: Transnational Families and Polymedia.* New York, NY: Routledge.

Mahdavi, Pardis. 2011. *Gridlock: Labor, Migration and Trafficking in Dubai.* Stanford, CA: Stanford University Press.

———. 2013. "Gender, Labour, and the Law: The Nexus of Domestic Work, Human Trafficking and the Informal Economy in the United Arab Emirates." *Global Networks* 13(4): 425–40.

Mahmood, Saba. 2011. *Politics of Piety: The Islamic Revival and the Feminist Subject.* Princeton, NJ: Princeton University Press.

Makulec, Agnieszka. 2014. "Philippines' Bilateral Labour Arrangements on Health-Care Professional Migration: In Search of Meaning." ILO Asia Pacific Working Paper Series. Manila, Philippines: International Labour Organization.

Mangulabnan, Bernard Paul, and Carl Rookie Daquio. 2018. "A Review of Bilateral Labor Agreements Concluded by the Philippines with Countries of Destination: Toward a Framework for Monitoring and Evaluation." ILS Discussion Paper Series. Manila, Philippines: Institute for Labor Studies.

Marcus, George. 1998. *Ethnography through Thick and Thin.* Princeton, NJ: Princeton University Press.

Marx, Karl. 1987. *Economic and Philosophic Manuscripts of 1844.* Buffalo, NY: Prometheus Books.

Medenilla, Samuel. 2019. "DOLE Seeks Justice for Death of OFW Constancia Dayag in Kuwait." *Business Mirror* (May 16). Available at https://businessmirror.com. ph/2019/05/16/dole-seeks-justice-for-death-of-ofw-constancia-dayag-in-kuwait/. Accessed December 28, 2020.

Mendez, Jennifer. 1998. "Of Mops and Maids: Contradictions and Continuities in Bureaucratized Domestic Work." *Social Problems* 45(1): 114–35.

Mill, John Stuart. 2001 (1859). *On Liberty*. Kitchener, ON: Bartoche Books.

Murray, Heather. 2013. "Hope for Reform Springs Eternal: How the Sponsorship System, Domestic Laws and Traditional Customs Fail to Protect Migrant Domestic Workers in GCC Countries." *Cornell International Law Journal* 45(2): 461–86.

National Economic and Development Authority [NEDA]. 2017. The International Migration Almanac. Available at http://www.neda.gov.ph/the-international-migration-almanac-2017/. Accessed December 28, 2020.

Newbould, Chris. 2018. "Former Miss Lebanon on Sondos Al Qattan: "How Can Anyone Be OK with Slavery? But the Backlash Is Also Bullying." *The National* (July 29). Available at https://www.thenational.ae/arts-culture/film/former-miss-lebanon-on-sondos-al-qattan-how-can-anyone-be-ok-with-slavery-but-the-backlash-is-also-bullying-1.755184. Accessed December 28, 2020.

Nozick, Robert. 2013 (1974). *Anarchy, State and Utopia*. New York, NY: Basic Books.

Ocampo, Anthony. 2016. *The Latinos of Asia: How Filipino Americans Break the Rules of Race*. Stanford, CA: Stanford University Press.

O'Connell Davidson, Julia. 2010. "New Slavery, Old Binaries: Human Trafficking and the Borders of 'Freedom.'" *Global Networks* 10(2): 244–61.

———. 2013. "Troubling Freedom: Migration, Debt and Modern Slavery." *Migration Studies* 1(2): 176–95.

O'Neill, John. 2011. "Varieties of Unfreedom." Manchester Papers in Political Economy, Working Paper No. 4. Centre for the Study of Political Economy: University of Manchester.

Ortiga, Yasmin. 2018. "Learning to Fill the Labor Niche: Filipino Nursing Graduates and the Risk of the Migration Trap." *RSF: The Russell Sage Foundation Journal of the Social Sciences* (4)1: 172–87.

Palmer, Phyllis. 1991. *Domesticity and Dirt: Housewives and Domestic Servants in the United States, 1920–1945*. Philadelphia, PA: Temple University Press.

Panaligan, Marisse. 2019. "OFW Who Was Tied to Tree by Saudi Employer Now Back in PHL." *GMA News Online* (May 27). Available at https://www.gmanetwork.com/news/pinoyabroad/news/695790/ofw-who-was-tied-to-tree-by-saudi-employer-now-back-in-phl/story/. Accessed April 20, 2021.

Pande, Amrita. 2012. "From 'Balcony Talk' and 'Practical Prayers' to Illegal Collectives: Migrant Domestic Workers and Meso-Level of Resistances in Lebanon." *Gender & Society* 26(3): 382–405.

———. 2013. "'The Paper that You Have in Your Hand Is My Freedom': Migrant Domestic Work and the Sponsorship (Kafala) System in Lebanon." *International Migration Review* 47(2): 414–41.

Parreñas, Juno. 2018. *Decolonizing Extinction: The Work of Care in Orangutan Rehabilitation*. Durham, NC: Duke University Press.

Parreñas, Rhacel Salazar. 2011. *Illicit Flirtations: Labor, Migration and Sex Trafficking in Tokyo*. Stanford, CA: Stanford University Press.

———. 2015 (2001). *Servants of Globalization: Migration and Domestic Work*. Stanford, CA: Stanford University Press

———. 2017. "The Indenture of Migrant Domestic Workers." *Women's Studies Quarterly* 45(1&2): 113–27.

Parreñas, Rhacel, Krittiya Kantachote, and Rachel Silvey. 2020. "Soft Violence: Migrant Domestic Worker Precarity and the Management of Unfree Labour in Singapore." *Journal of Ethnic and Migration Studies*. Online First on April 2, 2020. Available at https://www.tandfonline.com/doi/abs/10.1080/1369183X.2020.1732614.

Parreñas, Rhacel Salazar, Rachel Silvey, Maria Hwang, and Carolyn Choi. 2019. "Serial Labor Migration: Precarity and Itinerancy among Filipino and Indonesian Migrant Domestic Workers." *International Migration Review* 53(4): 1230–58.

Parveen, Nazia, and Patrick Wintour. 2018. "Matthew Hedges: British Academic Accused OF Spying Jailed for Life in UAE." *The Guardian* (November 21). Available at https://www.theguardian.com/world/2018/nov/21/british-academic-matthew-hedges-accused-of-spying-jailed-for-life-in-uae. Accessed January 2, 2021.

Paul, Anju Mary. 2012. "Stepwise International Migration: A Multi-Stage Migration Pattern for the Aspiring Migrant." *American Journal of Sociology* 116(6): 1842–86.

Pettit, Philip. 1996. "Freedom as Antipower." *Ethics* 106(3): 576–604.

———. 2002. "Keeping Republican Freedom Simple: On a Difference with Quentin Skinner." *Political Theory* 30(3): 339–56.

Philippine Overseas Employment Administration. 2010. Philippine Overseas Employment Administration OFW Deployment by Occupation, Country, and Sex—New Hires, 2010. Available at http://www.poea.gov.ph/ofwstat/deppercountry/2010.pdf. Accessed December 29, 2020.

Philippines Statistics Authority. 2015. Integrated Survey of Households. Available at https://psa.gov.ph/sites/default/files/FIES%202015%20Final%20Report.pdf. Accessed December 28, 2020.

———. 2018. 2018 Survey on Overseas Filipinos. Available at https://psa.gov.ph/statistics/survey/labor-and-employment/survey-overseas-filipinos/table. Accessed April 21, 2021.

Pido, Eric. 2017. *Migrant Returns: Manila, Development and Transnational Connectivity*. Durham, NC: Duke University Press.

Polanco, Geraldina. 2019. "Competition Between Labour-Sending States and the Branding of National Workforces." *International Migration* 57(4): 136–50.

Polanyi, Karl. 2001 (1944). *The Great Transformation*. Boston, MA: Beacon Press.

Ponce de Leon, Janice. 2019. "Filipina Maid Bids Goodbye to Dubai Family after 29 years." *Gulf News* (June 15). Available at https://gulfnews.com/uae/filipina-maid-bids-goodbye-to-dubai-family-after-29-years-1.64625567. Accessed December 28, 2020.

Portes, Alejandro, and Rubén G. Rumbaut. 2006 (1996). *Immigrant America: A Portrait.* 3rd ed. University of California Press.

Portes, Alejandro, and Min Zhou. 1993. "The New Second Generation: Segmented Assimilation and Its Variants." *Annals of the American Academy of Political and Social Science* 530 (November): 74–96.

Pratt, Geraldine. 2012. *Families Apart: Migrating Mothers and the Conflicts of Labor and Love.* Minneapolis, MN: University of Minnesota Press.

Qatar. 2017. Law No. 15 of 2017 concerning Domestic Workers. Available at https://www.ilo.org/dyn/natlex/natlex4.detail?p_lang=en&p_isn=105099&p_count=8&p_classification=22. Accessed December 28, 2020.

Rafael, Vicente. 2000. *White Love and Other Events in Filipino History.* Durham, NC: Duke University Press.

Ramos, Christia Marie. 2019. "DOLE Asks NBI to Locate Companion of Kuwait OFW Found Dead in Employer's Home." Available at https://globalnation.inquirer.net/176141/dole-asks-nbi-to-locate-companion-of-kuwait-ofw-found-dead-in-employers-home. Accessed January 4, 2021.

Ray, Raka, and Seemin Qayum. 2009. *Cultures of Servitude: Modernity, Domesticity and Class in India.* Stanford, CA: Stanford University Press.

Redden, Elizabeth. 2015. "Persona Non Grata." *Inside Higher Ed* (March 18). Available at https://www.insidehighered.com/news/2015/03/18/nyu-professor-denied-entry-uae-where-university-has-campus. Accessed January 1, 2020.

Republic of the Philippines. 1974. Labor Code of the Philippines. Available at https://blr.dole.gov.ph/2014/12/11/labor-code-of-the-philippines/. Accessed December 28, 2020.

———. 1995. Republic Act No. 8042 (Migrant Workers and Overseas Filipinos Act of 1995). Available at http://www.poea.gov.ph/laws&rules/files/Migrant%20Workers%20Act%20of%201995%20(RA%208042).html. Accessed December 28, 2020.

———. 2009. Republic Act No. 10022 (Amendment of Migrant Workers and Overseas Filipinos Act of 1995). Available at https://www.officialgazette.gov.ph/2010/03/10/republic-act-no-10022-s-2010/. Accessed December 28, 2020.

Rey, Aika. 2018. "Philippines and Kuwait Sign Agreement Protecting OFWs." *Rappler* (May 11). Available at https://www.rappler.com/nation/202303-kuwait-philippines-memorandum-agreement-signing-protection-ofw. Accessed December 28, 2020.

Reyes, Victoria. 2020. "Ethnographic Toolkit: Strategic Positionality and Researchers' Visible and Invisible Tools in Field Research." *Ethnography* 21(2): 220–40.

Robertson, Shanti. 2019. "Migrant, Interrupted: The Temporalities of 'Staggered' Migration from Asia to Australia." *Current Sociology* 67(2): 169–85.

Rodriguez, Robyn. 2010. *Migrants for Export: How the Philippine State Brokers Labor to the World.* Minneapolis, MN: University of Minnesota Press.

Rollins, Judith. 1985. *Between Women: Domestics and Their Employers.* Philadelphia, PA: Temple University Press.

Romero, Mary. 2002. *Maid in the U.S.A.* New York, NY: Routledge.

Sabban, Rima. 2012. *Maids Crossing: Domestic Workers in the UAE*. Saarbrücken, Germany: LAP Lambert Academic Publishing.

Said, Edward. 1978. *Orientalism*. New York, NY: Pantheon Books.

Saldaña-Portillo, Maria Josefina. 2003. *The Revolutionary Imagination in the Americas and the Age of Development*. Durham, NC: Duke University Press.

Sankar, Anjana. 2013. "UAE Maid Rules 'Stacked against Sponsors.'" *Gulf News* (August 21). Available at https://gulfnews.com/uae/uae-maid-rules-stacked-against-sponsors-1.1222644. Accessed December 28, 2020.

Shenon, Philip. 1995. "Filipinos Protest Singapore Death Sentence." *New York Times* (March 16). Available at https://www.nytimes.com/1995/03/16/world/filipinos-protest-singapore-death-sentence.html. Accessed December 28, 2020.

Skinner, Quentin. 1997. *Liberty Before Liberalism*. Cambridge, UK: Cambridge University Press.

Scott, James. 1985. *Weapons of the Weak: Everyday Forms of Peasant Resistance*. New Haven, CT: Yale University Press.

———. 1990. *Domination and the Arts of Resistance*. New Haven, CT: Yale University Press.

Secorun, Laura. 2018. "The Perils of Housecleaning Abroad: Domestic Migrant Workers in the Middle East Continue to Face Confinement and Abuse." *New York Times* (August 6). Available at https://www.nytimes.com/2018/08/06/opinion/international-world/domestic-workers-middle-east.html. Accessed December 28, 2020.

Shouk, Ali Al. 2019. "Two on Trial after Locked Up Maid Dies in Dubai." *Gulf News* (September 11). Available at https://gulfnews.com/uae/crime/two-on-trial-after-locked-up-maid-dies-in-dubai-1.66358289. Accessed January 4, 2021.

Silvey, Rachel. 2007. "Unequal Borders: Indonesian Transnational Migrants at Immigration Control." *Geopolitics* 12(2): 265–79.

Silvey, Rachel, and Rhacel Parreñas. 2020. "Precarity Chains: Cycles of Domestic Worker Migration from Southeast Asia to the Middle East." *Journal of Ethnic and Migration Studies* 46(16): 3457–71.

Sonmez, Sevil, Yorghos Apostolopoulos, Diane Tran, and Shantyana Rentrope. 2011. "Human Rights and Health Disparities for Migrant Workers in the UAE." *Health and Human Rights* 13(2): 17–35.

Stenum, Helle. 2011. *Abused Domestic Workers in Europe: The Case of Au Pairs*. Brussels, Belgium: European Commission.

Swidler, Ann. 1986. "Culture in Action: Symbols and Strategies." *American Sociological Review* 51(2): 273–86.

Testaverde, Mauro, Harry Moroz, Claire H. Hollweg, and Achim Schmillen. 2017. *Migrating to Opportunity: Overcoming Barriers to Labor Mobility in Southeast Asia*. Washington, DC: World Bank.

Tyner, James. 2009. *The Philippines: Mobilities, Identities, Globalization*. London, UK: Routledge.

United Arab Emirates. 2017. Federal Decree No. 10 of 2017 (1438) on Domestic Workers. Available at https://www.ilo.org/dyn/natlex/natlex4.detail?p_lang=en&p_isn=107727&p_count=5&p_classification=22. Accessed December 28, 2020.

United Nations (League of Nations). 1926. Slavery Convention. Available at https://www.ohchr.org/en/professionalinterest/pages/slaveryconvention.aspx. Accessed December 28, 2020.

United Nations. 2000. Protocol to Prevent, Suppress and Punish Trafficking in Persons Especially Women and Children, supplementing the United Nations Convention against Transnational Organized Crime. Available at https://www.ohchr.org/en/professionalinterest/pages/protocoltraffickinginpersons.aspx. Accessed December 28, 2020.

Vora. Neha. 2013. *Impossible Citizens: Dubai's Indian Diaspora*. Durham, NC: Duke University Press.

Wasmi, Naser Al. 2018. "Kuwaits Call Sondos Al Qattan's Video an 'Embarrasment.'" *The National* (July 26). Available at https://www.thenational.ae/lifestyle/kuwaitis-call-sondos-al-qattan-s-video-an-embarrassment-1.754455. Accessed December 28, 2020.

Willen, Sarah. 2007. "Exploring 'Illegal' and 'Irregular' Migrants' Lived Experiences of Law and State Power." *International Migration* 45(3):177–81.

———. 2014. "Plotting a Moral Trajectory, *Sans Papiers*: Outlaw Motherhood as Inhabitable Space of Welcome." *Ethos* 42(1): 84–100.

Wimmer, Andreas, and Nina Glick Schiller. 2002. "Methodological Nationalism and Beyond: Nation-State Building, Migration and the Social Sciences." *Global Networks* 2(4): 301–34.

World Bank, 2018. "Access to Electricity, Rural (% of Rural Population)." Available at https://data.worldbank.org/indicator/EG.ELC.ACCS.RU.ZS. Accessed December 28, 2020.

Xiang, Biao, and Johan Lindquist. 2014. "Migration Infrastructure." *International Migration Review* 48(1): S122–S148.

Yeoh, Brenda, and Shirlena Huang. 1998. "Negotiating Public Space: Strategies and Styles of Migrant Female Domestic Workers in Singapore." *Urban Studies* 35(3): 583–602.

Zelizer, Viviana. 2000. "Fine Tuning the Zelizer View." *Economy and Society* 29(3): 383–89.

———. 2005. *The Purchase of Intimacy*. Princeton, NJ: Princeton University Press.

———. 2007. "Pasts and Futures of Economic Sociology." *American Behavioral Scientist* 50(8): 1056–69.

———. 2012a. "How I Became a Relational Economic Sociologist and What Does That Mean?" *Politics & Society* 40(2): 145–74.

———. 2012b. "Talking about Relational Work with Viviana Zelizer." Interview by Nina Bandelj and Fred Wherry. Available at https://orgtheory.wordpress.com/2012/09/06/talking-about-relational-work-with-viviana-zelizer/. Accessed March 15, 2020.

Index

Ingram Content Group UK Ltd.
Milton Keynes UK
UKHW010900220323
418972UK00006B/280